The greening of
British party politics

Issues in Environmental Politics

series editors Tim O'Riordan *and* Albert Weale

already published in the series

Environment and development in Latin America: The politics of sustainability   David Goodman and Michael Redclift eds.

The politics of radioactive waste disposal   Ray Kemp

The greening of
British party politics

Mike Robinson

Manchester University Press
Manchester and New York
Distributed exclusively in the USA and Canada by St. Martin's Press

Published by Manchester University Press
Oxford Road, Manchester M13 9PL, UK
and Room 400, 175 Fifth Avenue, New York, NY 10010, USA

Distributed exclusively in the USA and Canada
by St. Martin's Press, Inc., 175 Fifth Avenue, New York,
NY 10010, USA

British Library Cataloguing-in-Publication Data
A catalogue record for this book is available from the British Library

Library of Congress Cataloging-in-publication Data
Robinson, Mike, 1960–
  The greening of British party politics/Mike Robinson.
    p.   cm.—(Issues in environmental politics)
  Includes index.
  ISBN 0–7190–3198–2.—ISBN 0–7190–3199–0
  1. Environmental policy—Great Britain.   2.Green movement—Great
Britain.   3. Political parties—Great Britain.   I. Title.
II. Series.
HC260.E5R63   1992
363.7'056'0941—dc20   91–44099

Typeset in Great Britain
by Northern Phototypesetting Co. Ltd, Bolton.

Printed in Great Britain
by Bell & Bain Ltd, Glasgow

Contents

Figures and tables

Figures

Tables

Acknowledgements

In researching this book, over sixty interviews were conducted between 1986 and 1990 with politicians from each of the major UK parties. My thanks go to all of them for sharing their valuable time with me. The interviews were at various times humorous, tense and often hurried, but were all highly enjoyable to conduct and full of interest.

I would particularly like to thank the following individuals for their ideas, advice, interest and hospitality at various stages of the research: John Bates, Ray Buckton, Tom Burke, Dr David Clark MP, Dr John Cunningham MP, Nigel Forman MP, Robin Grove-White, Nigel Haigh, Peter Hain, Robert Hutchinson, Tony Paterson, Stan Rosenthal, Sir Hugh Rossi MP, Richard Sandbrook, Jim Slater, Chris Smith MP, Andrew Sullivan and Adrian Watts.

Especial thanks go to Professor Tim O'Riordan of the University of East Anglia for his encouragement and comments; to Richard Purslow and Manchester University Press for their patience; and to Judith, to whom this book is dedicated.

Introduction

'It is clear that every Minister, every Department, must take on board environmental responsibilities for its own activities – obvious examples are transport, agriculture, health, housing, planning, defence. Concern for our environment has got to be part of the fabric of all our policies. It is the most political of all problems facing modern society.'[1] This could well be an extract from the Conservative Government's White Paper 'Our Common Inheritance', published in September 1990, which proposed that each government department should have a minister responsible for environmental policy. Such ideas had been put forward by the major opposition parties some five years earlier. In fact, it is an extract from a Labour Party policy document entitled 'The Politics of the Environment', published in 1973. Why has it taken so long for such an idea to come to fruition, and how do such ideas sit within the realms of party politics? These questions were the starting point of this book in 1986.

From a rise in public consciousness regarding environment, issues during the 1970s, the 1980s saw rising expectations amongst environmental groups, and the development of apparently long-standing political interest in the environment by the major parties. A cursory glance at the quality press and various journals throughout that time revealed unprecedented interest in the environment amongst politicians, and 'the greening of British politics' became the popular media phrase which seemed to describe this phenomenon.

After years of relative neglect, it now seemed as if politicians of all parties wanted to be environmentalists. Take, for example, the following statement: 'The war which man is now raging against nature is not only foolhardy, it is downright dangerous. We can't go on polluting the atmosphere and poisoning the sea, we can't go on slaughtering our wildlife forever.'[2] This particular piece was a product of the National Front in its attempt to cultivate a 'green' image. Not surprisingly, there were no mass defections from the Green Party, but bold pieces of rhetoric of this kind have now become woven into contemporary mainstream politics.

Beneath the journalistic appeal of the 'green' label, there lies a host of socio-political questions that require analysis. The motivations and workings of the British political parties is a well researched area with fairly clearly defined boundaries. Environmentalism, however, is still a relatively new area of research which overlaps with a multitude of disciplines. Research into the UK environmentalism/ politics interface has expanded in recent years and now forms an increasingly important area for study. However, work has largely tended to focus upon issues, the role of government and contributions of the pressure groups. This book focuses upon the major parties themselves, including the party of government, and seeks to get behind their rhetoric, offering explanations as to how and why they are responding to the challenge of environmentalism. It is therefore not a book solely about environmental issues and the role of the environmental movement, although these clearly feature. Nor is it an in-depth study of British party politics. It is about the complex and unfolding relationship between the two.

The book is based upon research conducted chiefly between 1986 and 1990, which included over sixty interviews with politicians of the major political parties. These included Members of Parliament, ministerial advisers, opposition spokesmen, party strategists, policy makers, trade union leaders, pressure group leaders and prospective parliamentary candidates. The interviews were undertaken to provide an insider perspective on the attitudes of leading party politicians toward the environmental movement and its 'green' element.

In order to supplement the information gained through the interviews, analyses were made of official and quasi-official party policy statements, 'green' briefing documents, speeches and key articles. Early interviews covered a great deal of new ground, providing new information on why and how party 'greening' was occurring, and identifying the various factors which could impede its development. As the interviews progressed, further information emerged until many of the later interviews began to repeat, and in effect verify much of what had been communicated earlier.

Party political concern for the environment is certainly nothing new. However, as public concern for the environment became increasingly sophisticated, government and party responses have matured. Throughout the 1970s, environmental issues explicitly emerged as political issues, but were consequently largely managed in an *ad hoc* way by government, and given some consideration by the opposition parties. This recent history forms an important back-cloth. Chapter 1 looks at the emergence and context of environmental concern in British party politics and the rise in power of the word 'environment' – power to stimulate legislation, create new institutions and widen political horizons to European and global perspectives. The chapter looks at how the parties, during the 1980s, have had to respond to a growing, more mature and pervasive environmental movement.

Chapter 2 examines the variety that is inherent in the environmental movement, in terms of its ideological foundations and the numerous groups which constitute it. Environmentalism has manoeuvred itself into the position of being a major force for change in British society. It is examined as a particularly British social movement, operating in a political culture which specialises in accommodation and reform rather than challenges and conflicts. It is a social movement which does not possess the relatively clear-cut structure of a European Green Party or the single purpose of a UK pressure group, but has a variety of organisational forms and a range of component ideologies.

The 1980s witnessed the development of the 'green' element of environmentalism, – that which had a radical intellectual edge and provided a new political alternative. The word 'green' has come to be synonymous with environmental concern, but despite obvious links, the concept of 'greenness' is quite distinctive in its meaning and social, moral and political focus. To clarify such distinctions, we employ the idea of a 'green datum' by which the activities of the major political parties can later be evaluated. Given the often over-generous way the 'green' label is utilised, chapter 2 attempts to shed light on the Greens within the environmental movement and the way they are shaping contemporary intellectual, social, economic and political debates.

In chapter 3 we take a macro-view of how environmentalism as a social movement interacts with government and the parties. The 'greening' of government and of the parties involves interchange at three interdependent levels. Initially 'greening' may be evidenced by nothing more than carefully-chosen rhetoric. Action in the form of new policy initiatives or alterations to existing policy positions indicates a deeper commitment to environmental concern. However, the ultimate challenge for the environmental movement is to see environmental concern integrated with the ideologies of the parties, so that proaction becomes a matter of course.

Given that there exists little in the way of established theoretical material to draw upon, chapters 4 to 6, which focus on the how and why of the 'greening' process, are written chiefly as narrative from the information accumulated from the interviews. Much of the information eventually used in the discussion was conveyed by perhaps five or six key interviews with members of each of the main parties. Each interview provided a different perspective by virtue of the interviewee's party position, age, political experience and so on. Quotations have been sparingly used in the text, mainly to emphasise points brought about by wider discussion, and so as not to interrupt the narrative. Those used provided a slightly different perspective because they either seemingly went against the party line, or they appeared to conflict with the position of the respondent at the time.

The conventional interpretation used to explain why the political parties respond to the environmental movement has centred upon a 'pressure–response' mechanism, as explored, for example, by Downs and Solesbury.[3] Relating mainly to the party of government, this suggests that the parties will tend to alter their policies and rhetoric if sufficient external pressures are applied and 'force' them to do so. This constitutionally flattering interpretation is explored in chapter 4, in relation to the various sources of pressure from inside and outside the environmental movement.

It is argued that the nature and extent of changes taking place under the banner of party 'greening' represents something much deeper than mere reaction to a series of unco-ordinated pressures. In chapter 5 a complementary interpretation is put forward, as being increasingly influential. This suggests that the 'greening' of the parties is also driven by internal factors relating to the actions and positions of key personalities, and to ideological developments within the parties. It is argued that through the work of a growing number of 'green' activists, and because of a necessity for party ideologies to adapt to the wishes of an environmentally aware electorate, the major parties are increasingly receptive to the environmental movement and proactive to an unprecedented degree.

Against interpretations as to how and why the main parties are 'going green', chapter 6 examines the array of constraints which operate to prevent this process, or at least metamorphose it into an ideologically acceptable outcome. The inputs of 'green' party activists is severely constrained by wider considerations relating to party strategies, particularly near a general election, and ideology. In order for environmental concern to be acceptable to the parties, it has to conform to the needs and goals of party members. This results in a selective screening of issues and calculated approaches to policy, which may highlight some areas and neglect others. As long as the demands of the environmental movement are channelled through the major political parties, compromises will be made.

Chapter 7 examines the marginal role of the Green Party in UK politics. Whereas the Greens and the Green Party may be said to have made a strong intellectual contribution to the environmental movement, they have presented little in the way of a political challenge because of internal ideological and organisational tensions, and the constraints imposed on them by the traditional political system. Using the conceptual yardstick of the 'green datum', it is argued that what is widely referred to as the 'greening' of British party politics actually bears little relation to the concept of 'greenness'. Because of constraints of ideology, and the way British party politics functions, what may sound like a process of radical transformation can be no more than a series of piecemeal adjustments in policy, together with ideological accommodation and compromise.

The dominance of the party system in the UK means that the future of environmental concern and the environmental movement in the UK, including the Greens, is bound up with changes in the main parties, with the pressures that act upon them, with ideological developments and the influence of key personalities. The 1980s saw considerable developments in the way the parties tackled environmental questions. It is likely that throughout the 1990s such developments will continue, although in politics there are few certainties, and the pace of change can vary considerably. Chapter 7 concludes by assessing recent developments in British environmental politics and prospects for the future.

Being an exploration of a relatively new subject, this book can only say so much. The 'greening' of British party politics involves complex and highly dynamic processes which are extremely difficult to research. However, it is hoped that the purpose of this study is fulfilled if the reader leaves its pages with some knowledge and understanding of an important and increasingly relevant phenomenon.

Notes and references

1 Labour Party, 1973. *Politics of the Environment*. The Labour Party.
2 Quoted in: Benton, S./Edwards, R. 1984. 'The Greening of the NF.' New Statesman, 26.10.84. 16–17.
3 Downs, A. 1972. 'Up and Down with Ecology – The Issue–Attention Cycle.' *The Public Interest*, 28. 38–50; Solesbury, W. 'The Environmental Agenda.' *Public Administration*, 54. Winter. 379–97.

1

Environmental concern in UK politics

Emergence and context

British party politics has always possessed an environmental dimension. However, interpretations of this dimension have changed, particularly since the early 1970s. The terms 'environment' and 'environmental', used in reference to an area of policy, have taken a long time to find their way into the language of British politics. It was not until 1970 that the general election manifestos of the main political parties specifically employed the term 'environment' to refer to a particular section of policy. This practice has continued to the present, albeit in an often inconsistent way, which has reflected the evolutionary impact of the environmental movement upon the British polity and the steady, but lengthy, process by which the concept of environment has permeated society. This process has essentially involved the establishment of 'environment' as a label. Yet the substance beneath the label, the objective problems relating to the quality of people's surroundings and their relationship to the human condition, now referred to as 'environmental' issues, have been part of party rhetoric for a much longer period.

The Liberal Party manifesto of 1923 called for the 'national credit' to be protected and restored, particularly in the rural sector where concern was shown, not just for the amount of land in agricultural production, but also for the 'quality' of the land, and for the housing and amenities of the people who are dependent upon it.[1] In a similar vein, the 'Programme of the Labour Party' of 1937 declared that land should be properly utilised, with the qualification that this would involve not only the reorganisation of agriculture, but also:

problems relating to the best grouping of communities with reference to economic needs and opportunities and the provision of transport, social services and amenities; the preservation of natural beauty; the provision of national parks and facilities for recreation; and, indeed, a whole range of problems affecting the efficiency of the nation, the conservation of our resources and the well-being of the people.[2]

Despite the long history and cosy rhetoric of this genre of party political concern, its essence is part of the ideology of contemporary environmentalism. At the time however, such statements were not referenced by any 'environmental' label.

Similarly, substantive pieces of party policy and government legislation which address what we would now call 'environmental issues' have long histories. Torren's Artisans' and Labourers' Dwellings Act of 1868 and the subsequent Improvement Act of 1875 attempted to deal with perhaps the most fundamental of environmental problems, that of public health and sanitation. These Acts represented a degree of political recognition that the quality of the physical environment directly affected the quality of the human condition. Governments repeated this theme throughout the twentieth century in a wide variety of social legislation, culminating in the town and country planning statutes of Attlee's post-war administration. These established permanent legal mechanisms for the articulation and resolution of environmental and social problems.

The development of environmental concern in the realm of British party politics has largely been seen as a programme of reaction to pressures, in an ongoing dynamic of socio-economic trial and error. Political parties have not been portrayed as having environmental concern as an inherent part of their ideologies, but rather as targets of environmentalist pressure. The historical evolution of these pressures has tended to pre-empt specific articulation of political concern through policy; indeed, the process has laid the foundations of the contemporary environmental movement.[3]

There are two main strands in the development of the environmental movement.[4] The first has involved public health reform and the sanitary revolution, which sprang primarily from the report of the 1834 Poor Law Commission.[5] These improvements, founded upon utilitarian ideals, dealt with the basic environmental concerns of an expanding urban working population. Chadwick, the leading reformer in this area, summed up many of the concerns of contemporary environmentalists in a statement made in 1886, near the end of his life. He suggested that the following questions remained to be asked about the areas he had surveyed:

Are the great canals properly purged and cleansed? Is the breath of the place sweet and wholesome? Is it free, or is it infested with vermin? Is the circulation of what goes in and out of the town orderly and regular? Is the water with which it is supplied of good and proper quality? Is the food sufficient in regards quality and quantity? Is the place supplied with pure air or does mist hang over it morning and evening like a fog?[6]

The second strand, and one particulary well documented academically, is the amenity movement which can be traced back to the formation of the Commons, Open Spaces and Footpaths Preservation Society in 1865.[7] Current concerns of amenity groups revolve around landscape and habitat preservation, together with improved and extended public access in both rural and more recently in urban areas. In relation to the concerns expressed by Chadwick, the platform of groups such as the National Trust, the Civic Trust and the Council for the Protection of Rural England may be viewed as relatively elitist, dealing predominantly more with aesthetic preferences rather than human needs. Despite these differences, however, the two strands have to an extent been bound together by the the post-war development of a planning ethos, though this has been primarily directed at the built environment.

Whether in terms of rhetoric or concrete policy, environmental concern is far from being an original actor in the stage play of party politics. The name is novel – just some two decades young – and the costume may have been adapted, but in terms of the physical and human environment as an object of political attention, the essential character of concern has been little altered since the nineteenth century. Yet from the late 1960s until the early 1980s, substantive political changes have accompanied the labelling process. These changes sowed the seeds of what we may tentatively call 'party political environmentalism'. A number of interdependent features seem to characterise this period.

Public interest, 1970 to 1981

Against a background of expansive social changes, the late sixties and early seventies are widely cited as the years of peak public interest in the environment. Evidence for this seems to be unequivocal. Content analysis has shown that British media coverage of environmental issues reached a peak between 1972 and 1973, although similar media research has not been carried out in the United Kingdom post 1982.[8]

Although the character of media coverage is far from being an accurate guide to public concern as defined as 'active participation' over the long term, it nevertheless provides an indication of the public mood. Moreover, it establishes a background climate for changing political opinion.[9] Though media attention to the environment declined after 1972, it still remained higher and more intense than during any past decade. Indeed, it has been suggested that environmental protection became one of the 'lasting concerns' of the American public in the 1970s, and despite inevitable differences in circumstances, this was perhaps an accurate description of British public feeling at the end of the decade.[10]

The increase in public awareness both stimulated activity in established environmentally-orientated groups and also encouraged the growth of new groups seeking channels of access to political decision makers. This growth of the environmental lobby in terms of membership, numbers of groups and their wholesale political effectiveness has received much attention.[11] Lowe and Goyder give the period 1966–75 as being that of the greatest expansion in the number (not membership) of national environmental groups. The period since, however, has seen a decline in the number of groups, but a consolidation of membership and organisation.[12] In terms of influencing the political climate, the 1970s saw a convergence between the so-called 'attentive public' and organised groups, and the latter increasingly became able to mobilise the former. This introduced a new feature, seen as some as a thorn, into all levels of the policy making procedure, that of the 'environmental consideration'. 'Taking the environment into account', though neither a continuous nor an uncontentious input into the political process, established itself as a significant political move, particularly in the run-up to a General Election. The role of public opinion in the political system is, however, a function of the nature of that system, and as a result ebbs and flows with the tides of political culture. The 1970s saw a general extension of the ethos of pluralism and public accountability which paralleled and complemented the rise of environmental awareness at national and local level.

Institutional provisions

The diffusion of environmental awareness throughout an arbitrarily outlined 'public domain' and the growth of the environment lobby stimulated definitive institutional responses from successive governments in the 1970s and early 1980s. There were administrative provisions for the handling of environmental problems prior to 1970, but problems were not dealt with comprehensively nor by a comprehensive agency under a defined banner of environmental concern. It could be argued that this did not matter as long as the problems were successfully handled. Yet a new bureaucratic approach was implemented, and it has remained since as testimony to a significant political reaction to the wider social changes that were occurring at that time.

The establishment of the Department of the Environment (DOE) in November 1970 was central to these administrative provisions. In 1969 the Labour Government discussed the need for a new multifocus department and the succeeding Conservative administration acted upon its ideas. The 1970 October White Paper on the 'Reorganisation of Central Government' stated: 'It is increasingly accepted that maintaining a decent environment, improving people's living conditions and providing for adequate transport facilities all come together in the planning of development.'[13] The fusion of the Ministry of Housing and Local Government, the Ministry of Public Building and Works and the Ministry of Transport (made separate in 1976) took place the following month, and following Prime Minister Edward Heath's wishes, it was called the Department of the Environment. Peter Walker, the first Secretary of State, addressed his staff on the department's first day:

The merger is going to enable us to deal more comprehensively with environmental problems and to create a better synthesis of requirements and resources. The tasks before us are complex and demanding: the reward is to make the country a better place for people to live, work and enjoy themselves. Our Department is 'the Department' most concerned with improving the quality of living in our country.[14]

The creation of the DOE represented something more than formal recognition of a new wave of public concern about essentially old environmental problems. It symbolised the advent of a new political awareness which recognised the socio-economic significance of environmental concerns and the fact that environmental issues were interwoven with other policy areas. The new governmental structure also placed the fledgling term 'environment' in politicians' well-demarcated vocabulary, allowing them to contemplate its substance. In retrospect, the DOE was perhaps seen by both politicians and public as an institutional panacea for environmental problems. They failed to see how environmental responsibilities were spread throughout other ministries and agencies, or the tension which existed between the DOE's environmental protection duties and its adjacent remit for environmental development.

Other major institutional developments in the period 1970 to 1982 included the establishment of the permanent Standing Royal Commission on Environmental Pollution in 1970, the Health and Safety Commission in 1974 and the Select Committee on the Environment in 1979, as part of the reform of the Select Committee system. The Royal Commission on Environmental Pollution encapsulated the increasing political trend toward scientific assessment of environmental problems via a system of quasi-judicial inquiry. Although the Commission has a significant and prestigious pedigree which obliged governments to respond to, if not to accept, its recommendations, it has remained an advisory body, albeit an influential one. Significantly, the Royal Commission on Environmental Pollution was established on a permanent basis, suggesting that government saw pollution as a far from transitory problem.

The Select Committee on the Environment was set up as part of a larger measure to achieve a greater degree of parliamentary control of the Executive by overseeing and investigating the activities of the fourteen government departments. The interpretation of 'control' in this sense, however, is more in terms of influence rather than American Congressional-type power.[15] The early concerns of the committees were focused upon housing policy, council house sales and local government, although some attention was given to the problems of the inner cities and the tasks of urban renewal.[16] The importance of the formation of the Environment Select Committee lay in the creation of the opportunity to introduce the concept of environment directly into the House of Commons. It brought the concerns of the DOE to the attention of a continually changing group of eleven or so cross-party back benchers. Individuals who may not have had previous contact with the intricacies of environmental issues were given a forum in which to explore DOE expenditure, administration and policy, from either the perspective of a member of the opposition attacking government policy, or as government back benchers defending the department.

Legislative measures

The construction of environmentally orientated legislation during the 1970s did not stem from any new-found environmental concern across the political spectrum. Laws concerned with environmental protection pre-date the advent of the environment label by over a century.[17] The statutes that were introduced clung closely to the newly created administrative framework. New environmental laws and policies lagged slightly behind levels of public interest, and the legislation conceived was done so in spite of political and public sensitivity. This legislation was important in two ways: firstly, in its achievements, whereby environmental protection was enhanced and pressure groups were pacified, and secondly, in its failures, which provided the pressure groups with future targets to aim at.

The Control of Pollution Act (COPA) stands out as the 1970s' main piece of UK-initiated environmental legislation. At the introduction of the Control of Pollution Bill (first introduced as the 'Protection of the Environment Bill') by the Labour administration in 1974, Mrs Thatcher, then the opposition spokeswoman for the environment, stated her support for the Bill, declaring that it was 'likely to have a greater, more lasting impact on the quality of life in many parts of Britain than most other measures'.[18] The Act was strongly influenced by the early reports of the Royal Commission on Environmental Pollution. It centred on co-ordinating and tidying up existing control provisions for four main sectors – air pollution, noise nuisance, land waste disposal and water pollution. In the main, the Act sought to reinforce procedures which had been laid down in an array of previous statutes, and which were handled by the Central Directorate on Environmental Pollution within the DOE. Although the Act provided for separate control procedures for each of the four sectors, the overall approach allowed the environment to be handled, for the first time, in a comprehensive and co-ordinated manner.[19] But the importance of the Act also lay in the business it did not finish. Part II of COPA, dealing with water pollution – arguably the most important issue – was not implemented until 1984. This delay gave critics of government policy, both outside and inside Parliament, opportunities for repeated political attacks.

The other major piece of 'environmental' legislation which attempted to go some way to being comprehensive on countryside matters was the 1981 Wildlife and Countryside Act. The Callaghan administration introduced a Countryside and Wildlife Bill in 1979, a required response to the EEC Directive on Rare Birds passed the same year. The Bill fell with the election of the Conservatives, only to be pushed through amidst enormous political rancour in 1981 with a much extended remit, attempting to conciliate the interests of both the agriculture and conservation lobbies.[20] The Act sought to link various aspects of past countryside law in a consolidated whole and there was an expectation that it would be well received in parliament. In fact, the passage of the Act elicited lengthy Parliamentary dispute, and laid down the gauntlet to the increasingly organised conservation lobby, which fervently rose to the challenge.

It would be wrong to see the period 1970–81 as marked by only two pieces of environmental legislation.[21] The above acts were by far the most important indicators of a different genre of legislation, though as always, other measures had implications for the environment, either directly as part of a wider statute, or indirectly through having a 'knock-on' environmental effect. These measures were not part of a co-ordinated effort to deal with the environment in some kind of holistic or planned fashion. They had particular objectives and focused upon the protection of particular aspects of the environment, or allowed for administrative developments which had environmental applications.

The European dimension

With the passing of the European Communities Act of 1972, Britain agreed to hand over certain powers to the European Commission and the Council of Ministers. From then on, concern for the environment was to be influenced by Britain's membership of the EEC, and the government's acceptance of 'a common [i.e. European] interest in developing a harmonised approach toward the protection and improvement of the environment', and desire 'to make a full contribution in such an approach'.[22]

The Treaty of Rome itself contained no explicit provision for environmental policy, but after the Paris Summit of October 1972 (inspired by the United Nations Stockholm Conference earlier that year) the European Community adopted an environment policy centred upon a series of 'action programmes', and introduced a new variable into the workings of British politics. Britain was directly involved in these Community policies which created the Environment and Consumer Protection Service (now including nuclear safety) within the European Commission, and the Environment, Public Health and Consumer Protection Standing Committee of the European Parliament in 1973.

In 1977, the Community outlined eleven principles intended to guide environment policy. These included the 'polluter pays' idea, the ethos that 'prevention is better than cure' and the concept of environmental action at the 'appropriate level'.[23] Although readily seized upon by British pressure groups as welcome parts of the process of environmental policy formulation, these principles made no sudden impression upon the thinking of the main political parties. The articulation of public environmental concern is a function of the particular national base from which it emanates. In Germany and France since the 1970s the most appropriate channels of pressure have been through electoral participation at local, regional and national levels, although the then newly formed 'ecology' parties achieved little national political influence before the 1980s. In Britain, where the electoral system militates against new parties, pressure has chiefly been directed into the existing political parties via traditional lobbying arrangements.

Inevitably, tensions between Community environmental policy and national policy began to emerge as environmental directives were issued.[24] Directives are the chief type of legislative power administered by the European Community, calling for legislation to be binding upon each member state, though they leave the methods of implementation to the national authorities. Policy conflicts can occur not only between different approaches to environmental policy, but also between environmental directives and other national imperatives. The relevance of such tensions between the European Community and what are seen to be priorities of the UK lies not only with government, but also with the main political parties. Whether a defensive posture was to be taken or a line of political attack developed, party strategies now had to take the European perspective into consideration.

The international context

The 1970s also witnessed the beginnings of a shift in political environmental policy positions from a long-established parochial perspective toward an international understanding of the environment and its problems. Although international concerns remained predominantly economic and patriotic, the idea of the environment as a global entity gained political acceptance. Aided by the growth of a scientifically informed knowledge-base and the increasing dissemination of this knowledge through media channels, the concept of 'spaceship Earth' began to establish itself.[25]

The landmark of the period which attempted to crystallise this increased concern was the United Nations (UN) Conference on the Human Environment held in Stockholm in June 1972. The conference adopted a Declaration for the preservation and enhancement of the human environment, and an action plan with 109 recommendations for international action. It set up the United Nations Environment Programme (UNEP), with a small secretariat based in Nairobi, supported by a voluntary environmental fund, with the DOE responsible for the UK's contribution. The conference brought a new line to environmental thinking in the political parties both in and out of government. It highlighted the complex interrelationships within the world ecosystem, and it stressed the human dimension.[26] Moreover, it also brought home the interdependence of the global economy and the fragility of international resource bases.

For the conference, the British Secretary of State for the Environment, Peter Walker, had set up four working parties to produce reports on the state of public opinion toward environmental matters in the UK. The reports considered: immediate urban planning problems; the management of natural resources; the control of pollution, and the role of voluntary environmental pressure groups.[27] These reports were significant in that they were the first to address formally the British attitudes towards environment/conservation issues, and they provided the Secretary of State with an information base to take with him to the June conference. However, the Conservative Government's response to the conference was double edged. One report stated that: 'Her Majesty's Government accepts the paramount need to join with other nations so that together, we may more wisely manage our world environment, and especially the great common estates of the air and the ocean. Without worldwide collaboration, we know that all our efforts in the end will avail nothing.' Meanwhile in the same report it was stated that: 'The UK believes that many cases of environmental management and pollution control are best left to national governments to deal with in the light of their historic, geographic and economic circumstances.'[28]

This ambiguous response was attacked by the opposition parties as a sign of the government's unwillingness to enter into a programme of international action and co-operation to protect the global environment.[29] Certainly the British government was critical of many of the twenty-six Stockholm resolutions on the grounds that they were 'too political' and therefore did not lend themselves to international action.[30]

International conferences, increasingly with an environmental emphasis, punctuated the 1970s, and each presented new insights into the global ecosystem and laid down new challenges to UK politics. A series of UN conferences on population, world food, human settlement, water, tropical rainforests and new and renewable energy, plus smaller-scale, conferences continually forced the UK government and the various political parties to evaluate their own positions on these issues, whilst seeking politically neutral solutions. In 1980, the World Conservation Strategy attempted to co-ordinate all of these issues in a programme of international conservation action based upon the concept of 'sustainable development'. Yet this too shied away from prescribing the political and economic changes necessary for achieving the goals it set out.[31] Yet in retrospect, whatever the failures of these international programmes, the growing global approach continued to influence the UK's political handling of environmental issues in an indirect, if not a direct, way.

A changing political approach

Growing national and international interest in environmental issues influenced the ways in which ideas are formulated and expressed, policy is approached, and party politics are practised. How issues are handled in politics is a function of the political culture, the views of the individuals involved and the nature of the issue in question. The new concept of 'environment' had to fit into a system which was used to dealing with a standard set of issues around which it could readily draw boundaries. Politicians understand these boundaries and they largely work within them. Certainly, issues will always arise which can be handled in line with a characteristic 'crisis–response' approach. The 1956 Clean Air Act, set up in response to the infamous London smogs, is a good example. Yet such was the growth in public interest in the environment and the 'quality of life' in the 1970s, that this *ad hoc*, responsive approach began to be called into question.

Political response to environmental concerns was rapid in the early 1970s. This was particularly the case in the field of pollution control, where within a five-year period from 1970 to 1975 some fifteen separate pieces of primary and secondary leglislation were passed. The rapidity of reaction can perhaps be seen to be indicative of the novelty value of the pollution issue at the time. Moreover, enforcement procedures laid down in the field of pollution control and other areas tended to follow the British pattern of being voluntary, discretionary and 'practicable'.

On the other hand, moves such as the formation of a permanent Standing Royal Commission on Environmental Pollution and the political commitment evident in the creation of the new 'super' DOE and the Central Directorate of Environmental Pollution within it, can be seen as indicating the beginnings of a deeper, more long-term policy approach toward the environment. Initially, however, despite the establishment of an administrative framework, the style of investigation and policy formulation followed trends laid down in the 1960s. The trend toward centralisation in environmental decision making, the emphasis on good environmental 'management' and 'technological-fixes' were to provide the key solutions to environmental problems.

Throughout the seventies, prominence was also given to the development of a scientific base for environmental policy. All the major parties supported and encouraged this development. However, 'pure' technological solutions were soon seen as inadequate in themselves, and increasingly environmental problems were recognised as having a socio-economic dimension in terms of both cause and remedy. This realisation mirrored an overall shift in understanding amongst protest groups and organisations with environmental interests. Within the OECD, for instance, the Environment Committee restructured its programme in 1975 and began to look at energy, industry and the city, rather than just at water management and air pollution.[32] In the UK, the party political approach to environmental issues changed in the years following the 1973 oil crisis, and widened its horizons to move away from an orientation toward pollution control to take in more issues based on social problems. In its Statement to Conference in October 1978, Labour's National Executive Committee (NEC) exemplified how far political perceptions of the environment had changed. It began:

Our purpose in this Statement is to set out the basis of a new approach to the problems of the environment – an approach which will not only be relevant for today, but for the eighties and beyond. We are concerned here not merely with the prevention of pollution and the protection of our cities and country-side from spoliation – important though these are. For the problem of the environment goes far wider than issues of this kind: it concerns the very values and priorities which determine the nature of our society.[33]

Politicians were drawn into a more interdisciplinary mode of discourse, and began to see environmental problems as generic rather than isolated. Nevertheless, throughout the 1970s environmental policy was largely made to fit into the traditional sectoral pattern of the political agenda. Election manifestos contained tightly defined sections on the environment, with no mention of the term in any of the other sections. The dilatory manner in which environmental legislation was implemented accentuated this fragmentation of policy, as did the administrative structures. Although the DOE went some way toward intergrating policy areas, it still remained in relative competition with other departments with different objectives, and the lack of departmental co-operation and co-ordination is still the case.

Pro-environmental public opinion levelled off after 1973, and the response of the politicians altered from one of rapid reaction to events to one that was more cautious. Environmental policy formulation was drawn into the wider developments of public consultation within the established planning framework. The socio-economic implications of environmental issues, on a national and local scale, were aired through new arrangements, such as commissions of inquiry and public hearings. Furthermore politicians, in their rhetoric at least, increasingly turned their attentions to future possibilities rather than current problems. A 1978 Cabinet paper entitled 'Future World Trends' focused upon Britain's future capacity to obtain imported food and materials from the rest of the world.[34] In the same paper, however, it was emphasised that Labour's policies should be re-shaped toward the prevention of those future disasters linked with increasing global industrialisation, rather than mere post-event response. However, the traditional pragmatic approach which deals with environmental problems when they have occurred, remained dominant. The style of implementing legislation and the form and remit of administrative arrangements tended to reinforce this approach.

Changes in the British political experience have occurred through both global and local pressures, and have in turn influenced events both at the local and the global level. Emphasis quite rightly has been placed upon government and its role as the formal respondent to the environmentalist challenge. Yet in a democratic party system where legislative power and influence are constantly competed for, the positions of the other parties are also of relevance. In parallel to its growth in wider society, environmentalism established a significant political base in the UK in the 1970s. We now need to identify the changes that have taken place since 1982.

Changing to green, 1982–91

The developments outlined above essentially took place outside the internal dynamics of the British party system. The creation of administrative structures, the extension of existing remits, and the enactment of legislation, all with an environmental target, were processes occurring outside the UK's key political workings. The way party politics conducts itself, government/party relations and their expression, and the contesting of elections at local and national level proceeded in its established manner, the emergence of the environmental motif acting rather like a series of overlays, trying to fit itself upon an established landscape. In this way, environmental issues and the body of environmentalist pressure groups were largely treated as ephemeral irritants by both government and opposition, acted upon through political expediency, but otherwise seen as removed from the conventions and concerns of party politicking. Although each party had developed its own particular environmental policy position, general elections were fought on the established policy fronts of defence, employment, housing and health, and the members and organisational structures of each party were drawn up to do battle over familiar territory.

The 1979 General Election manifestos of the three main political parties nevertheless addressed environmental policy. The Liberal Party in a lengthy manifesto allowed one-and-a-half sides to the 'Conservation of Resources and the Environment', and of the three main parties, gave by far the most comprehensive and enthusiastic coverage of the topic.[35] The Labour Party's manifesto, written by Mr

Callaghan's personal staff at 10, Downing Street, was swiftly imposed upon the party's national machine to minimise conflicts between the rightist leadership and the leftward NEC.[36] The contents reflected the traditional concerns of the Labour Party right, and the section on the environment fell into this frame. Six proposals for environmental action were outlined, including the idea of introducing an annual 'State of the Environment' report to Parliament.

The Conservatives produced a radical political manifesto, sharply breaking tradition with the policies of previous post-war governments. However, amidst the attempt to promote a new wave of self-confidence and self-reliance under a monetarist system, scant attention was paid to 'environment' in the manifesto in any 'radical' sense. Within the eight lines given over to 'Protecting the Environment', the Conservatives emphasised their record of achievements in the environmental field and declared that: 'We shall continue to give these issues a proper priority.'[37] In the event, the Conservative victory at the polls seemed to indicate that eight lines were an adequate reflection of party and public priority at the time of the election.

Mrs Thatcher's first term of office did not see any major changes in the way environmental issues were handled by the political parties. The legacy of the 1978/79 'winter of discontent', a soaring inflation rate, and a disturbing three million peak in the number of the unemployed, determined the agenda for the majority of politicians. The head of the Prime Minister's Policy Unit, John Hoskyn's call for a significant toning down of the environmental voice in planning decisions was, it would seem, justified by both contemporary events and his personal commitment to a radical, unfettered, free-enterprise solution to the deepening economic spiral.[38] Michael Heseltine as Secretary for State for the Environment was committed to streamlining planning controls through the Local Government and Planning Act, particulary in urban areas, so as to stimulate re-generation and avoid further stagnation of the building trade. The Falklands crisis in 1982 helped to direct public attention away from the economic situation, and also moved the agenda even further away from matters environmental.

However, by the time of the 1983 General Election, some major steps had been taken in the environmentalist direction. One, for example, was the important but controversial passing of the Wildlife and Countryside Act in 1981 discussed earlier. Another was the announcement by Tom King, then Minister at the DOE, in May 1981, that the government sought to reduce the amount of lead in petrol to 0.15 grams per litre by 1985. This move was not, however, stimulated by any marked change in the government's attitude to environmental issues; rather, it typified the existing way such issues were handled. Mr King's announcement to the House of Commons was primarily a result of a letter to Whitehall chiefs (later leaked to *The Times*) by the senior medical officer at the Department of Health and Social Security, Sir Henry Yellowlees. In his letter, Yellowlees strongly indicated the risks of atmospheric lead pollution to public health, and urged that the 'simplest and quickest' thing the government should do was to reduce or remove the lead content of petrol. The initial decision to reduce the lead content of petrol and not to introduce lead-free petrol *per se* was later seized upon by the well-organised pressure group CLEAR (Campaign for Lead-free Air), established in January 1982.[39] The continued politicisation of the inadequacies of the government's position by CLEAR was aided by publication of the eighth report of the Royal Commission for Environmental Pollution in April 1983.[40] Within one hour of the report's publication and less than two months away from a General Election, Tom King, then Secretary of State for the Environment, promised to seek a European-wide ban on lead in petrol by 1990. The above two occasions can be seen as response events and not part of any structured attempt by the political parties voluntarily to bring environmental issues to the fore. Yet forced or otherwise, these issues became part of the agenda close to the General Election of 1983.

Environmental issues did not feature at all highly in the 1983 General Election campaign. Out of a range of press conferences called by the three main parties throughout May, only the Conservatives focused upon 'The Environment and the Rates'. Attended by the Prime Minister and Tom King, the emphasis at the meeting was almost exclusively on local government spending. However, the environment as an area of policy was once again covered in the manifestos of the main parties, thus indicating a level of internal environmental concern, or at least some understanding that public concern for environmental issues did exist to a politically significant degree.

The Conservative manifesto substantially increased its now established section on environmental policy by incorporating the topics of 'Reviving Britain's cities', 'Public transport', 'Rural policy and animal welfare', 'Controlling pollution' and 'Arts and the heritage', under the heading of 'Improving our environment'.[41] Apart from the pollution control aspect – the core of any party political outline of an environment policy – and public transport (not addressed in 1979), these topics had previously been listed separately in the 1979 manifesto in a way unconnected with the environment. This new approach stemmed from the more comprehensive way the Conservatives defined the environment in their manifesto, as 'a clumsy word for many of the things that make life worth living'. However, given the environment section had significantly expanded, there was no mention of environmental aspects in the rest of the policy proposals, including the sections on energy, farming and fishing.

Influenced by its period out of office and internal leftward pressure, the Labour Party's manifesto for the 1983 General Election contained a well outlined and radical set of environmental policy proposals in relation to the 1979 document.[42] A specific section on 'The environment' proposed amongst other things to: enact a new Wildlife and Countryside Act; implement the outstanding Section II of the 1974 COPA; set a date after which all new cars will be able to use only lead-free petrol, and increase resources for the Countryside Commission and the Nature Conservancy Council. The manifesto broke with tradition in the sense that it addressed the environmental aspect of some of the more conventional sections of policy. The sections on transport, rural areas, 'Leisure for living' and 'Planning for people' all contained some recognition of possible environmental costs and benefits. Most significant, however, were the policy fields of energy and agriculture. In the former there were proposals for increased spending on the development of renewable energy sources, combined heat and power schemes and a programme of energy conservation. Furthermore, following trade union pressure and a perceived loss in public confidence, the Labour Party opted for a definite end to the Conservative Pressurised Water Reactor (PWR) programme and a reassessment of the whole British nuclear programme based on the Advanced Gas-cooled Reactors (AGR). In the area of agricultural policy, the environment was promised 'new priority' by making all agricultural aid and development subject to environmental criteria.

In comparision with the Liberal General Election manifesto of 1979, that of the Alliance in 1983 was rather more limited and vague.[43] Linkages with other policy areas were made under an environment heading particularly with the areas of transport, land use, animal welfare, farming and conservation; the need to extend pollution legislation was also emphasised. In other policy areas environmental considerations were given little or no room, apart from the energy sector, which promised to invest in renewable energy sources and to research into the disposal of nuclear waste. The Alliance manifesto stated its opposition to the PWR programme, but did not address the future of the AGRs.

The comparative blandness of the Alliance's environmental policy position had two main causes. The first related to the structural composition of General Election manifestos and affects all the main parties in more or less the same way. A limited amount of space is made available for a party to get its particular ideas and programme across. In the case of the Alliance – a newly created party seeking a radical approach to the way politics is conducted – much of the manifesto was given over to trying to establish an identity with the voters by spelling out the more fundamental policy proposals. Secondly and more specifically, the shallowness of the environment section was a function of the SDP's control over the content. The manifesto itself was hurriedly written by the SDP's Chris Smallwood and quickly rushed through in order that it should be the first manifesto out. This rush was uncharacteristic of the Liberals (although it was supported by David Steel at the time), and at the revising of the first draft many Liberals called for stronger sections on the environment, agriculture and minority rights. When the manifesto was published on 12 May 1983, Liberal members of the party's Standing Committee expressed their discontent that the manifesto was too much an SDP platform.

In the context of the overall political climate at the 1983 General Election, and given the 'tradition' factor in the way party politics is carried out, the environment as a focus for concern fared extremely well at the manifesto stage in comparision to 1979. With the Alliance searching for electoral credibility, the Labour Party entering a major period of introspection both sides of the election, and the Conservatives seeking to develop their concept of long- term governance, policy as a whole seemed to play second fiddle to party profile. Real evidence of environmental concern within the parties, expressed through actions to colour-in the outlines of the manifesto rhetoric, were in short supply. Environmental issues were now firmly established within party agendas, despite intense political distractions.

Yet from the position of the environmentalist, political concern for the environment was nothing more than 'token' decoration, there to look good, but achieving little.

The four-year period from the General Election of June 1983 to that of June 1987 saw a number of changes in the way environmental issues were handled by the main political parties, the way environmental policy was formulated, and the way environmentalism as a concept was understood in political terms.[44] It is within this specific period that the phenomena referred to as the 'greening of British politics' can be said to have taken place, although this period cannot be seen in isolation from what came before and after it.

Apart from the 1985 Wildlife and Countryside Amendment Act, introduced by Dr David Clark MP, Labour's Environment Spokesman, which closed gaps left by the 1981 Act, and the 1986 Agriculture Act which established Environmentally Sensitive Areas, Mrs Thatcher's second term saw little significant environmental legislation. However, the period did see a dramatic increase in party political rhetoric centred on the environment. Attention was paid to environmental issues in speeches by leading party figures and spokesmen. Articles declaring new environmental priorities and ideas appeared within a wide range of journals and periodicals from *Marxism Today* to *Woman's Realm*, by a seemingly new breed of 'earth caring' politicians. The media who had consistently reported environmental events and environmentalist concerns for over fifteen years found themselves in the position of reporting the reactions and concerns of the political parties to environmental questions. Words and phrases such as 'green growth', 'sustainability' and 'ecologically-based community regeneration' entered political circles, and references to Schumacher by the major parties reached a new height.

Conference debates, whilst often being an opportunity to express rhetoric rather than real commitment to an issue, do provide a guide to party feeling. The very fact that an issue is placed on what is usually a busy conference agenda reflects the status of that issue at the time. As with the development of election manifestos, the environment as an area of policy became established at annual party conferences in this 1983 to 1987 period. Although the Liberal Party had debated environmental issues at their conferences as early as 1971, the Labour Party and the Conservatives had seldom touched upon such 'minority' interests. In 1983 the Labour Party Conference addressed twenty-five environmentally-related resolutions. Given this was out of a total of 560, it nevertheless represented nearly twenty-five more than were held up at the previous conference. By the 1986 Labour Conference the number of anti-nuclear resolutions alone totalled 194. A precedent was also set at the 1984 Conservative Conference with a debate held on 'Conserving the environment' at which Environment Minister William Waldegrave confidently asserted that: 'Rallying the Conservative Party to the cause of conservation ought to be like putting down a motion at the Society for the Advancement of Arithmetic urging the leadership to reaffirm that two plus two equals four.'[45]

The 1983 to 1987 period also saw the publication of a series of policy documents and discussion papers by the main parties taking the environment as their theme. This contributed to the development of each party's position on the environment and was the most conspicuous indication of a new focus of political attention. The authors involved in this process of pamphleteering included constituency party activists, back bench MPs and some party leaders. Although the views expressed by some of the authors were not always in line with contemporary party policy, they generally contained non-controversial ideas. As such, they were generally well received within their respective party ranks, and they helped to disseminate environmental ideas both inside and outside the parties.

Three features distinguished the rhetoric of this period. Firstly, there was emphasis upon integrating environmental policies with other policy areas. This broke with the pre-1983 perspective of seeing environmental problems as single issues, and was directed to establishing an agenda for the environment rather than leaving it as an add-on policy consideration. Neil Kinnock, in the preparation of the 1985 Labour 'Charter for the Environment', indicated that the party was: 'quite deliberately placing our environment policies in the context of our major economic campaign'.[46] Similarly William Rodgers, at the launch of the SDP 1985 policy statement 'Conservation and Change', announced that: 'Environmental policy is not an optional extra, but part of the warp and weft of our society.'[47] And William Waldegrave told the 1985 Conservative Party Conference that 'environmental concern isn't an add on, optional extra policy like a sun roof on a new car'.[48]

The idea of attempting to blend an environmental dimension into all areas of party policy entailed the beginnings of a breakdown in a key area of political psychology which held that environmental policy was essentially antagonistic toward a process of economic growth. This idea overlaps with a second feature of this spate of rhetoric, which was that of incorporating selected environmental innovations into party policy. The three main parties employed the term 'green growth' and began to discuss conducting environmental audits, producing annual 'state of the environment' reports and either altering the existing remit of the DOE or creating a new ministry in order that it be more responsive to environmental issues. A third feature was that the parties appeared to adopt environmental agendas which were proactive rather than reactive, with an emphasis on environmental protection. Party activists pushed for a new policy style that included increased provision for environmental improvement and anticipatory planning. By the time the General Election was announced in May 1987 the 'greening' process had led the main parties into unprecedented environmental policy positions. Yet these were not articulated to any significant degree during the General Election campaign by any of the major parties. Indeed, in terms of coverage in the 1987 party manifestos, environmental issues did not fare well in comparision with 1983, taking into account the interest shown particularly since 1985.

Both the 1987 Labour Party and SDP Liberal Alliance manifestos contained statements on future environmental action, yet these were somewhat diluted and did not seem to reflect the discussions that had been held previously.[49] The Conservative manifesto was a two-part publication.[50] The first part, cosily entitled 'Our first eight years', listed the achievements of the Conservative administrations since 1979 and contained a separate section on 'Protecting the environment'. The only substantive achievements of the second administration listed were the establishment of Her Majesty's Inspectorate of Pollution, and a £600 million programme to cut sulphur emissions from power stations. The manifesto proper, 'The Next Moves Forward', contained a section on 'Planning and the environment', but this also did not seem to match up to the some of the environmental debates that had previously been held by some Conservatives. So although covered in the main party manifestos, the environment was not accorded priority, and the optimism of many environmental groups prior to the election was soon lost as the major issues of the economy and defence dominated the hustings once again.

The advent of Mrs Thatcher's third term heralded a lull in party political interest in the environment. The 1987 party conferences were generally quiet with regard to the environment, although Neil Kinnock made reference to the importance of the environment in his conference speech for the first time as party leader. Debates on the environment were held, but other more pressing party issues dominated proceedings.

With the Labour Party undertaking its own post-mortem regarding its third successive General Election defeat, and the Liberal/SDP Alliance crumbling under the strain of its highly unsuccessful attempt to break the mould of British party politics, it was not surprising that environmental thinking took a back seat. The Conservative Government did nothing to advance the environmental cause, and through a cabinet reshuffle added to the inactivity by removing the respected and effective Environment Minister, William Waldegrave, and replacing him with junior ministers from the House of Lords.[51]

However, the post-electoral quiescence in UK environmental politics was broken abruptly with Mrs Thatcher's speeches to the Royal Society in September 1988 and to the party conference in the following month when she suddenly declared the Conservatives to be green.[52] These largely unexpected announcements meant that the environment was led rapidly back into a political ascendancy, and thus began a late mid-term phase of environmental interest.

This renewed interest was exhibited in four main ways. Firstly, Mrs Thatcher displayed an apparent willingness continually to speak out for an area of policy which she had previously shown little interest in. Secondly, the Environmental Protection Bill was introduced, which was intended to provide a comprehensive framework to address a range of matters including waste disposal, pollution control and nature conservation. Thirdly, the government White Paper 'This Common Inheritance' was published, which is the most comprehensive attempt yet to develop a national environmental policy.[53] Fourthly, both the Labour Party and the Liberal Democrats produced major environmental policy documents in the wake of the White Paper respectively entitled 'An Earthly Chance' and 'What Price our Planet?'[54]

Mrs Thatcher's departure and the election of John Major as Prime Minister with no apparent interest in environmental matters, together with the crisis in the Middle East, has brought a period of uncertainty for UK environmental politics. Yet it would seem fair to suggest that political interest in the environment is merely temporarily obscured by wider issues. Indeed, the courses of the major political parties have been fixed by major statements of policy which reflect a higher level of political interest than ever before.

The political developments throughout the 1980s as outlined above have seen the environment move from the margins of party politics to mainstream party thinking. The former passive and negative attitudes of the major parties toward the environment have been transformed into active and positive attitudes. The environmental rhetoric of the main parties is now well developed, and policy positions have increased both in number and sophistication. This is the 'greening' of British party politics; a process which has at its root the relationship between the environmental movement and the major political parties. It is this relationship which is at the heart of this book. As a starting point to examining this relationship, we must first come to terms with the complex and dynamic nature of the environmental movement. The next chapter looks at the beliefs and structure of environmentalism as an increasingly potent social movement in the UK.

Notes and references

1   Liberal Party. 1923. 'Liberal General Election Manifesto – A Call to the Nation' in *Pamphlets and Leaflets for 1923*. London: Liberal Publication Department.

2   Programme of the Labour Party. 1937. *For Socialism and Peace*. The Labour Party. This document includes many environmentally orientated policies, although the word 'environment' is nowhere to be seen.

3   See Lowe, P./Goyder, J. 1983. *Environmental Groups in Politics*. Resource Management Series. London: Allen and Unwin. Because of the emphasis given to the pressure groups, one is perhaps led to the conclusion that government and the political parties care nothing at all for the environment and would do nothing about it independently of the environmental movement.

4   See: Macrory, R. 1986. *Environmental Policy in Britain: Reaffirmation or Reform?* International Institute for Environment and Society. IIUG. dp 86–4. Berlin.

5   For a good account of the public health theme in the early environmental movement see: Cassell, E. J. 1971. 'Nineteenth and Twentieth Century Environmental Movements.' *Archives of Environmental Health*, 22. Jan. 35–40.

6   Quoted in: Ashworth, W. 1954. *The Genesis of Modern British Town Planning*. London: Routledge and Kegan Paul. Chadwick's analysis of the conditions of urban areas in Victorian England and the work of other health

philanthropists, such as Farr and Simon, can be seen as early pioneering attempts to address the interface between environmental conditions and the development of the human condition.

7   See for instance: Brookes, S. K./Richardson, J. J. 1975. 'The Environmental Lobby in Britain.' *Parliamentary Affairs*, 28, 312–28 and note 3, *op. cit.*

8   Brookes, S. K. *et al*. 1976. 'The Growth of the Environment as a Political Issue in Britain.' *British Journal of Political Science*, 6. 245–55. The authors are quite specific in highlighting 1972 as the climax of British media interest in the environment, irrespective of the data limitations in their investigations. Also McHugh, P. R. 1984. 'Changing Environmental Awareness in the Light of Two Distinctive Analyses of *The Times*.' Newcastle Polytechnic, in an unpublished dissertation, followed the pattern of content analysis used by Brookes and Richardson and showed that media coverage of environmental issues steadily declined until 1982 when coverage dropped dramatically to 35 per cent less than that of 1973.

9   See Lowe, P./Morrison, D. 1984. 'Bad News or Good News: Environmental Politics and the Mass Media.' *Sociological Review*, 32. 75–90.

10   Anthony, R. 1982. 'Polls, Pollution and Politics: Trends in Public Opinion on the Environment.' *Environment*, 24, No. 4. May. 14–20, 33–4.

11   See for instance: Kimber, R./Richardson, J. J. (Eds.) 1974. *Campaigning for the Environment*. London: Routledge and Kegan Paul; Wootton, G. 1978. *Pressure Politics in Contemporary Britain*. Massachusetts: Lexington Books.

12   Note 3 *op. cit.*

13   Taken from the White Paper, *The Reorganisation of Central Government*, 15 October 1970, Cmnd 4506. Section 31 of this document further pointed out: 'There is a need to associate with these functions, responsibility of other major environmental matters: the preservation of amenity, the protection of the coast and countryside, the preservation of historic towns and monuments, and the control of air, water and noise pollution – all of which must be pursued locally, regionally, nationally and in some cases internationally.'

14   Draper, P. 1977. 'Creation of the DOE.' *Civil Service Studies*, 4. London: HMSO.

15   See for instance: Greer, I. 1985. 'Right to be Heard: A Guide to Political Representation and Parliamentary Procedure'. Ian Greer Associates. Private Publication.

16   See accounts by: Englefield, D. (Ed.) 1984. *Commons Select Committees: Catalysts for Progress?* Essex: Longman, and Drewry, G. (Ed.) 1985. *The New Select Committees. A Study of the 1979 Reforms*. Oxford: Clarendon Press.

17   Note 4 *op. cit.*

18   Taken from: Pearce, F. 1986. 'Dirty Water Under the Bridge.' In Goldsmith, E./Hildyard, N. (Eds.) *Green Britain or Industrial Wasteland?* Cambridge: Polity Press.

19   This is expressed by Gilg, A. 1986. 'Environmental Policies in the United Kingdom.' In Park, C. (Ed.) 1986. *Environmental Policies: an Inter-*

national Review. London: Croom Helm. 145–79.

20 Good accounts of the passage of the 1981 Wildlife and Countryside Act are given by: Cox, G./Lowe, P. 1983. 'A Battle Not the War: The Politics of the Wildlife and Countryside Act.' In Gilg, A. (Ed.) *Countryside Planning Year Book, Vol. 4.* 48–76; Adams, W. M. 1984. *Implementing the Act.* London: The British Association of Nature Conservation and World Wildlife Fund.

21 The environmental legislation of this period is discussed in detail by: Hughes, D. 1986. *Environmental Law.* London: Butterworths.

22 Taken from Haigh, N. 1987. *EEC Environmental Policy and Britain. Handbook.* (2nd Ed.) London: Longman.

23 Outlined in Ellington, A./Burke, T. 1981. *Europe: Environment, The European Community's Environmental Policy.* London: Ecobooks.

24 Note 22 *op. cit.* for a comprehensive itinerary of EC environmental directives.

25 The 1970s saw an exponential growth in the number of nations with authoritative institutions involved with environmental managment from 15 in 1970 to 115 in 1980. Quoted in Sandbrook, R. 1984. 'Opening the Environmental Debate.' In Wilson, D. (Ed.) *The Environmental Crisis.* Chap. 2. London: Heinemann Educational Books.

26 An extensive number of writers emphasise the links between global environmental degradation and human misery. Of these, one of the most powerful remains Eckholm, E. P. 1982. *Down to Earth: Environment and Human Needs.* London: Pluto Press.

27 Department of Environment. 1972. *Human Habitat. 'How Do You Want to Live?'* HMSO; Department of Environment. 1972. *Organisations and Youth. '50 Million Volunteers.'* HMSO; Department of Environment. 1972. *Natural Resources. 'Sinews for survival.'* HMSO; Department of Environment. 1972. *Pollution: Nuisance or Nemesis?* HMSO.

28 Taken from: Department of Environment. 1972. *The Human Environment: The British View.* HMSO.

29 See Hansard, 14.6.72 and 5.7.72. House of Commons.

30 Comments made in: United Nations. 1975. *Yearbook of the United Nations.* New York: The Office of Public Information.

31 A criticism strongly put over by Redclift, M. 1984. *Development and the Environmental Crisis.* London: Methuen.

32 These changes are documented in OECD, 1975. Activities of OECD in 1975. Report by the Secretary General. OECD.

33 Labour Party. 1978. *Labour and the Environment.* Statement to Annual Conference. The Labour Party.

34 Department of Environment. 1978. *Future World Trends.* Cabinet Paper.

35 Liberal Party. 1979. General Election Manifesto. The Liberal Party.

36 Labour Party. 1979. *The Labour Way is the Better Way.* Manifesto. The Labour Party.

37 Conservative Party. 1979. *The Conservative Manifesto.* The Conservative Party.

38 In July of 1979, a few weeks only after the Conservative election

victory, John Hoskyns, then the head of Mrs Thatcher's Policy Unit, had urged the government to reduce its 'oversensitivity to environmental considerations' in planning matters. Taken from: Paterson, T. 1984. 'Why True Blues must go Green'. *The Times*, 6 October.

39   A first-hand account of the politicisation of the 'lead in petrol' issue is given in Wilson, D. 1984. *Pressure: The A to Z of Campaigning in Britain*. London: Heinemann.

40   Royal Commission on Environmental Pollution. 1983. *Lead in the Environment*. 9th Report. Cmnd 8852. London: HMSO.

41   Conservative Party. 1983. *The Challenge of Our Times*. Manifesto. The Conservative Party.

42   Labour Party. 1983. *The New Hope for Britain*. Manifesto. The Labour Party.

43   SDP/Liberal Alliance. 1983. *Working Together for Britain*. Manifesto. SDP/Liberal Alliance.

44   Owens, S. 1986. 'Environmental Politics in Britain: New Paradigm or Placebo?' *Area*, 18(3), September, highlights that within these years 'environmental consciousness' in British politics was raised to a new threshold.

45   Waldegrave, W. 1984. Conservative Party Conference speech.

46   Labour Party. 1985. *Labour's Charter for the Environment*. The Labour Party. Walworth Road. London. This was part of Labour's 'Jobs and Industry' campaign. See Kinnock, N. 1985. 'Turning over a New Leaf'. *New Ground*, No. 5. 4–5.

47   SDP. 1985. *Conservation and Change. Policy for the Environment*. July. The Social Democratic Party.

48   Waldegrave, W. 1985. Conservative Party Conference speech.

49   Labour Party. 1987. *Britain Will Win*. Manifesto. The Labour Party. SDP/Liberal Alliance. 1987. *Britain United: The Time has Come*. Manifesto. SDP/Liberal Alliance.

50   Conservative Party. 1987. *The First Eight Years/The Next Moves Forward*. Manifesto. The Conservative Party.

51   Waldegrave was replaced by Lord Belstead who was in turn replaced by the Earl of Caithness.

52   Thatcher, M. 1988. Speech given at a Royal Society Dinner. Tuesday 27 September and Speech to Conservative Party Conference. October.

53   The Conservative Government. 1990. *This Common Inheritance*. White Paper. Cmnd 1200. London: HMSO.

54   Labour Party. 1990. *An Earthly Chance*. The Labour Party; Liberal Democrats. 1990. *What Price our Planet? – A Liberal Democrat Agenda for Environmental Action*. The Liberal Democrats.

2

The changing face of the environmental movement

Environmentalism is far more than a series of unconnected actions and events based upon shallow opinions and ephemeral ideas. It is widely understood as a social movement with a long history and a political edge.[1] As a social movement concerned with shaping the patterns and direction of social change, environmentalism possesses an informing and dynamic ideology and an organisational make-up that exhibits variety. It is international in character and constituency, it has an increasingly huge following, and its impact upon societies in both the developed and developing world is only beginning to materialise. Such a vast and important movement which critically examines social, economic and moral norms and challenges them on a local and global scale has inevitably begun to make its mark on the world's political systems.

Before we can discuss the impact of the UK environmental movement on the UK's polity, we need to understand the beliefs and organisation behind the challenge that the environmental movement is making.

Beliefs: an ideological cocktail

The ideology the environmental movement holds and manipulates, the line of thinking that gives the movement identity, status and purpose is a subjective phenomenon: subjective in the sense that it resides in the very consciousness of the movement itself and does not rely upon appeals to objective and logical analysis. To look for some complete objective framework for this ideology is to miss the point: the environmental movement's primary aim is to change society, not to study it.

It would be hard to assess the 'originality' of individual belief components present within the ideology of environmentalism. The constituent ideas and beliefs can be traced as far back in history as one would care to go. Central environmentalist assumptions, such as the 'interdependence of life', may have been empirically resolved via contemporary ecological science. However, what may be termed the 'ideological roots' of such a concept were discussed in pre-Socratic Greece.[2]

Analyses of the origins of environmentalist beliefs have been carried out in attempts to understand contemporary positions.[3] By and large, these have been piecemeal and selective. This is hardly surprising when one considers the breadth of influences that have been available. Indeed, historical investigations of environmentalism leave many gaps and offer intellectual 'green-field sites' for multi-disciplinary studies.

It is the history of environmental ideology, with its diverse background of ideas and beliefs, which has encouraged the eclecticism of the present environmental movement.[4] Environmentalist rhetoric has drawn inspiration from such diverse ideological wells as Christian, Buddhist, Hindu, Taoist and Pagan religious belief systems, Anarchist, Marxist and Conservative political ideologies, the critical rationalist tradition in science from ecology to quantum physics, and the romantic reactions to post-Enlightenment social changes from Keats to Kerouac. Some environmentalists have found no problem in bastardising old ideologies in order to support or develop their message, justifying present-day actions by philosophies such as romanticism, socialism, Taoism, Buddhism, North American animism and Christianity.[5]

Epistemological problems in differentiating such a diffuse range of beliefs seem to be deliberately overlooked in order to emphasise some unity of purpose toward a 'better' environment. As one self-styled 'Pagan Ecologist' put it: 'Different paths suit different people, but they all meet on the same mountain top.'[6]

The eclectic element of the environmental movement's ideology gives it a marked degree of flexibility, undermining possible criticisms that it is too exclusive. Principles of action are given increased scope and support by being able to draw on a variety of worldviews. Eclecticism in environmentalism extols the virtue of choice and guards against over-specialisation and elitism. Source beliefs are treated in instrumentalist terms, used to support actions and positions in the here-and-now, and there is a strong feeling that no 'single' belief system is solely right nor wholly adequate to achieve the variety of goals sought by the environmental movement.

Ideologies are notoriously fraught with problems of categorisation and remain constantly contentious.[7] Eclecticism, whilst giving the environmental movement choice, does cause problems of incoherence. With such a variety of influences, it is sometimes difficult to identify what the movement stands for, yet, adherents seem to prefer the wisdom of many influences to the narrowness of just one philosophy.

The ideology of the environmental movement is also imaginative. The philosophical basis of deterministic, neo-Malthusian rhetoric, prevalent in the environmental movement of the late 1960s and early 1970s, has become described as 'escapist, defensive and socially regressive'.[8] Yet the negativity of the environmental movement's ideology at this time, as illustrated in the propensity of doomsday merchandising, was largely because no alternative system of beliefs had been developed and future directions had not been mapped out.

New directions for change have been established by the environmental movement through creativity and intellectual ingenuity, stimulated by courage and dedication. Existing ideologies, ingrained in contemporary culture, have been questioned for their relevance to a society increasingly awake to global environmental problems. Some elements of the environmental movement have called for revolutionary shifts in the traditional beliefs of western society, but the majority have sought a more traditional path, whereby old beliefs are not rejected outright but are re-examined and adapted to fit a changing society.[9] This creative component of the environmental movement has enhanced its credibility, drawing it away from the empty realms of reactionism and 'false consciousness'.[10] This change from enthusiasm to realism, based upon a developing environmentalist critique, is not a tidy, readily accessible or unanimous declaration of beliefs and values, but rather it manifests itself through social action and political engagement.[11]

A further feature of environmentalist ideology has been its increasing relevance to society. It exists as an intellectual reservoir, enabling people to draw upon it for support, inspiration and explanation, lending them reasons for action in times of drought. Relevance has evolved within a wider framework of social change as 'new' beliefs have provided 'new' directions in an age of accelerated socio-economic transition. Porritt has pointed out that, what is seen to be 'new' may merely be 'the rediscovery of old wisdom made relevant in a very different age' as old belief systems are attacked as being anachronistic and increasingly inappropriate.[12]

The ideology of environmentalism provides a basis for alternative actions, and although its exact nature may be difficult to capture, its relevance is borne out by the very existence of what O'Riordan has termed the 'fourth environmental revolution'.[13] Although the term 'revolution' is misleading, the reservoir of environmentalist ideas, fed from its vast network of historical and cultural tributaries, seems to be feeding an increasing number of people in a rapidly changing society.

Organisation; an expanding coalition of groups

A social movement should possess a 'minimal degree of organisation'.[14] What this 'degree' should be is not clear, but it seems inevitable that it ranges between the extremes of a sophisticated bureaucracy of well-organised groups and the informal activities of individuals. Variation in the organisational structure of environmentalism is predominant a function of the eclectic and hence diverse nature of the ideologies embraced. Variations in assumptions, values, goals and principles for action manifest themselves in the structure and tactics employed by the environmental movement.

The environmental movement can be seen to consist of two interrelated sections.[15] The first, the environmental groups, are what Lowe and Goyder term 'the organisational embodiment of the movement'. These are akin to Weber's 'closed' groups, identifiable by concise core beliefs and particular principles of action.[16] The second section of the environmental movement is termed by Lowe and Goyder 'the attentive public' and corresponds to Weber's 'open' groups. Although they may not be held together by any sense of communal purpose and ideology, they still participate in and share the ideologies of the formal groups at given times and for given issues. Put another way, one does not have to be a member of Friends of the Earth (FoE) or the Council for the Protection of Rural England (CPRE) to be an environmentalist. But in seeking an answer to the question 'who are the environmentalists?', it would seem easier to identify members of organised groups than to ascribe any accurate magnitude to the 'attentive public'.

The organisational core of the environmental movement is characterised by groups such as Friends of the Earth and the National
Trust. But between such obvious environmental groups (and even
within the groups themselves, as between national and local level) lie
marked differences in organisational style and effectiveness in the
socio-political forum. In the literature such groups are usually discussed as pressure, interest or lobbying groups. Here we shall use the
term 'pressure group', firstly because it has an established place in
political science literature (even though the politicians and press may
attach a negative value to it), and secondly because it implies the
necessary attribute of 'pushing' against the institutions of government. Moran provides a workable and relatively uncomplicated
definition of a pressure group as being 'any group which tries to
influence public policy without seeking the responsibility of government'.[17]

The classification of pressure groups has attempted to reveal
differences in their structure, aims and strategies, and activity has
'become a veritable cottage industry among political scientists'.[18]
Jordan and Richardson observe the necessary caution involved in
classifying groups, but highlight perhaps the most basic and effective
axis of classification, distinguishing 'sectional' interest groups and
'promotional' cause groups.[19] Sectional groups seek to 'protect' and
advance the interests of their members by acting as spokesmen and
negotiators for relatively clearly defined sections of the social and
economic structure. In this category would fall business interests or
members of a trade union. Such groups tend to be defensive and are
drawn into the activities of government institutions by virtue of their
interests which tend to be primarily economically bound. Promotional groups, on the other hand, are those groups which seek to
advance or defend particular causes and principles which are
reflected in, and shared by, the wider but less clearly defined
membership.

Dividing pressure groups up on the basis of group aims is not, as
one might expect, a clear-cut task. It raises questions such as: what is
an interest, what is a point of principle and how can the two be
separated, particularly if the former is shrouded in the rhetoric of the
latter? Jordan and Richardson help to clarify matters by developing
Grant's categorisation of groups by virtue of the strategies they
adopt as well as their aims.[20] Group strategies are divided as being
either 'insider' or 'outsider'. The term 'insider' refers to those which

act, or seek to act, 'responsibly' toward government. The 'responsible' activities adopted by the groups may culminate in their being regularly consulted by government on appropriate issues, or at the very least recognised as being 'approachable'. Some environmental groups, such as the Ancient Monuments Society, the Georgian Group and the Victorian Society have developed insider status to the point where they have to be consulted as a matter of statute by the local planning authorities before a listed building is altered or demolished.[21] A group with 'outsider' status may have deliberately chosen to keep its distance from government as a matter of principle, while other groups may aspire to insider status but lack the resources to develop such a role. However, the most likely reason for a group having outsider or insider status derives from the attitudes of government institutions themselves. Government attitudes may derive from a single key individual, civil servant or minister, whose core beliefs may face in precisely the opposite direction to those perceived to be held by a group.

Certain groups can be classified more readily than others as either insiders of outsiders. Greenpeace, for instance, is an environmental group which has deliberately sought to promote the environmentalist cause via outsider, high-media profile tactics.[22] In contrast, the Green Alliance is a low-profile insider group, working within the 'establishment' which seeks to set political agendas favourable to the environment. The strategy of FoE, however, has developed with ambiguity, and whilst maintaining a distance between themselves and government, FoE has accepted invitations to sit on departmental advisory committees.[23] Variations in FoE tactics make it difficult to categorise the group as either outsiders or insiders. Jordan and Richardson suggest a mediating 'threshold' classification to account for the activities of groups such as FoE. Figure 1 illustrates this categorisation of pressure groups on the basis of both aims and methods using environmentally related groups as examples.

The majority of core groups of the environmental movement can be described as promotional, although exceptions do exist. Many local groups, for instance, are motivated by the protection of specific, non-economic interests such the amenity of an area. Even with promotional groups, interests can be keenly defended and alternative values put forward. Lowe and Goyder suggest the existence of two sub-types of promotional group.[24] The first seeks to emphasise and promote existing values: groups such as the Civic Trust and

National Trust which possess aims which do not necessarily conflict with wider social values, but rather attempt to 'fit in' with them. The second type of group actively seeks to change existing social values and to promote new values. Such groups are brought into conflict with government and the dominant social institutions of an industrial society and also with the more conservative environmental groups.

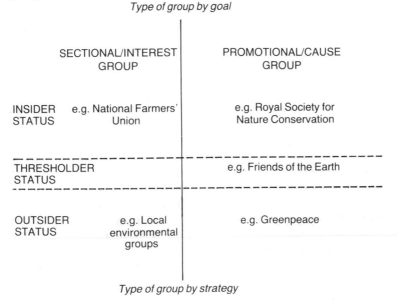

Type of group by goal

SECTIONAL/INTEREST GROUP   PROMOTIONAL/CAUSE GROUP

INSIDER STATUS   e.g. National Farmers' Union   e.g. Royal Society for Nature Conservation

THRESHOLDER STATUS   e.g. Friends of the Earth

OUTSIDER STATUS   e.g. Local environmental groups   e.g. Greenpeace

Type of group by strategy

Fig. 1   Classification of pressure groups using goal-strategy axis

Source: adapted from Jordan and Richardson (1987)

The distinction between promotional groups is basically one between reformists and radicals, although clear-cut divisions are not so apparent in reality. Aims overlap as well as strategies, with a group like FoE prepared to support the preservationist aims of, say, the National Trust in relation to the designation of Heritage Coast. Parallel to differences in the aims of the promotional groups are differences in strategies, the general tendency being that 'emphasis' groups are closer to insider status than those groups promoting more radical changes in social values. However, though possessing insider status may provide access to government, this is not the same as possessing influence. Outsider groups such as Greenpeace believe that hard-hitting publicity stunts can have at least the same level of influence on government policy by means of public pressure as that exerted by insider groups through direct consultations.

Furthermore, promotional groups can change both character and intention over time, relating to the wider developments in the society in which they operate. Three options are open for the development of both reformist and radical types of group. As new values become assimilated into wider society, the *raison d'être* of the more radical environmental groups is lost and they may emerge as defenders of the changes they have brought about. If resistance within society is too strong, or alternative values are not adequately articulated, a more radical group may merely fade away due to lack of success. Finally, a conservative group may revert to actively promoting values rather than emphasising them if circumstances change and those values come under threat.

Because the range of pressure groups occupying the central ground of the environmental movement is so vast, it would seem inevitable that tensions exist between them. This may suggest doubts as to how such a collage of groups can come to be referred to as a single movement. Surely it would be more accurate to see such groups as each pursuing individual objectives founded upon discrete belief systems, and thus reference could be made to, say, the amenity movement or the conservation of wildlife movement. However, although differences in specific aims, emphasis and tactics of the core groups may produce tensions between them, all can be seen to possess coherent ideologies orientated toward a given aspect of the environment. Reformist groups such as the CPRE, or radical groups such as Greenpeace may focus upon a range of environmental issues. Other groups such as the Ramblers' Association can be seen to be to specialise in countryside access issues. But whatever specific concerns may exist, the common denominator of group ideologies is the concept of environmental concern, providing a certain amount of reticulation amongst the groups, particularly when a specific issue is focused upon. 'Trespassing' into another group's territory is welcome if it brings support, and lines of close association, friendship, and social ties can be formed amongst group leaders and members, speakers and organisers, allowing the dissemination of information and the maintenance of informal but effective coalitions.[25]

The concept of the environment can be interpreted in different ways: is it simply a question of aesthetics, or does it involve the development of the human condition? The diversity in environmental perceptions helps to account for variation in the core beliefs of environmental groups and variations in organisation and strategy. Yet despite extremes of interpretation, they are all, as it were, seeing different images of the same object.[26] Whether concerned with protection or improvement, reaction or proaction, each group is motivated by some aspect of the concept of environment; the breadth of the term allows different groups to stress different elements at different times.

Despite conceptual problems, one can consider environmentalism as being a coalition of groups with a singular, intrinsic ideological link. The link may not operate all of the time, but nevertheless it exists. However, it would be misleading to see the environmental movement as merely an amalgamation of *environmental* pressure groups. The terms of reference for the movement are broad enough to encompass cells of other groups whose ideological motivations are not derived from the sole perspective of environmental concern. Thus, a promotional group such as the Royal Society for the Prevention of Cruelty to Animals (RSPCA), established in 1824, may not see itself as an 'environmental' group with its narrow set of core beliefs centred upon its aim of 'seeking to prevent cruelty and promote kindness toward all animals'.[27] But to many environmentalists, the RSPCA is seen to be pursuing aims which are compatible with and arguably integral to general environmental concern.

Promotional groups such as the Automobile Association (AA) can also take an interest in environmental matters but only when group beliefs do not seriously conflict. The concern of the AA with issues such as road construction, siting, and safety means that from time to time they overlap with identifiable environmental groups. At both local and national level, the AA may join with other environmental pressure groups to oppose road construction plans damaging to a local environment, though a coalition may not be possible if the plans go against the primary interests of the AA, which include the provision of good roads and services for members. Furthermore, the AA is concerned with keeping motoring costs at a minimum for its members, a goal which has tempered its contributions to the debates on lead in petrol and the role of NO_x emissions in the formation of acid rain.[28]

The environmental movement also draws support from 'sectional' or 'interest' groups. Trade unions and those groups representing the interests of industry, commerce and professional organisations are in this category. As with the promotional groups, their primary rationale is not environmentally orientated; their core beliefs originated in a 'pre-environmentalist age', and their goals and strategies lie in the opposite direction to those adhered to by the environmentalists. However, the idea of the environmental movement being dramatically opposed to the representatives of industry and business (and, by extrapolation, against the dominant values of the majority of society which they represent) has been both persistent and highly damaging to the credibility of the environmentalists in their attempts to become a coherent movement.

Broadly speaking, groups representing the interests of labour have seen the environmental movement as an adversary, their objectives in environmental protection contradicting policies focusing upon the protection and maximisation of employment.[29] This perception has been accentuated by an accompanying perception of environmentalists as being predominantly drawn from the non-productive middle classes.[30] Furthermore, in the USA at least, pitting environmentalists against workers and consumers has been a deliberate and effective corporate strategy, particularly against the more powerful unions.[31] Reciprocally, however, some environmental groups have tended to portray their relationship with a majority of the trade unions as being based upon seemingly inescapable conflicts of interest. This view has been perpetuated by some of the more radical thinkers in the movement. Porritt, for instance, comments on the role of trade unions (with no distinction made between them) as possessing an 'insistence for propping up the formal economy at all costs and enthusiastically endorsing the philosophy of industrialism which they perceive to be the only way of defending their members' interests'.[32]

Groups representing the interests of capital and industry, from the umbrella organisations such as the Confederation of British Industry (CBI) and the British Institute of Management, to more specific bodies such as the House Builders' Federation, have also seen environmental groups as adversaries. Whilst relatively unconcerned about environmental groups' social constituency, sectional groups representing the interests of capital have expressed concern over the activities of the more radical environmental groups, which they see as undermining central capitalist values which promote the maximisation of profit and the minimisation of cost. Whilst acknowledging growing pressures for environmental controls, groups such as the CBI have resisted moves which seem to threaten central, neo-classical, economic rationalities. A CBI statement on 'British Industry and the Environment' made in 1980 at the peak of economic recession attempted to re-emphasise the central tenets of business ideology in an atmosphere of increasing environmentalist pressure:

The need for sensible environmental control is acknowledged but trade and industry is concerned that some regulations and rights designed to protect the environment are having significant and unforeseen effects resulting in increased industrial and commercial operating costs. In certain circumstances environmental controls which have not been fully thought through can inhibit international trade and can even prevent proposed industrial development taking place or result in existing industrial activity being closed down with adverse effects on the local or national economy.[33]

In the cases of both capital and labour representation, underlying beliefs and motivations of actions seem to leave little room for establishing coalitions with core environmental groups. However, coalitions have been forged, particularly between environmental groups and the trade unions. Historically, more common ground exists between the trade unions and the environmentalists, chiefly on the issues of health and safety, than between environmentalists and the guardians of business and industrial capital. Established themes in trade union policy, such as the health and safety of the workforce, run parallel to environmental concerns, and this has accounted for union sympathy on some environmental issues. Links between the two types of groups may be founded upon a specific issue, where objectives overlap. The 1983 ban on the dumping of nuclear waste by the National Union of Seamen (NUS), aided by ASLEF and the TGWU, showed how unions could respond to the campaigning of environmental groups, in this case chiefly Greenpeace and FoE, on a particular issue.[34] Co-operation on one issue sows a seed for further joint activity on others, perhaps outside the unions' traditional remit.

The potential for voluntary relations between environmentalists and major business groups may be limited, but it seems inevitable that corporate bodies, as participators in problems such as air and water pollution or misplaced land development, will be drawn into the environmental arena. Selective 'voluntary' efforts have been made by interest groups. In March 1987, for instance, the Chemical

Industries Association (CIA) launched the idea of the 'Green Code' with the aim of encouraging environmentally-sound management practices in the UK chemical industry. The objective of the code was to emphasise the responsibility of management within the chemical industry for short- and long-term environmental protection. Whilst the CIA acknowledges the dangers of environmental hazards, it has acted in response to pressure-group campaigning and public opinion. Since environmental concern was definitely not the ideological focus of the CIA when it was established in 1966, the Green Code was set up as part of 'good business practice', in line with the predominant rationale of the group. Here, an influential sectional body appeals not to any one specific environmental group with which it has struck some sort of 'environmental contract', but rather to the public directly.

By taking the environmental movement as a number of organised cause and interest groups, we can consider ideologies. Closed groups can be distinguished by their belief systems and principles of action. Some groups have environmental concern in general as their prime motivation; others have at least one aspect of the concept as their rationale. Other groups have been drawn into the movement as the extensive meaning of 'environment' continues to unfold, while others voluntarily contribute to the movement out of self-interest. Indeed, the idea of an 'identity frame' encounters an impasse when applied to the social movement of environmentalism.[35] It becomes difficult to avoid placing all seemingly pertinent group ideologies into a framework, yet equally unsatisfactory not to leave some out.

At first glance one would not consider groups such as the trade unions or multinational companies as part of the environmental movement. Yet via their pro-environmental activities and coalitions with recognisable environmental groups over specific issues at specific times, and despite their non-environmental ideologies, one can argue that they contribute to the phenomenon of the environmental movement. Like clouds of free electrons and protons within a dynamic of stable and excited states, group ideologies clash and coalesce, expand and contract, merge and emerge within an ever-changing socio-economic and political sphere. The process is not random, although chance may play its part in the coming together of some groups. Ideological selectivity operates, and the boundaries of group beliefs tend to be flexible rather than rigid.

Lowe and Goyder estimated the membership of the 53 national

and local environmental groups they surveyed in 1983 to be approximately three million.[36] Throughout the mid-1980s, the three million figure was often quoted by politicians despite being an underestimate. Membership of environmental groups has continued to grow apace. Table 1 illustrates the growth in membership of seven major voluntary environmental groups in the UK over two decades.

Table 1 *Membership of UK environmental voluntary organisations, 1971–1990*

| | Membership (thousands) | | | |
	1971	1981	1986	1990
Civic Trust*	214	–	241	300
Friends of the Earth (except Scotland)	1	–	28	200
National Trust (excluding Scotland)	278	1046	1417	2031
Ramblers' Association (including N. Ireland)	22	37	53	82
Royal Society for Nature Conservation	64	143	179	212
Royal Society for the Protection of Birds	98	441	506	885
World Wildlife Fund	12	60	106	110

* Figures refer to the aggregate membership of all local amenity societies registered with the Trust.
Source: Social Trends (18) 1988. London: HMSO. Organisations concerned.

That vague sector of society called 'the attentive public' constitutes the bulk of the environmental movement. Robert Peel's portrayal of the public as 'that great compound of folly, weakness, prejudice, wrong feeling, right feeling, obstinacy and newspaper paragraphs' is outmoded in an age of extensive and rapid information flow. The public is now better informed on the range and nature of environmental issues and problems than ever before, which goes some way to explaining the message behind Table 1. But although many people can be conveniently compartmentalised into groups, many more remain as an amorphous mass acting as a potential well of support, and we should consider them part of the social movement. Unlike the members of the formal environmental pressure groups, the attentive public are irregular participants in the movement. Lowe and Goyder indicate the kind of people constituting this mass, and include 'the readership of various environmental magazines, students of environmental studies in schools, colleges and universities, sympathetic members of the design and land-use professions and the many people, who through their personal convictions, behaviour and life-styles, express their concern for the environment'.[37]

Whereas the constituents of the organised environmental groups have been shown to be predominantly white, young and middle-class, the social constituency of informal participants is much broader.[38] Opinion poll data has shown that concern for issues such as pollution and amenity use is shared by a cross-section of social classes.[39] Working-class concern for environmental degradation suggests that working-class people are the ones primarily affected; indeed, it would seem to indicate that they are an underrepresented element of the attentive public. However, as Lowe and Goyder's list suggests, there still may be some ground for seeing environmental concern as a pre-occupation of the better-educated and those in a position to afford environmental magazines. There is simply no satisfactory method for surveying such a dynamic and vast proportion of the population.

Weber's idea of 'open groups', mentioned at the start of this section, gives us perhaps the best way to characterise the environmental movement's informal mass. Essentially this means that, in terms of the informal side of environmentalism, anyone can be an environmentalist; it does not require one to join a group, or hold a definitive environmentalist ideology. The idea of environmentalism as an *organised* social movement hinges on the interpretation of 'organisation'. Certainly, the movement has a central organised formal core, consisting of identifiable but fluctuating groups able to coalesce with other groups in given circumstances. However, part of the social movement idea is that it is deliberately unorganised, decentralised and diffuse in terms of its mass support.[40] The important point is that environmentalism possesses the necessary spread of support from which it can potentially draw *when required*.

Movement within movement: the greens

The 1980s saw sweeping developments in the structure and organisation of the environmental movement. 'Post-material issues' such as feminism, animal rights and peace have long histories, and each can lay claim to social movement status. However, to try and bind these newly expressed beliefs into some cohesive ideology around the central concept of 'environment' was a dramatic innovation. Perhaps more dramatic still was the accompanying politicisation of this eclectic and intrinsically unstable collage of beliefs. Drawing upon the more radical ideas of environmentalism, and overlapping with its radical groups, the 'green' dimension of the environmental movement has emerged. Inglehart's 'silent revolution' in values has become increasingly evident.[41] Partly in reaction to the dominant reformism of the environmental movement, and partly by representing the maturity and integrity of their ideas, the Greens have sought to emphasise personal action as opposed to institutional theory. As one Working Group Convenor of the UK Green Party commented on the reformists of the environmental movement: 'We are growing up through the floorboards while they are gazing through the window.'[42]

The 'greening' of the British political parties, a convenient, media-manufactured phrase, has within it a dual implication. It implies on the one hand something substantive outside the boundaries of the British party political system which is 'green'. On the other hand it implies an active process by which there is interaction between this outside 'green something' and the system itself. The mainstream political parties are not assumed to be green, but rather engage in a process of becoming green to varying degrees. The development of the green component in environmentalism is in a state of flux and this entails difficulties in establishing the true meaning of the term. This is further complicated by its varied and popular use. It is therefore important to establish some base-line of interpretation for the term 'green', so that we can assess its use in the environmental movement and in a party political context.

The colour green has often been used as a derogatory symbol for a state of immaturity and naivety. To say someone is 'green' is to imply that he or she is unaware of the intricacies of a situation owing to his or her youth, status and overall lack of knowledge. Related to this is the antithetical notion of green as being reflective of a refreshing, new and innovative approach to a situation, an approach brought about precisely by one's youth. The colour green is associated with spring-like, fresh feelings of hope and optimism. Parallel to such interpretations has been the metaphorical use of green to promote images of nature. From Blake's moral equation about what is 'green' and what is 'pleasant', to the stark contrasts between the 'brown mud of war' and the green fields of peace employed by Wilfred Owen, the colour has come implicitly to evoke Boucherian images of rural idylls seen to be prevalent in the pre-industrial era: psychological escape from the grey and the black, symbolic of two centuries of industrialisation and urbanisation.[43]

The green label also carries with it a value component which correlates with feelings of goodness and, by implication, right.[44] Even within a largely urban society, pastoralism, rurality and greenery are extolled as being good and in danger of being lost to the soul-destroying forces of industrial progress. That rural harmony was essentially a myth is beside the point. The 'green language' has played a central part in the depiction of many social utopias, and moral indignation is never more apparent than when 'green belt' land is threatened by a new town or retail development.

The metaphorical use of the term 'green' to refer to the new edge of environmentalism has been a calculated choice by those who use it. The self-styled Greens have attempted to cultivate positive images of nature and the moral high ground that goes with it. Furthermore, the colour green acts as a new political symbol, which many Greens would argue is removed from both the traditional red of socialism and the blue of conservatism.

The Greens are frequently seen as constituting a social movement, as though they were separate from the rest of the environmental movement.[45] Perhaps a more appropriate interpretation is to see the Greens as the radical wing of environmentalism, attempting to give their ecocentric ideology political expression. Their attempts to link feminism and peace issues to the environment, for example, can be seen as a reaction to the politically acceptable, technocentric reformism that dominates the environmental movement.

Although the name may be novel, the radical ideological position the Greens have adopted has been an ever-present feature of societal development; it is the romantic reaction to the Enlightenment and the industrial revolution – the call upon nature to amend and atone for man's folly.[46] In the past, however, this reactive force has seldom developed into anything other than an abstract system of ideas, more attractive to poets than politicians. However, a distinctive feature of this 'new' radical edge to environmentalism has been the politicisation of eco-topian ideas through a new politics which does not lie easily with traditional political activity in a democratic system.

Table 2 *Porritt's minimum criteria for 'being green'*

A reverence for the Earth and all its creatures

A willingness to share the world's wealth among *all* its peoples

Prosperity to be achieved through sustainable alternatives to economic growth

Lasting security to be achieved through non-nuclear defence strategies and considerably reduced arms spending

A rejection of materialism and the destructive values of industrialism

A recognition of the rights of future generations in our use of all resources

An emphasis on socially useful, personally rewarding work, enhanced by human scale technology

Protection of the environment as a precondition of a healthy society

An emphasis on personal growth and spiritual development

Respect for the gentler side of human nature

Open, participatory democracy at every level of society

Recognition of the crucial importance of significant reductions in population levels

Harmony between people of every race, colour and creed

A non-nuclear, low-energy strategy, based on conservation, greater efficiency and renewable resources

An emphasis on self-reliance and decentralised communities

Source: Porritt, J. 1984. *Seeing Green – The Politics of Ecology Explained.* Oxford: Basil Blackwell

A green datum

The concept of 'being green' lacks a pure expression or single theoretical basis; it has emerged in the work of various thinkers in a rather jumbled way. In the words of Davy, 'being green' means: 'It is in such a seemingly insignificant activity as this, a walk in the woods, turning over a compost heap, or observing dandelions forcing their way through the cracks in a concrete playground which personally renew my awareness of our close inter-relationship with nature. One which is spiritual as well as physical'.[47] Table 2 gives Porritt's 'minimum criteria for being green'. Although these criteria are Porritt's personal expression of 'green first principles', we can take them as typical of what most Greens believe. Porritt's criteria are by no means exclusive and consist of a mix of ethical statements and specific policy positions, which for Greens correspond closely.

The morality of the Greens is a distinctive element of their guiding philosophy. It is a morality which has emerged with the growth of ecology as a science which, in conjunction other biological concepts, has become implanted in contemporary sociology as a legitimate form of explanation for human/societal relations.[48] However, the Greens have moved away from the technocentrically-based ecology of the 1960s toward a deeper and more spiritual interpretation of central ecological precepts. Symbolic recognition of this came in September 1985, when a motion to change the name of the British Ecology Party to the Green Party was passed at their biennial party conference and annual general meeting by a two-thirds majority. The decision was chiefly based upon the belief that 'ecology' as a scientific name was not comprehensible to the ordinary citizen, and that the Green name would popularise the party. The decision was welcomed by many members who no longer wished to be associated with an scientifically orientated ecology.[49]

At the centre of the Greens' conception of ecology is a description of the earth as a huge ecosystem, akin to Darwin's notion of the 'web of life'. The key idea within this description is that of holism: the belief in interdependence and interrelatedness. Holism goes against the dominant worldview inherited from western Renaissance science and its emphasis on specialisation; paradoxically, contemporary science seems to be increasingly moving toward ideas of 'inter-connectedness'.[50]

The principle of ecological interconnectedness is something more substantial for the Greens than a mere description of the world; it permeates their morality. Ecology informs the Greens that everything is morally relevant, relevance being determined by how far the functioning of the ecosystem is affected by any action. Ecological morality, in the eyes of the Greens, maintains balance, dynamism and diversity within the ecosystem and keeps it whole and complete. In the words of Porritt, it is 'the wisdom of ecology that now begins to re-instruct us about the crucial importance of balance and the holistic interrelatedness of life on Earth'.[51] A belief in social responsibility and a commitment to social justice are rooted in the Greens' acceptance of a morally-bound ecology.[52] A Green Party Working Group Discussion Paper on Social Welfare policy illustrates the driving force of ecological thinking: 'The concept of

"inter-connectedness" in nature with its notion of mutual responsibility transposes into the relationships between individual and state/
community . . . the connections on a larger scale, between individual
well-being and state systems e.g. housing, education and transport
etc.'[53] Ecological thinking is not a prisoner of the abstract for the
Greens, but a practical method of social liberation, and although
there may exist a minority of Greens happy to 'opt out' of society, the
majority seek its basic restructuring.

In this aim, the Greens' position overlaps with that of socialism.
Socialists have been consistently critical of the neglect that environmentalism has shown for basic socio-economic and political relations in society and the concentration of attention that has been
given to nature and ecology.[54] In response to this criticism, the
Greens address the issues of social responsiblity and egalitarianism
in harness with their distinctive commitment to an ecological
worldview, arguing that the two are not mutually exclusive concerns
but interdependent, and that negative effects upon the ecology of the
earth causes human death and social disintegration.

Putting the ecological message across to the public is not an easy
task for the Greens. Jo Robins, a Green Party candidate for New-
castle-upon-Tyne in the 1987 General Election, campaigned in the
blighted high-rise council estates and highlighted the problems
faced:

I would knock at doors and people would feel like I was talking a different
language. I think the Green Party slogan 'think globally and act locally' is so
important, but in fact you've got to be reasonably secure to be able to think
globally; if all you can think about is the fact that you're unemployed, how
can you worry about the planet?[55]

The problems of communicating wide-ranging global ecological
issues 'in the field', whilst also pressing for more conventional social
objectives, does not detract from the Greens' desire to achieve these
dual goals. For Greens, society is not isolated from the future nor
from the complexities of the global ecosystem, but is rather seen as
an integral part of the whole. While traditional Marxists and
socialists may lay claim to a strong platform on questions of
egalitarianism and social responsibility, the Greens see the ecological
dimension of socialism as underplayed or absent altogether. For
them, injustices in society are not merely an inevitable function of
capitalism, but are the product of a much deeper cause that alienates

man physically and spiritually from nature and the wisdom of ecology.

The long-term perspective the Greens give to questions of social and economic planning derive from the time-scales employed in ecology, which deal with generations. They argue that extending responsibilities and rights into future society should be a cornerstone of policy, and that present worldviews, both capitalist and Marxist, are characterised by a short-term, irresponsible, hedonistic outlook which restricts policy to the immediate. The idea of extending rights to future generations is not orginal.[56] However, it has been adapted by the Greens and given an ecologically-based moral imperative in place of the utilitarian, rather instrumental approach usually taken in theories of intergenerational equity.[57] Thus, the Greens are keen to apply the principle of rights for future generations to contemporary environmental issues such as the development of nuclear power, toxic chemical waste disposal and the increase in atmospheric carbon dioxide levels.

The Greens' commitment to the concept of social responsibility and their critique of industrial rationality is inherently economically bound. Although capitalist mechanisms of profit and market forces, characterised by intense institutionalisation, may be held responsible for an individualistic and fragmented society, the Greens also see no hope for Marxist alternatives which seem to rest upon the promise of a post-revolutionary future of industrial abundance, where resource limits are either ignored or assumed to be extendable by the application of technological prowess.

Moving from the present economic system to an alternative one compatible with central Green principles involves the development of a 'new economics'.[58] This goes beyond the environmental economics put forward by Pearce, which essentially applies existing economic theory to questions of environmental management and regulation by assigning prices to environmental benefits based on how much people are prepared to pay.[59] Although still in an embryonic stage, the 'new economics' seeks not only the redistribution of wealth, but also the redefinition of wealth itself, by switching the emphasis from society's wants to society's needs.

The recognition of society's basic needs and mechanisms to ensure their equitable distribution requires an economy which works within a framework of equal rights, care, co-operation and obligation for each other's mutual welfare. The Greens' desire to transform the economy in this way is distinctive in the fact that it is more than simply giving everyone equal shares. Material equality alone does not imply an ecologically sustainable society. The Greens also argue for the recognition of spatial and temporal limits to the resource capacities and waste sinks of the global ecosystem, although these limits are perceived not to be as rigid or so near at hand as suggested in the neo-Malthusian environmentalist rhetoric of the early 1970s.

The ecological thinking of the Greens which stresses diversity and social equality has helped attract other movements seeking to alter some aspect of social organisation and the direction of socio-economic policy. The Greens' desire for a more equal, liberal and just society is stimulated by the ideologies held by these other movements, which to various degrees lend their support and adapt ecological premises to fit their own goals. Two of the more distinct and established social movements which have to some degree merged with the green dimension of environmentalism have been those which advance the causes of feminism and peace.

Congruency between the womens' movement and the Greens is strong. Feminists have pointed to the links between the Greens' desire to oppose all forms of exploitation and have drawn parallels between the domination of nature and the domination of women. A symbiotic relationship has developed between the two movements, with the Greens adopting the feminist commitment to an equalisation of the sexes in a post-patriarchical future. Dubiel expresses this commitment thus: 'We must adopt "female" values like compassion and co-operation even though our conditioning tells us to reject them . . . it will take a long time and a lot of work, until we can think in terms of a new identity. First we must destroy the old one and its long and painful history.'[60] The overlapping social goals of Greens and feminists have to some extent allowed the development of a mutually self-supporting platform. However, tensions exist between feminists who point out that practical sexual equality, even within their own organisations, lags behind well-intentioned principles, and Greens who suggest that in the process of adopting a feminist profile, a type of inverted sexism may be being introduced.

The Greens' commitment to a peaceful world has entailed a close relationship with the peace movement, although the thaw in the cold war and recent controls on nuclear weapons proliferation has meant that support for the peace movement has waned. The Greens' concept of peace, however, extends much deeper, starting from an

individual level where peace within oneself is seen as a moral guide
for action. From this personal level, peace extends to an inter-
personal level between all human beings; in the desire for social
harmony coupled with diversity, Greens believe in tolerance between
social groups.

Violence is interpreted in green thinking as more than physical
action. It includes concepts such as alienation, exploitation and
oppression, particularly as they apply to the more vunerable members of society — women, children, racial and cultural minority
groups. The Greens' critique of contemporary society highlights
what Capra and Spretnak term 'structural violence' — the neglect of
basic human needs, the unemployment and economic exploitation
affecting these groups which can lead to emotional and spiritual
turmoil.[61] Following the rationality of the peace movement, the
Greens are anxious to employ means that are concurrent with ends,
and so adhere to the ideas of education and active social resistance.

Purity, pragmatism and profit

The establishment of green radicalism within the environmental
movement was an important feature in its development through the
1980s. However, as such a diverse social movement, environmentalism is open to other ideological influences which continue to
shape its direction and political focus. We now briefly consider three
of these influences, given their relevance to the relationship between
the environmental movement and the major political parties.

Gaia: the new metaphor?
For the fundamentalist Greens in the environmental movement, the
concept of Gaia has emerged as a metaphor for the development of
society. Gaia was the name the ancient Greeks gave to the Goddess of
the Earth; more than a symbolic deity, she was 'a living creature, one
and visible, containing within [herself] all living creatures'.[62] From
Gaia came a morality based upon the laws of nature beyond human
appeal.

Despite being rooted in legend, the rediscovery of the Gaian idea
holds strong appeal for radicals in the environmental movement. For
those in search of an universal bio-ethic, Gaianism emphasises a
moral order based upon a non-anthropocentric view of the earth.
Pedlar, for instance, argues that the concept of Gaia is particularly

relevant to the contemporary environmental 'crisis', and that once the earth is seen as a living entity, life's actions are given reason in a quasi-religious sense leading us toward a sustainable and eco-logically compatible lifestyle.[63]

Such ideas have found ready acceptance amongst some Greens, particularly those who have argued the need for a 'new moral order' over and above political action. The ecological morality that Gaianism offers has been readily taken up by the 'eco-anarchists' who, in Porritt's words, have 'fallen foul of that particular streak of chronically unrealistic escapism over the last couple of decades'.[64] The Gaian idea may well provide an important spiritual element for the green movement, but it is far removed from any political reality and does not offer a practical foundation for the majority of environ-mentalists.

There is another side to the Gaian concept put forward by the geo-chemist, James Lovelock.[65] His work has kept clear of mysticism, concentrating upon Gaianism as a science, capable of being computer modelled and proved in some fashion. Lovelock defines Gaia as: 'A complex entity involving the earth's biosphere, atmosphere, oceans, and the soil; the totality constituting a feedback or cybernetic system which seeks an optimal physical and chemical environment for life on this planet.'[66] What Lovelock is suggesting is that the earth is capable of rejuvenation and therefore it does not matter how badly we pollute and destroy the oceans and the land, since the earth will seek to regain a state of equilibrium, independent of mankind if necessary. Given the earth's capacity to regenerate, this may lead us to adopt an attitude of complacency which is compatible with the central motivations of environmentalism. How-ever, Lovelock does suggest that certain areas of the earth are par-ticulary sensitive to ecological disturbance (the continental shelves, wetlands and the rainforests) and thus demand special protection in the interests of the greater good.

Whilst Lovelock's concept of Gaia possesses scientific credibility, for many in the environmental movement it lacks an important ethical dimension. Politically, the extreme interpretations of Gaianism are likely to be unacceptable. It is the combination of hard science with a new emphasis on ecological ethics which is likely to influence the environmental movement the greatest.[67] This hybrid Gaianism appears capable of providing a new model for a global strategy of sustainable development: a model which points not only to complex and finely-tuned ecological relationships, but also to the necessity of maintaining them.

The Red/Green debate
Socialism is a more pragmatic ideological influence upon the environmental movement. Unlike Gaianism, it is inherently political in nature and more acceptable to those in the environmental movement who seek practical influence rather than a moral revolution. The so-called 'Red/Green' debate is the manifestation of socialist influence revolving around a trade-off between its potential contribution to the environmentalist cause and the role of green thinking in the future development of socialism.[68]

On the surface, the long-term aims of the environmental movement would seem compatible with those of socialism. In the words of Ashton: 'The sort of society envisioned by Greens is not dissimilar from that espoused by at least the radical left, which has some roots in syndicalism – the idea of decentralised self-managed society with production geared to social need through local democratic forums.'[69] There are also overlaps between 'red' and 'green' in terms of commitment to social justice and equality, the redistribution of wealth, and the need to protect the weak. However, because both ideologies are open to wide interpretation, there is a marked degree of selectivity regarding how each views the environment. The majority of Greens would seem to welcome socialism as advocated by William Morris, but distrust the 'state socialism' of Attlee and later Wilson, complete with nationalisation, centralisation and a commitment to industrial growth – policies which are seen as the very antithesis of 'green' ideas.

It is socialism's apparent sole concern with industrialism and materialism that is the main ideological hurdle for the Greens. Despite a certain amount of common ground regarding social goals, the Greens reject the socialists' apparent willingness to exploit the earth's resources in order to achieve these, together with their preoccupation with class warfare and the continuing drive for economic growth.[70] Indeed, the 'super-ideology' of industrialism is perceieved to be shared by socialist and capitalist alike. However, the antagonism that Greens feel toward socialism is based upon a narrow view of post-war state socialism. It overlooks the fact that more than a century ago Engels had provided one of the most devastating critiques of the joint forces of industrialisation and urbanisation and the miserable living conditions which resulted. It also overlooks how socialist thinking has moved on. Many socialists today would probably agree that the processes of industrialism have been central to physical and human environmental degradation. In the same way, not all socialists adhere to the idea of centralised, massive, state intervention as the way to advance environmentalist aims. Robin Cook, Labour's opposition spokesman for Health and Social Security, has argued for instance that: 'Neither the market capitalism of America nor the state capitalism of the Soviet Union has produced an economic model which respects the fine tolerances of nature or grants self-respect to labour.'[71] What many socialists now seem to be arguing is that, the environmental movement's goals are perfectly compatible with a democratic, decentralised socialism which draws upon syndicalist/anarchistic traditions, rather than the Soviet-inspired, outmoded state communism once advocated. However, this eco-socialism still centres upon a critique of the worst excesses of capitalist industrialism rather than the industrial process itself.

As the environmental movement has matured, criticisms from the left relating to the once prevalent neo-Malthusian perspective have faded.[72] From a socialist point of view, the major problem with the Greens' position, is the failure to identify the function of capital and the realities of class. Whilst the majority of Greens see social change as an idealistic process revolving around new theories, ideas and values extending from the individual, socialists view it from a materialistic perspective, arguing that environmental problems are primarily a class struggle against the might of national and international capital. Anderson, for instance, argues that the development of a 'new' economics by the Greens places far too little emphasis upon the realities of a capitalist economic system in favour of stressing the theory of economic growth. 'In other words,' says Anderson, 'it's about time they [the Greens] discovered capitalism.'[73]

The more extreme ideas held by some Greens, such as 'withdrawing from industrial society', are highlighted as pure escapism by socialists.[74] Furthermore, the Greens find it difficult to shake off the socialist claim that they are predominantly drawn from the white middle classes. The Greens insist that the ecosystem is not merely the preserve of any one social class, and that solving the problem of socio-economic inequality by handing over the means of production to the working classes does not necessitate that environmental questions will even be considered.[75] However, for an ideology centred around the notion of class differentiation, socialism ultimately rejects such a reply. In the words of Ashton: 'A middle class family resident in rural suburbia may not escape the ravages of air and water borne contamination, but will be more protected than a working class family from the environmental degradation of inner cities, poor working conditions and housing.'[76]

There is no inevitable relationship between 'red' and 'green'. But in the words of Stretton, there does exist 'a tangle of common, overlapping and conflicting interests, and plenty of opportunity for negotiation'.[77] Common ground is being established through events such as the National Green and Socialist Conference held in May 1988. Increased dialogue of this sort helps dispel myths; Greens can see that not all socialists are in favour of rampant industrial growth, and socialists can see that the image of all Greens as 'bourgeois liberals' is an outdated caricature.

Green capitalism and green consumerism

The interpretation given to the term 'green capitalism' is dependent upon one's ideological view point. From the point of view of both Green and socialist alike, the phrase is a contradiction in terms. For the socialists, capitalism itself is taken to be a soul-destroying evil, whilst for the Greens, it joins state socialism in being a corrupting influence on any attempt to achieve a post-industrial 'eco-topia' via a new ideology. From these inevitably cynical standpoints, the 'greening' of capitalism is seen as nothing more than a process of superficial readjustment to, and camouflaging of, an inherently environmentally damaging and socially dominant ideology. The addition of a trendy prefix does nothing to stop environmental degradation or alter global resource inequalities. This may or may not be true, but it is argued here that the development of green capitalism and the rise of green consumerism are inevitable consequences of the dominant influence of capitalism, accentuated by a decade of Thatcherism and the worship of the free market economy. The key question which arises is; what is being changed – the structure and direction of the environmentalist movement, or the nature of capitalism itself?

During the 1980s, British business and industry climbed out of a major recession under a Conservative administration arguably the most committed ever to a self-reliant, entrepreneurial, private enterprise capitalist economy. The monetarist and liberalistic economics of Friedman and Hayek which so inspired Mrs Thatcher's administrations had little to say of the need to extend environmental concern into industry and corporate enterprise. Indeed, the idea of the free market acting as a self-regulating mechanism for a society of individuals seemed to be the antithesis of the key beliefs of environmentalism. But in recent years, some of the structures of capitalism have responded to the pressures of public opinion and the environmental groups.

The 'green' message has made some impression on those organisations previously held to be culprits of social and physical environmental despoliation. This has occurred independently of direct government controls and arguably because of a deliberate lack of government intervention. Elkington suggests that 'green' capitalists and environmentalists alike 'recognize that no government, or collection of governments, can cope with the environmental agenda in isolation'. He continues: 'The role of the non-governmental sector, and increasingly of the new breed of environmental entrepreneur, is likely to be an essential ingredient in the transformation which is beginning to take place in the economies of most major industrial nations.'[78] Reformist environmental groups have in general welcomed this transformation with the realisation that economic growth and improved environmental quality are not incompatible.

At the centre of the 'greening' of capitalism is a process of image reconstruction. In an increasingly sensitive consumer society and against a political climate where competition is encouraged, public relations for companies is given considerable emphasis. After years of cultivating an image of ignorance, insensitivity, negligence and battling with the environmental lobby, British companies are now keen to stress their concern for the environment. British Gas, Shell UK, ICI and British Nuclear Fuels Limited (BNFL) are amongst some the larger companies who have undertaken massive advertising campaigns to highlight the benefits of their products and services and the consideration they give to the environment in terms of health, welfare and aesthetics. Nuclear and non-nuclear power stations around the country have invested in visitor centres and community relations ventures to highlight their concern for the environment. ICI advertising campaigns emphasise environmentally-friendly products, and British Gas have sponsored a major series of independent commentaries on various environmental issues as their contribution to the environmental debate.

Smaller companies, too, are engaged in changing to a 'greener' image. Robinson Brothers Ltd., an old-established chemical firm in the Black Country has, along with many other companies in the UK, begun to reverse the negative image of the 'smokestack' industries and to promote a positive profile of environmental concern and consideration. They have opened their doors to the local public, designed events and tours to stress the safeguards that have been installed in their production process and to show off their new landscaped setting for the plant.[79]

The 'greening' of capitalism, however, is more than the development of a new image. A climate of awareness is being cultivated in board rooms and on the shop floor, which equates good environmental practices with profit. The UK Centre for Economic and Environmental Development (CEED), for instance, has been particularly active in establishing dialogue between those within industry and business, and those concerned with establishing sound environmental policies. As Nicholson-Lord suggests, what CEED seems to be unashamedly proclaiming is, 'there's money in greenery'.[80] This money is generated in three main ways.

Firstly, savings can be made where, as result of environmental thinking, projects are undertaken which minimise waste and hence expenditure. J. Sainsbury, for instance, now uses heat generated by its refrigeration plants to heat its supermarkets, whilst the latest in microcomputers control store conditions to ensure optimal conditions for customers and staff for minimum energy consumption. The new Sainsbury stores now use 40 per cent less energy than the stores of 1975, saving £7 million a year in running costs. Secondly, capital is created via the selling of new technologies and equipment for environmental protection. Johnson Matthey Chemicals Limited, for instance, now build and supply new air pollution control equipment which can remove fumes and recover energy from a variety of industrial processes. Thirdly, money is generated through possessing an environmentally-friendly image. This image may be passive, in the sense that a company adheres to existing health and safety standards and generally maintains a good appearance; or it may be active, where a company develops an environmental motif as a selling point. In this way, a company can latch on to increasing concern amongst consumers for healthy foods, or for naturally-produced and cruelty-free cosmetics, areas for ethical investment and products which do not pollute or degrade the environment. As 'green consumerism' increases, it stimulates further demand for greener products and more environmentally-friendly methods of production.

In June 1980, the Confederation of British Industry (CBI), representing large and small businesses alike, issued a cautious statement on 'British Industry and the Environment' in which it recognised the increasing pressures of the demands for protection of the environment, particularly from the EEC, upon the operating efficiency of British trade and industry.[81] It acknowledged the need for 'sensible environmental control', but also emphasised that new regulations were having increased industrial and commercial operating costs and that careful consideration should be given to these costs and the implications for international trade. In 1983 the CBI, acknowledging the increasing pressure of the environmental lobbies, took a more positive line in its environmental policy. It made the following recommendations:

i) that the CBI itself should make a major effort to achieve public recognition of the responsive and responsible role already played by industry in environmental protection;

ii) that, recognising that the CBI can be effective only in general terms, it should actively encourage its members to pursue the same objective, both nationally and locally, by all appropriate means; and

iii) that the committee should actively seek to extend constructive working relationships with responsible environmental organisations.[82]

Such changes in CBI policy, as well as the recently formed Business in the Environment private sector initiative, embracing the idea that a well-conceived environmental policy is just part of good management, and numerous examples of companies who have adopted a 'cradle to grave' approach to environmental issues, would seem to reflect a substantial change in the attitude of UK industry toward the environment. However, there is still a long way to go. A survey conducted by the Institute of Directors in 1990 showed that companies were still paying lip service to environmental issues and revealed a 'surprising degree of complacency or ignorance'.[83] Companies still struggle with the problem of how they can balance their responsibility to society and their shareholders. The Environmental Protection Act of 1990 with its emphasis on the 'polluter pays' principle will help industry focus its mind on its wider responsibilities, but given such an accumulation of problems, the large amount of capital required and a period of recession, industry is likely to struggle with its loyalties for some time to come.

.The 'greening' of capitalism marks a dramatic departure in the evolution of environmentalism. It is a move which has been encouraged by reformists in the environmental movement and stimulated by over ten years of Thatcherism. It is inevitable that a political and economic ideology as strong as this has influenced the environmental movement. However, Greens and 'green' socialists do not see this as a positive influence, but as a process of subconscious surrender where the Pied Piper of capitalism still plays the loudest and most pervasive tune for the environmental movement to dance to.

The environmental movement continues to develop under the wide range of influences outlined above. In doing so, internal tensions increase, but ironically, the appeal of the movement becomes wider as a result, and its central message is given more force and political credibility. In the following chapter we examine how environmentalism as a diverse social movement presents a challenge to the British party political system.

Notes and references

1 See: Marsh, A. 1981. 'Environmental Issues in Contemporary European Politics.' In Goodman, G. T./Kristoferson, L. A./Hollander, J. M. (Eds.) *The European Transition from Oil: Societal Impacts and Constraints in Energy Policy.* London: Academic Press. 121–54.

2 The interdependence of life relates to the concept of Gaia, the Greek name for the Goddess of the Earth.

3 See for instance: Attfield, R. 1983. *The Ethics of Environmental Concern.* Oxford: Blackwell; Passmore, J. 1974. *Man's Responsibility for Nature.* London: Duckworth; Thomas, K. 1983. *Man and the Natural World: Changing Attitudes in England 1500–1800.* London: Allen Lane.

4 Sessions, G. 1985. 'Ecological Consciousness and Paradigm Change.' In Tobias, M. (Ed.) *Deep Ecology.* San Diego, CA: Avant Books. 28–44.

5 See for instance: Capra, F. 1975. *The Tao of Physics.* London: Fontana; Capra, F. 1982. *The Turning Point.* London: Fontana; Robertson, J. 1978. *The Sane Alternative.* London: Private publication.

6 Pye, T. 1986. 'The Role of Paganism in the Ecology Movement', *Green Line*, 42, 11–12. Pye is representative of the more spiritual side of the environmental movement, searching for a better environment through religion.

7 Manning, D. J. (Ed.) 1980. *The Form of Ideology.* London: Allen & Unwin.

8 Pepper, D. 1985. 'Determinism, Idealism and the Politics of Environ-

mentalism – a Viewpoint.' In *International Journal of Environmental Studies*, 26. 11–19.

9 Porritt, J. 1984. *Seeing Green: The Politics of Ecology Explained.* Oxford and New York: Basil Blackwell.

10 Enzenberger, H. N. 1974. 'A Critique of Political Ecology.' *New Left Review*, 84. March/April. 3–31.

11 Morrison, D. 1980. 'The Soft Cutting Edge of Environmentalism.' *Natural Resources Journal*, 20. April. 275–98.

12 Note 9, *op. cit.*

13 O'Riordan, T. 1984. 'Future Directions for Environmental Policy.' IIUG Discussion Papers dp 84–14. WZB.

14 See: Wilkinson, P. 1971. *Social Movement.* London: Pall Mall.

15 As put forward by: Lowe, P./Goyder, J. 1983. Environmental Groups in Politics Resource Management Series. London: Allen & Unwin.

16 Weber, M. 1964. In Parsons, T. (Ed.) *The Theory of Economic and Social Organisation.* New York: Free Press.

17 Moran, M. 1985. *Politics and Society in Britain.* London: Macmillan.

18 Alderman, G. 1984. *Pressure Groups and Government in Great Britain.* London: Longman.

19 See: Jordan, A. G./Richardson, J. J. 1987. *British Politics and the Policy Process: An Arena Approach.* London: Allen & Unwin.

20 Grant, W. 1978. 'Insider Groups, Outsider Groups and Interest Group Strategies in Britain.' Working Paper No. 19. Dept of Politics, University of Warwick.

21 Note 15, *op. cit.*

22 See: Steward, F. 1985a. 'Growing Greens.' *Marxism Today*, November. 17–19;. Steward, F. 1985b. 'Rainbows and Warriors.' An interview with S. Sawyer. *Marxism Today*, November. 20–22.

23 Note 19, *op. cit.*

24 Note 15, *op. cit.*

25 Blowers, A. 1984. *Something in the Air.* London: Harper & Row.

26 Gerlach, L. P. 1971. 'Movements of Revolutionary Change: Some Structural Characteristics.' In Freeman, J. (Ed.) *Social Movements of the Sixties and Seventies.* New York & London: Longman. 133–47.

27 Entry taken from: Barker, M. J. C. 1986. Directory for the Environment: Organisations in Britain and Ireland 1986–87. London: Routledge & Kegan Paul, 2nd ed.

28 See for instance the AA's evidence given to the House of Commons Environment Select Committee on Acid Rain: House of Commons. 1984. July. Fourth Report from the Environment Committee. Acid Rain Vols. I and II. HMSO. 446–1.

29 A classic North American case study of the conflicts between the trade unionists and employers is given by: Schnaiberg, A. 1983. 'We Almost Lost Detroit: Three Cheers for Environmentalists?' Report prepared for the annual meeting of the Society for the Study of Social Problems, Detroit, August 1983. See also: Siegmann, H. 1985. *The Conflicts between Labor and Environmentalism in the Federal Republic of Germany and the United*

States. WZB – Publications. Gower. Aldershot.

30 Cotgrove, S./Duff, A. 1980. 'Environmentalism, Middle-Class Radicalism and Politics.' *Sociological Review*, 28. No 2. 333–51.

31 See: Heffernan, P. 1975. 'Jobs and the Environment.' Sierra Club Bulletin, 60. 25–9.

32 Note 9, *op. cit.*

33 CBI. 1980. 'British Industry and the Environment': CBI Statement June, C 39, 80.

34 See account by: Slater, J. 1986. 'North Sea Dumping.' In Hilyard, N./Goldsmith, E. (Eds.) *Green Britain or Industrial Wasteland.* Policy Press.

35 See: Du Preez, P. 1980. *The Politics of Identity.* Oxford: Basil Blackwell. 67–9.

36 Note 15, *op. cit.*

37 Note 15, *op. cit.*

38 For discussions of the range of participants in the environmental movement see: Bouchier, D. 1978. *Idealism and Revolution: New Ideologies of Liberation in Britain and the United States.* London: Edward Arnold; Morrison, D. E./Dunlap, R. E. 1986. 'Environmentalism and Elitism: a Conceptual and Empirical Analysis.' *Environmental Management*, 10, No. 5. 581–9.

39 Public opinion on the environment would seem to be recession-proof in that support has remained high during periods of high unemployment. However, a high rank in an opinion poll is no indication that some-one will change their vote at the opportunity of a general election.

40 Note 1, *op. cit.*

41 Inglehart, R. 1971. 'The Silent Revolution in Europe: Intergenerational Change in Post-Industrial Societies.' *American Political Science Review*, 65, 991–1017;. Inglehart, R. 1977. *The Silent Revolution: Changing Values and Political Styles Among Western Publics.* Princeton: Princeton University Press.

42 Personal Communication.

43 The idea of greenery as a social escape is discussed by: Weiner, M. J. 1981. *English Culture and the Decline of the Industrial Spirit: 1850–1980.* Cambridge: Cambridge University Press.

44 Williams, R. 1973. *The Country and the City.* London: Hogarth Press. Williams explores literature and social commentary of the romantic era from which emerged the belief that the 'natural state' was perfection.

45 See for instance: Langguth, G. 1984. *The Green Factor in German Politics: From Protest Movement to Political Party.* Boulder & London: Westview Press; Papadakis, E. 1984. *The Green Movement in West Germany.* London & Australia: Croom Helm; Porritt, J./Winner, D. 1988. *The Coming of the Greens.* London: Fontana.

46 Galtung, J. 1986. 'The Green Movement: A Socio-Historical Exploration.' *International Sociology*, 1, No. 1. March. 75–90.

47 Davy, A. 1985. 'People, Nature, Hope: What Green Means to Me.' *Green Line*, No. 35. 6–7.

48 For a discussion see: Buttel, F. H. 1986. 'Sociology and the Environment: the Winding Road Toward Human Ecology.' *International Social*

Science Journal, 109. Environmental Awareness Issue. Basil Blackwell/ UNESCO.

49 244 members voted for, 93 voted against and 11 abstained in relation to the change of name from Ecology Party to the Green Party, notably some two years after the German Green Party came to political prominence. See: Carpenter, J. 1985. 'Change of Name, Change of Heart?' *Green Line*, No. 36. October. 17.

50 See: Henderson, H. 1983. 'The Warp and the Weft: The Coming Synthesis of Eco-Philosophy and Eco-Feminism.' In Caldecott, L./Leland, S. (Eds.) *Reclaim the Earth*. Women's Press. 203–14.

51 Note 9, *op. cit.*

52 Capra, F./Spretnak, C. 1986. *Green Politics*. (2nd ed.) London: Hutchinson.

53 Green Party, 1986. *Social Welfare – a Start to Discussion*. The Green Party Social Welfare Policy Working Group.

54 See for instance: Pepper, D. 1984. *The Roots of Modern Environmentalism*. London: Croom Helm; Weston, J. (Ed.) 1986. *Red and Green: The New Politics of the Environment*. London: Pluto Press.

55 Robbins, J. 1987. 'The Women in Green.' *Guardian*, 27.01.87.

56 For instance see: Callahan, D. 1971. 'What Obligations do we Have?' *American Ecclesiastical Review*, 116. 265–80; Partridge, E. 1981. *Responsibilities to Future Generations: Environmental Ethics*. Buffalo, NY: Prometheus Books; Rawls, J. 1971. *A Theory of Justice*. Cambridge: Harvard University Press.

57 Kirsch, G. 1986. 'Solidarity Between Generations: Intergenerational Distributional Problems in Environmental and Resource Policy.' In Schnaiberg, A./Watts, N./Zimmermann, K. (Eds.) *Distributional Conflicts in Environmental Resource Policy*. Aldershot: WZB-Publications. 381–405; Turner, R. K. 1988. 'Wetland Conservation: Economics and Ethics.' In Collard, D./Pearce, D./Ulph, D. (Eds.) 1988. *Economics, Growth and Sustainable Environments*. London: Macmillan. 121–61.

58 A compendium of papers on the 'new economics' is available in: Ekins, P. (Ed.) *The Living Economy: A New Economics in the Making*. London: Routledge & Kegan Paul.

59 Pearce, D. 1989. *Blueprint for a Green Economy*. London: Earthscan.

60 Dubiel, J. 1987. 'In Search of Real Man.' Green Line, No. 49, February.

61 Note 52, *op. cit.*

62 Hughes, C. J. 1985. 'Gaia: a Natural Scientist's Ethic for the Future.' *The Ecologist*, 15, No. 3. 92–4.

63 Pedlar, K. 1979. *The Quest for Gaia*. London: Grenada.

64 Porritt, J. 1985. 'Updating Industrialism.' *Resurgence*, No. 112. Sept./Oct. 36.

65 Lovelock, J. 1979. *Gaia: A New Look at Life on Earth*. New York: OU Press.

66 Note 65, *op. cit.*

67 Weston, A. 1987. 'Forms of Gaian Ethics.' *Environmental Ethics*, 9,

No. 3. 217–31.
68   The use of the term 'green' is here used in its popular sense to refer to environmental matters rather than the radical philosophy.
69   Ashton, F. 1985. *Green Dreams and Red Realities.* NATTA Discussion Paper No. 2.
70   Bunyard, P./Morgan-Grenville, F. 1987. *The Green Alternative.* London: Methuen.
71   Cook, R. 1984. 'Let's Make the Red Flag Green.' *The Times.* 24.04.84. 12.
72   See for instance Simons, M. 1988. 'The Red and the Green – Socialists and the Ecology Movement.' *International Socialism*, 2:37. Winter. 49–91.
73   Anderson, V. 1987. 'Labour needs new economics.' *New Ground*, No. 14. 22.
74   Bahro, R. 1982. *Socialism and Survival.* London: Heretic Books; Bahro, R. 1986. *Building the Green Movement.* London: Heretic Books.
75   Glaberson, B. 1985. 'Class and the Greens.' *Green Line*, No. 35. 7.
76   Note 69, *op. cit.*
77   Stretton, H. 1976. *Capitalism, Socialism and the Environment.* Cambridge: Cambridge University Press.
78   Elkington, J./Burke, T. 1987. *The Green Capitalists: Industry's Search for Environmental Excellence.* London: Victor Gollancz Ltd.
79   Shinton, P. 1988. 'Public Image Ltd.' *Environment Now*, Dec. 87/Jan. 88. 20–21.
80   Nicholson-Lord, D. 1986. 'Will Industry Find Growth in Greenery?' *The Times*, 14.08.86. 10.
81   Confederation of British Industry. 1980. 'British Industry and the Environment.' *CBI Statement*, C 39, June 1980.
82   Confidential note from CBI Council on 'Positive Environmental Policies', C49 83.
83   Institute of Directors' Survey. 1990.

3

The challenge of environmentalism

Social movements can be categorised according to the strategies they adopt: withdrawal, protest, reform or revolution.[1] Elements of all these strategies are, or have been, apparent in the environmental movement from time to time. Currently, the movement's dominant strategy is that of accommodation and reform: of fitting into the existing structures of society, economy and politics, rather than attempting to overthrow them.

In the UK, which lacks the revolutionary tradition of other Western European states, the environmental movement in the main has not channelled its activities through a Green party. Instead, it is currently undergoing a process of absorption, whereby the existing parties adopt and shape its ideas to suit themselves. This process underlines both the diverse evolution and constituency of the environmental movement and the strength of the British political system. For most environmentalists, aside from Gaian purists and those within the Green Party, the most immediate and practical mechanisms available for achieving their demands are government and the existing political parties.

The environmental movement and British polity are intimately and unavoidably bound to each other, given that many environmental issues involve questions of physical resource distribution and allocation.[2] Indeed, it can be argued that many environmental problems have political causes and thus require political solutions.[3] Contemporary environmentalism considers questions of liberty, representation and social justice. These are far-reaching and sensitive issues and their arbitration is a political matter. Moreover, it is only through the established political framework that global environmental issues, such as transboundary pollution problems and changes in world climate, can be dealt with. The problem is, however, that much of politics involves short-term considerations, whilst environmental issues work on a much longer timescale. To a large extent, therefore, the environmental movement is drawn into the political system through social necessity.[4] The interaction between the political parties and the environmental movement can be portrayed as a fundamental and mutual ideological challenge. Each party's belief system represents a challenge to the environmental movement and vice versa. This two-way challenge is at the centre of the 'greening' process.

The role of party ideologies

The ideologies of the political parties differ from those within the environmental movement discussed in the previous chapter: their primary aim is the attainment of power under competitive conditions. However, once this power is secured, the party in government is forced to look outside the interests of its members to the wider problems in society. As a result, the ideologies of the political parties have to be wider in outlook than ideologies held by other closed groups.[5] Moreover, because a party is in competition with other parties, it has to consider the problems raised by the ideologies of its competitors. So, for instance, it could be argued that in the absence of an alternative socialist conception of a proper economic order, the Conservative Party would be less inclined to address the unemployment problem.

We should reject the cynical view that a party will accept any idea if it brings some tactical advantage. Similarly, we should reject the idea that parties resolutely hold to their principles for their own sake. As Michael Oakeshott has said, a politician cannot arise each morning with an empty mind ready to respond to whatever event or fancy may come his way.[6] At the same time Oakeshott also argued that political activity cannot emerge from abstract principles alone, but takes place with a knowledge of current events and their historical context. The ideology of the party is, however, its prime mover, the instrument which directs it to its changing destinations. The party which holds government dominates the wider processes of social change with aspects of its own ideology.

The ideology of a party is a manifestation of the party's history and tradition, and although not easy to state succinctly, it is discernible and relatively immutable.[7] Party members come and go, the voting opinions of the electorate may be capricious whims, but party ideologies seem to be solid and unchanging. But in the process of competing for power in the party system and the maintaining of that power by appeasing the electorate, party ideologies also have to be broad and flexible; rather than changing direction completely, they tend to veer with the winds of external pressures such as public opinion and party competition. They must also cope with the expectations of party members and consequently shift emphasis, not course.

The ideological component is therefore a powerful one within each party, and it has a series of functions which are relevant to the process of 'greening'.

i) *The boundary/identification function*
Party ideology delimits political territory. Although each is open to wide interpretation, we can nevertheless use ideologies to distinguish between parties. In the adversarial arena of the British polity, the differences between ideologies tend to be accentuated rather than diminished.

ii) *The order function*
If we accept that part of politics is concerned with the ordering of public affairs, then a party requires an image of 'proper' order if it is to persuade the electors that it is able to govern. Each party requires guidance across the existing constituted order, for one day it may be called to act in any domain of that order.[8]

iii) *The policy function*
The ideology of a party acts as a foundation for the formulation of policies. Although the exact terms of reference for the ideology may not be spelt out (nor wholly agreed by the party), it manifests itself in policy decisions and directions. If the electorate can recognise the broad ideological position of a party, it can then expect a certain policy orientation.

iv) *The rallying/legitimising function*
The existence of an underlying system of beliefs in a political party can be seen as part of the reason for its initial formation. These beliefs bind the party together and give a group within society a

particular direction. In the course of day-to-day party activity, ideologies are taken as read and are not commonly reiterated or justified. However at particular times, such as when controversial policy proposals are under discussion, or at conference time, the central beliefs of the party may be invoked to carry a decision, justify an action or mobilise support.

v) *The election function*
This is similar to the rallying function but is employed specifically in relation to the electorate at the time of elections. Electors respond to parties partly in terms of how the world is and partly as to how it should be: that is, in terms of a political ideology.[9] Parties therefore tend to highlight their principles during election campaigns to help voters make their decisions.

The challenge of environmentalism to the British political parties

A simplification of the interaction between the environmental movement and the political parties is represented in Figure 2. The diagram shows a balanced setting for the interaction between the two bodies. No one side is pushing or pulling toward the other and no one side has the upper hand. In reality, however, both sides continually react to each other simultaneously, and the relationship is heavily loaded in favour of government and the major opposition parties.

Interaction mainly takes place on three levels. Most superficially, but most often, it occurs at the level of rhetoric, where the two sides exchange statements about environmental issues or events; these tend to revolve around ends rather than means. It is at this level that consensus can be most readily achieved. A call from the environmental movement that 'green' concerns should take priority in policy decisions can simply be echoed in party statements from party members. It is at the policy level where imbalance between the two sides is most clearly evident. The dimensions of the arrow pointing to the right are substantially increased, for it is government within the context of the party system which possesses the legitimate mandate for formulating and controlling policy. However, the impact of the environmental movement is visible at the policy level and we have seen how the environmental pressure groups can influence policy outcomes. The most fundamental interactions take place at the ideological level. Exchanges at the level of policy may be piecemeal and transitory, but inroads made by the environmental movement into the beliefs which shape policy could be significant and perhaps permanent.

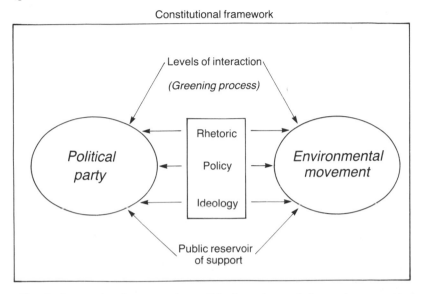

Fig. 2 Interaction between the political parties and the environmental movement

According to Smith, the relationship between a social movement and a political party can be viewed as a contest, with each as a contender for the support of the public.[10] This approach assumes that each is a fixed, discrete collective: in reality, the boundaries between a social movement, a political party and the public are often blurred. It may be that on one level both movement and party are acting in alliance. A party may have a movement dimension, and reciprocally, a movement may also have a party dimension. The adherents of each are to some extent influenced by the other's commitments, and in the case of a party, organised factions may form around the issues which generated the movement. Moreover, the forms of this public support are not directly comparable. A political party may lose some of the public vote at election time, yet still receive the support which comes from its own organisation and members. Thus, without overwhelming public support parties may still wield a degree of political power. On the other hand, a social movement may lay claim to widespread public support so long as it continues to operate within the constitutional framework, though it may not in itself possess the decision-making power required to realise its demands.

Smith's initial view of a conscious contest between party and movement may oversimplify the imbalance which exists between the two structures, but as he points out, this imbalance is related to the particular view of the public that a social movement and a political party hold. A movement requires active involvement and participation from the public, whereas a party treats the public (the electorate) largely as a passive reservoir of voting support. Thus, although parties and movements may have the same 'clientele', they may not be in direct competition. What is clear is that despite a skewed balance of power, social movements are seldom totally ignored by the political parties. The ability of a movement to mobilise a spread of public support for an issue or band of principles for any length of time sends out signals to a political party. The party may recognise that to support the demands of the movement may stabilise or increase their own support, and that if they ignore a movement's demands, then potential support may be lost to their competitors.[11]

Political recognition is the primary aim of a social movement. In the case of the environmental movement, various component groups have achieved a higher degree of political recognition than others and have gained 'insider status'. This process of comparative advantage is hard to explain, but is related to the personalities of the movement's spokespersons and audience. Well-presented and concisely articulated demands will tend to be recognised more easily in a political system where there is considerable competition between pressure groups for politicians' time and limited opportunities for putting forward demands. A high level of organisation and a united approach within a movement over specific issues help. But even the most exacting and eloquent presentations of demands often fail if they significantly challenge the prevailing orthodoxy and inherent vested interests. Lowe and Rudig quote Marsh to make the point that political recognition and formal consultation with environmental groups may occur, but that it may amount to little more than a symbolic sham.[12] In Marsh's words: 'while incorporation does not ensure influence, outsider status does not preclude influence'.[13] Thus, the environmental movement can incorporate both groups seeking to change policies by governmental participation, and those who wish to change the decision-making framework itself, as well as those who transcend the process of 'muddling through' by taking morally justified direct action.[14] The environmental movement thus presents a multi-pronged challenge to the political system. This can be seen as strategic weakness, as resources are applied in disparate and unco-ordinated fashion. It can also be interpreted as a strength, with the attack on the constitutional process being on more than one front, giving greater flexibility.

In order to translate ideas and demands into concrete legislation and policy programmes, environmentalism seeks to exercise a degree of political power beyond the initial process of recognition. Tawney's definition of power 'as the *capacity* of an individual, or group of individuals, to modify the conduct of other individuals or groups in the manner which he desires, and to prevent his own being modified in which he does not' (emphasis added) highlights the idea of power as an instrument for determining change. The access which the environmental movement has to political power is dependent upon the way one views constitutional relationships within the UK.

Lukes follows Dahl in making a distinction between actual and potential power.[15] In a pluralist model of the decision-making process, the environmental movement has the *potential* to influence every institution and every stage involved either directly or indirectly. This model asserts that no single elite group controls the political system and that power is widely dispersed between the different groups relative to resources (organisation, information and finance). A 'Whitehall' model of the constitution stresses the *actual* location of political power within the executive.[16] The reduction in the number of partaking institutions (and hence a reduction in the number of stages present in the decision-making process) accentuates an elitist view of the British polity. The model still allows for processes of participation and consultation, but in the knowledge that decisions can be taken independently. Between the two interpretations lies the notion that power is not solely resident in the hands of the elite, but is shared with larger, well organised groups, who have inevitably evolved through a programme of amalgamation. This is not a full corporatist conception of closed interests, but rather a more responsive marriage between the elite and the more influential groups.

Within the democratic framework of the British constitution, the environmental movement has potential access to the locus of governmental decision-making power, generally as part of the electorate and specifically via established arrangements for group representation. In this sense it can be seen as competing with other interest groups, which include the political parties in opposition, for the power to influence and modify the nation's decision-makers. It is the major (seat-holding) parties which have the most direct access to and strongest motivation for the power wielded by government. However, although competition can and does occur between the environmental pressure groups and the political parties, common interests have emerged. In order to develop overlapping aims and strategies, in the knowledge that the opposition parties of today may be the governments of tomorrow, and given that the evolution of an autonomous Green Party in the UK is hindered by the electoral system, the environmental movement actively seeks to influence the relevant decisions of the opposition parties as well as those taken directly by government.

The process of 'greening'

Before we try to explain why and how the political parties have responded to the challenge of environmentalism, it is useful to remind ourselves what we mean by the term 'greening'. It refers to a process in which ideas, attitudes, motivations, symbols and 'ways of thinking' are translated from the constituent cells of the environmental movement to the mainstream political parties in terms of rhetoric, policy and ideology. We can view the process as having three sequential and parallel stages: an uptake of environmentalist beliefs in a superficial rhetorical way; a more effective, but also possibly transitory, expression of concern in party policy; and a more permanent fusing of environmental beliefs into the realms of existing party ideology, thereby informing future policy decisions. No causal relationship exists between the stages. Rhetorical statements expressing concern for an environmental issue may not lead to the establishment of a policy position. Similarly, the existence of environmental policy may not involve any change in underlying party beliefs. Nevertheless, in a general sense, we can work on the assumption that there does exist an inferential relationship between the three stages and that it is reasonable to expect some form of linkage between what is said, what is done, and what is believed.

The outcome of the process can be compared against the 'green datum' outlined in chapter 2, though it should be stressed that this does not necessarily represent a 'perfect' or even 'better' position. 'Greening' is a dynamic process; a particular end state where the ideological framework and policy basis of the Conservative Party, for instance, became identical to that of the Green Party may never be attainable. However, 'greening' is a process of change which can be monitored in relation to the wider changes occurring in the political sphere and in society itself.

The translation of rhetoric

Rhetoric in this context refers to the use of language and literature for some specific effect. The emphasis is primarily upon display in order to present a selected image to listeners or readers. One interpretation assumes that what is being said is an affected or exaggerated position removed from the speaker's beliefs or intentions. Distinguishing rhetoric from reality is a complex process, and politicians perhaps exploit the difficulties. Party politicians are celebrated masters of rhetorical oratory, particularly when they communicate with the electorate. Whether they understand an issue or not, or whether they wish to engage in a particular policy field or not, politicians *have to be seen* to be concerned with those issues which concern elements of the population at any one time. It would be misleading to think of rhetoric just as unconsidered pronouncements, and similarly misleading to interpret it as lies. Politicians make statements which are well thought out, deep enough to pacify, but shallow enough to avoid commitments. They latch on to the words and phrases that are currently in fashion and freely borrow from the vocabulary of other groups.

The environmental movement too is well versed in the use of rhetoric as a form of communication.[17] It throws up a constant source of images and metaphors taken from the full spectrum of academic disciplines. Sooner or later these are passed on via the normative processes of political socialisation or through direct consultations, to the party politicians. As chapter 1 indicated, the term 'environment' was gradually integrated into the verbal armouries of the party politicians in the early 1970s. The use of the term 'green' as an identifier for environmental issues was developed in UK political parlance after the entry of the West German Green Party into European politics in 1983. Similarly, politicians' use of the term 'sustainable' post-dates the 1980 World Conservation Strategy when the concept of sustainable development received its first widespread airing.

On one hand, rhetorical exchange indicates that environmental issues have obtained some degree of political recognition, and in this sense the environmental movement may claim success. On the other hand, the use of rhetoric to express 'green' intentions does not indicate substantive changes in party policy or ideology. Indeed, in rhetorical terms alone, the major British parties have expressed remarkably similar concerns regarding the environment.[18] As Figure 3 shows, Greens tend to view this with a certain amount of cynicism, and claim instead the moral high ground of the 'pure' Green position. Statements such as: 'environmental policies are to be given high priority'; 'protection of the environment is a main aim of policy'; 'we are the only true green party', have been proffered in increasing profusion since the General Election of 1983. All these statements are interchangeable. All the parties, from the Green Party to the National Front, have made similar pronouncements, and each party could be saying any one of the statements. This would seem to indicate that the parties have at least responded to the challenge of environmentalism. The uncertain gap between what is said and what is done nevertheless remains. The rhetoric is concerned with idealised ends, and little is said about the means by which they may be achieved.

Policy participation

The greening of policy and the decision-making processes involves a more substantial and intimate interchange between the environmental movement and the political parties. It refers not just to the quantity of environmental policies, but also to the quality and the style in which they are constructed and administered. Furthermore, it refers to the whole spectrum of policy and not just to the conventional areas of countryside and conservation, for environmental thinking can be applied to any policy field.

Policies germinate in two ways. Firstly, a policy may take the form of an innovation and stem from an intellectual process in which parties (usually in a period of opposition) identify problems based upon previous experience in office or upon observation of

Fig. 3   The greening of the major political parties as seen by the Green Party
Source: Econews (1988)

contemporary socio-economic events. In this form, policy options
owe much to intellectuals and professionals.[19] Where professional
advice and information is not immediately available within the
party, policy makers may seek outside help via suitable and sympathetic (or at least impartial) individuals and groups. On the whole,
innovative policies tend to give way to the second and dominant
form of policy germination which is more reactive and incremental
in nature – what Lindblom terms 'muddling through'[20] – where the
parties and government respond to the issues thrown up in the daily
course of events.[21] Here the 'attentive public' and the environmental
pressure groups strive to get environmental issues on to the political
agenda, using the media as a magnifying glass. Parties in opposition
have more flexible agendas than governments, and can therefore
respond more easily to green issues brought up by the environmental
pressure groups, particularly if they are compatible with (or can be
made compatible with) party ideology or can be used for electoral
advantage. This reactive form of policy making is perhaps the most
highly charged politically. Assumptions, values and goals conflict as
ideological 'battle-lines' are made explicit in the consideration of
'policy facts'. It is here that the challenge of the environmental
movement is potentially at its strongest.

Policy formulation is the stage at which the ideas which have
germinated are transformed into structured policy proposals. For the
parties, the formulation of policy is usually carried out by officials
co-ordinated into some form of policy group or committee. In the
case of government, however, the formulation stage is slightly
different since ministers have the benefit of official advice provided
by the civil servants in their departments. The potential of the
environmental movement to influence this stage of the policy process
is considerably reduced. The basic interaction of beliefs between
environmental groups and party has probably already taken place,
although there may be room for a consultative role in the drafting
process, particularly when policy is being formulated in order to
introduce new legislation.

At the decision-making stage of the party policy process, the
potential for greening is at its least, since this is essentially a matter
for elected politicians. For parties in opposition, the process is
simple: the Shadow Cabinet either agree to or reject the policy
formulations put forward. Though this may require more than one
meeting, policy has generally been refined to a point where decisions

can be taken without much deliberation.

In government, decision making is a more complex activity and it is harder to make generalisations about the activities involved. Some decisions can be taken by individual ministers or their civil servants acting within their departmental remits. The more important decisions have to be taken by Cabinet or Cabinet committee. Normally, Cabinet decisions are taken fairly swiftly since the Prime Minister will usually have prepared the way by meeting with the specific minister concerned in advance of a full Cabinet meeting.

Though the environmental movement's potential for influencing policy at the crucial decision-making stages is low, it is not absent altogether. Environmental groups allied to a party or with privileged, long-standing access to ministers and senior officials influence policy outcomes particularly by advising on matters of detail. More indirectly, ministers, shadow ministers and senior officials remain open to contact with environmentally motivated individuals or groups outside the formal decision-making process. They may hold posts within environmental groups, or be involved in particular campaigns either through their personal interests or as MPs acting in the interests of their constituents. Labour MPs may be sponsored by a trade union supporting the demands of the environmental movement. Decision making therefore has a personal dimension in which environmental beliefs 'filter up' and influence individuals making policy decisions at the highest level.

The execution stage, when decisions on policies are implemented, is the litmus test of a government's effectiveness. After the objectives of policy have been decided within the party/government structures, civil servants and the relevant public bodies carry out the decisions. If a cabinet decision has legislative implications, it is the duty of ministers to pilot the legislation through Parliament. If new primary legislation is required to execute a government decision, civil servants undertake extensive consultations with experts and interested groups within and outside government. It is at this stage that elements of the environmental movement can influence outcomes most effectively. However, environmental groups tend to be consulted only when a given policy area is seen by government as having an environmental dimension. Moreover, consultation tends to centre on specific areas of policy rather than the principles of policy making. The executors of policy, decide which groups to consult, and select only those issues where they feel consultation is necessary. Environmental groups may therefore be counselled with reference to, say, transport policy, but not taxation policy.

The potential uptake of green ideas has previously been limited by this traditional process of selective screening. However, in recognition of the increasing role that environmental groups can play in government policy making, the 1990 Environment White Paper has promised that government will improve arrangements for consulting with environmental organisations. Furthermore, with a commitment to nominate a minister in every government department with responsibility for environmental policies, the potential exists for the wider involvement of environmental groups.

The final stage of the policy process is policy fulfilment. This refers to the extent to which the executed policy of the party or government pacifies or fulfils the demands of the electorate or pressure groups acting for part of the electorate. In many ways fulfilment is a rather abstract stage in the policy-making process. Until a general election is called, parties in opposition can only measure the success or failure of a particular policy artificially through opinion polls. The party in government, even with a substantial majority and after extensive consultations, cannot hope to pacify all those who clamour for different policy outcomes. Moreover, policy fulfilment does not operate within a fixed timescale, and the criteria against which outcomes are measured change rapidly with public opinion and the goals and strategies of the environmental movement.[22]

The greening of party ideology

The beliefs and values of each political party shape the policies that shape society: altering the ideologies of the parties is thus the environmental movement's ultimate challenge. Friends of the Earth, along with other environmental groups, are aware as that, as well exerting pressure to influence specific policy decisions, they are also seeking to establish new 'green' principles for government. It was hoped that the 1990 White Paper would assist this process of creating the right ideological climate for environmental policies to flourish. However, as we shall discuss in later chapters, getting the parties to change ideologies is not easy.

If we draw upon the 'balanced' view of interaction between the political parties and the environmental movement, we gain the impression that the ideologies of each faction are matched on equal terms. This is far from the case. The ideologies of the political parties function in relation to maintaining and achieving political power. Despite the tensions caused by a diversity of beliefs within a political party, ideologies are presented to voters as coherent homogeneous blocks. In the environmental movement, where the range of ideologies is vast, tensions have a more fragmentary effect.[23] Moreover, since the commitment to power and answerability to the voters is decidedly reduced in the environmental movement, the rallying/election function of an ideology is neither required nor present.

Party ideologies as 'ways of thinking' represent major obstacles to the environmental movement in the greening process. Although the Greens may seek some dramatic gestalt-like change in the workings of party politics, realistically the 'greening' of ideology has to be about achieving incorporation in the long term rather than replacement in the short term. The assumptions, values and goals expressed in the environmental movement are incorporated in existing ideologies of the political parties via a slow process of attrition in which pressures exerted by the movement's component groups are taken up in a piecemeal fashion. If the pressures continue, policies may increasingly take the environmental perspective, and ephemeral rhetoric may give way to more meaningful dialogue. We can then begin to speculate on some ideological alteration within a party. However, the time scale for this process is uncertain. It is difficult to say how long a party might take to alter its ideology in a way which allows it to incorporate an environmental way of thinking.[24] Even then, new beliefs may be excluded after a brief interlude. However, it is possible to identify the 'fit' between environmentalist beliefs and existing party beliefs and explore the possible areas of conflict, with the caveat that in normal circumstances, established party beliefs will always retain primacy.

The interaction between the environmental movement and the political parties seems in the first instance to be like any other confrontation, a battle between two sides, each with its own supporters and each striving to hold the reigns of power. Such an analogy is far too simplistic. Interaction takes place within a constitutional framework which has no fixed or agreed interpretation, and in a political style which seems to avoid consistency and formality. Although the parties are united through the conventions and rituals of democratic politics, they can never present an united front in terms of their ideologies. The task of the environmentalists is thus made more arduous, given that their 'opponents' are usually involved in some degree of ideological in-fighting.

There is also extensive overlap between each of the parties and the environmental movement. With debate cloaked in rhetoric, and with neither side able to define the causes it is fighting for in a manner its opponents can recognise, it is often problematic to differentiate challengers from the challenged, the right side from wrong, and ultimately it may be impossible to distinguish the victor from the vanquished.

Having established a framework within which the challenge of the environmental movement to party politics is taking place, from the rhetorical to the ideological level, we must now seek explanations as to why the parties have accepted the challenge and are engaged in the 'greening' process.

Notes and references

1   See: Gusfield, J. R. 1970. *Protest, Reform, Revolt: A Reader in Social Movements*. New York: John Wiley.

2   As Grove-White puts it: 'Every serious clash between amenity and development involves politics. The arguments advanced by either side are arguments about priorities, about what Roy Gregory (in 'The Price of Amenity') has called the "allocation of values and of costs" and that fact alone makes them political.' In Grove-White, R. 1975. 'The Framework of Law: Some Observations.' In Smith, P. J. (Ed.) *The Politics of Physical Resources*. Chap. 1. Harmondsworth: Penguin Education, Penguin Books Ltd.

3   Fernie, J./Pitkethly, A. S. 1985. *Resources: Environment and Policy*. London: Harper and Row.

4   Kolinsky and Paterson (1976) observe that: 'The interaction of movements and the political system is a two-way process. While considering the changes created by the impact of the movements on established political systems, one should not overlook the constraints imposed by the existing systems on the structure and orientation of movements.' In Kolinsky, M./ Paterson, W. E. (Eds.) 1976. *Social and Political Movements in Western Europe*. London: Croom Helm.

5   Increasingly, however, it is difficult for environmental groups not to have a perspective on affairs one would normally assume was outside of their concern. All aspects of life have a bearing on environmental concern.

6   Oakeshott, M. 1951. *Political Education*. Cambridge: Bowes and Bowes.

7   Within the Labour and Conservative Parties in particular there is a strong 'broad church' ideological tradition which each party is keen to emphasise. A range of beliefs are tolerated – possibly in exchange for party loyalty – making it difficult to be precise when referring to party ideologies.

8   Scarborough, E. 1984. *Political Ideology and Voting: An Explanatory Study*. Oxford: Clarendon Press.

9   Note 8, *op. cit.*

10   See: Smith, G. 1976. 'Social Movements and Party Systems in Western Europe.' In Kolinski, M./Paterson, W. E. (Eds.) *Social and Political Movements in Western Europe*. London: Croom Helm. 331–54.

11   The widespread protests that followed the introduction of the community charge were readily used by the opposition parties to gain support for themselves and erode support for the government.

12   Lowe, P./Rudig, W. 1986. *Political Ecology and the Social Sciences*. IIUG pre 86–2. Berlin: WZB.

13   Marsh, D. (Ed.) 1983. *Pressure Politics: Interest Groups in Britain*. London: Junction Books.

14   Watts, N./Wandesforde-Smith, G. 1980. 'Postmaterial Values and Environmentalism.' *Policy Studies Journal*, 9. 346–58.

15   Lukes, S. 1974. Power: A Radical View. London: Macmillan; Dahl, R. 1961. *Who Governs?* New Haven, Conn: Yale University Press.

16   This model rose in prominence under the administrations of Mrs Thatcher. See, for instance: Hennessey, P. 1987. 'The Quality of Cabinet Government.' In *British Politics: a Reader*. Burch, M./Moran. M. Manchester: Manchester University Press. 279–92.

17   Marxist critiques of the environmental movement readily delight in 'revealing' the real substance behind its use of rhetoric. See for instance the classic: Enszenberger, H. M. 1974. 'A Critique of Political Ecology.' *New Left Review*, 84. March/April, 3–31.

18   See: Brotherton, D. I. 1986. 'Research policy and review 8. Party Political Approaches to Rural Conservation in Britain.' *Environment and Planning A*, 18. 151–60; Owens, S. 1986. 'Environmental Politics In Britain: New Paradigm or Placebo?' *Area*, 18 (3) September.

19   Banting, K. G. 1979. *Poverty Politics and Policy*. London: Macmillan Press Ltd.

20   Lindblom, C. 1959. 'The Science of Muddling Through.' *Public Administration Review*, 19. 79–88.

21   Solesbury, W. 1976. 'The Environmental Agenda.' *Public Administration*, 54. Winter. 379–97.

22   In Forman's words: Politicians may imagine, especially when they have recently been returned to office with what they regard as a clear electoral mandate to carry out their policies, that they have become the undisputed masters of the political scene. Yet they would do well to remember that in modern political conditions they are bound to depend upon the co-operation of the pressure groups and the influence of other external forces for the fulfilment of their policies.' Forman, F. N. 1985. *Mastering British Politics*. London: Macmillan Press Ltd.

23   The extent of the ideological positions in the environmental movement may well be a function of its nascency. No single position has yet had time to emerge.

24   We can safely hypothesise that this would be a much longer process by adaptation than by revolution.

4

Responding to pressure

Party interest in the environment, matched by increasing political participation by the environmental pressure groups, points toward an unprecedented establishment of a 'green' agenda and a new environmental imperative to the political process. We now look at why this greening process has taken place within party politics during the 1980s.

Explanations for the greening of the political parties are inevitably party-specific. Variations in party structures, decision-making processes, intentions and political fortunes prevent the development of a single accurate and universally applicable model explaining why a party responds to the challenge of the environmental movement at any one time. Moreover, we have to bear in mind the important distinction between the 'greening' of the parties and the 'greening' of government. The way individual Conservative Party members react to social and political changes is coloured by the procedures of governmental decision making, the concept of responsible government, and a natural tendency to hold on to a powerful parliamentary majority.

However, we can establish broad interpretative models to explain why the 'greening' of the major political parties, including the party of government, is taking place. This chapter explores one such model which focuses upon the parties as institutions responsive to the pressures exerted and encouraged by the environmental movement.

The responsive account

A standard political model would suggest that government and the political parties respond to a range of dynamic pressures for change.[1]

These pressures emanate from various sources, are effective in different ways, and can precipitate a variety of outcomes. The main goal of the pressure groups is to change government or party policies. It is doubtful whether individual groups could change party ideologies, although the persistent pressures of coalitions of 'closed' and 'open' environmental groups may well alter party beliefs via a process of attrition.

We can understand the pressures acting upon the main political parties as both evolutionary and coincidental. Evolutionary pressures build up over a long period of time, although it is difficult to identify when exactly they may have originated; they just appear to have always existed 'in the background'.[2] Coincidental pressures seem to arise from nowhere and are transitory in character. These are related to the changing state of the physical and human environment and involve a strong element of chance. The line dividing the two types of pressure categories is artificial and fine, and what appears as a chance input may actually be the culmination of many years' pressure. In both cases, the pressures for change originate primarily, but not exclusively, from outside the political parties.

Figure 4 illustrates a 'pressure-response' model of party greening, adapted from the work of Downs (1972) and Solesbury (1976).[3] It links evolutionary pressures with coincidential pressures, and suggests that the greening process is a party's response to a variety of pressures applied at different times and under different circumstances. We now consider these pressures in turn, taking the evolutionary ones first.

The pressure of public opinion

Despite the fact that public opinion changes frequently, is difficult to measure and is often based more upon popular prejudice than any empirical knowledge of the facts, politicians of all parties still follow it closely. It represents some measure of objective feeling within the population which parties can heed or ignore. In a society increasingly politically aware, the majority of politicians include 'the mood of the people' somewhere in their policy-making calculations, and under 'normal circumstances' are ready to adjust party policy accordingly.[4] The influence of opinion polls tends to increase as a general election approaches. Early in an administration a government may be able to ignore public opinion, knowing that it

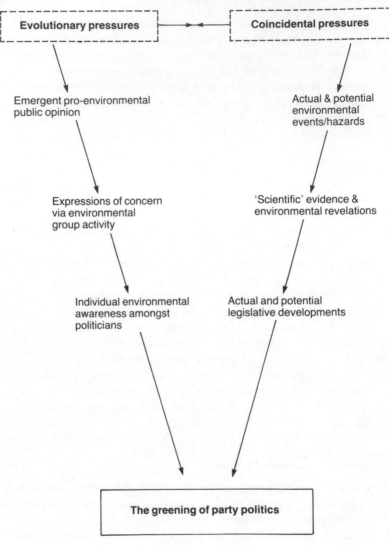

Fig. 4 The 'pressure-response' model of party greening

has three or four years to rebuild its popularity. Near an election, however, government tends to heed the public more intently, and each party is keen to demonstrate that public attitudes are properly taken into account.

Members of Parliament are informed of public opinion directly via letter. These predominantly address constituency or regional environmental matters and do not provide a good guide to national feeling. Furthermore, they do not guarantee a party response unless a significant number of MPs receive letters concerning the same issue. In 1983 eighty, mostly Tory MPs signed an Early Day Motion (EDM) protesting against draft circulars ambivalent in their commitment to protecting the Green Belt. The majority of signatories had been urged to take some form of action after receiving letters from their constituents living near the Green Belt itself. As with most EDMs, a debate was not forced on the issue, but it did make the minister concerned (in this case Patrick Jenkin) aware of the feelings of Tory back-benchers.

Public opinion as measured by the contents of an MP's mailbag increases environmental awareness of individual and groups of MPs and can start a 'domino effect'; if a sufficient number of MPs relay the feelings of their constituents to the relevant minister, then this may be taken note of by the party decision makers. It is unlikely, however, that party managers will immediately alter policy as a result of regionalised public opinion. A range of further questions will need to be addressed such as: what number is a sufficient number of MPs echoing the same opinion?; what is their majority?, and when is the next general or by-election?

National public concern for the environment is monitored through opinion polls which the parties regularly consult. The number of organisations requesting public opinion polls on environmental issues, and the number of bodies undertaking such polls, have steadily increased over the past twenty years. However, unlike a subject such as capital punishment where public opinion can be stated in a straightforward manner as a percentage for or against, the environment covers a wide range of issues, and the level of opinion tends to vary accordingly. In recent years environmental problems have been identified more specifically than broad headings such as pollution and the attractiveness of the countryside, and opinion polls now cover public attitudes to policy areas such as transport, energy, food, industry and taxation. Whereas politicians can be selective as regards what public opinion is, accentuating their concern for one issue and neglecting the level of concern for another, taken as a whole, public opinion on environmental issues now represents a weighty influence on party politics with parties and government wishing to maintain public goodwill.

Comparing levels of public concern over a period of time is difficult because polls do not always replicate their questions or cover the same issues. Nevertheless, despite such limitations, between 1983 and the present we can recognise a consistent increase in public concern for a range of environmental issues to levels in keeping with the rest of the European Community.[5] A Mori poll undertaken in 1983, for instance, did not address the issue of acid rain because it was not publically prominent at that time.[6] Some six years later, nearly 80 per cent of those interviewed were either 'quite worried' or 'very worried' by the issue.

Public opinion reflects the salience that specific issues have at any one time. A Mori poll undertaken for the pressure group CLEAR in 1982 at the height of their campaign showed that an extremely high percentage of the public were concerned about the issue of lead in petrol, with some 90 per cent believing it should be banned, 6 per cent adding that this was urgent.[7] In 1989, concern for this problem under the broader heading of 'traffic exhaust fumes' had fallen, with around 75 per cent saying they were either 'quite worried' or 'very worried'. In 1989, the global problem of the destruction of the ozone layer was included in the DOE survey for the first time, and over 75 per cent of respondents said they were either 'very worried' or 'quite worried'.

As one might expect, public concern for the environment masks a range of preferences and prejudices which ought to be taken into account when considering the opinion polls. There is a regional 'not in my back yard' (NIMBY) dimension to the public's opinions on pollution issues. Aircraft noise, for example, is thought to be a very serious problem mainly by those residing near large airports, and concern for dirt and noise from traffic registers high levels from those living in the larger metropolitan areas.[8] With regard to the country-side, concern for the preservation of amenity correlates to those who use it most, and similarly concern for property development or roadworks tends to correspond with those whose house values may suffer if development proceeds. Age, class and sex differences may also account for levels of public opinion toward the environment, and so too may party political affiliation. Thus, the life-long Conservative supporter may show little concern for the risks created by nuclear power generation, simply because it flies in the face of Conservative Party policy. This is not to view public opinion toward the environment solely as dependent on political ideology or personal interest, although the effects of these factors are rational, inherent and influential.[9] However, if public opinion does cut across other patterns of interest, then it may be of more significance than if it merely follows an established preference.

Despite changes in the type of environmental problems and allowing for public preferences, the environment has consistently ranked highly in opinion polls as an area of concern.[10] As a national issue of concern in 1990, the environment ranked second in the minds of the public behind the community charge – notably above issues such as education and the economy. Support also cut across a range of age and social income groups. To the politician this suggests two things: firstly, that public concern for the environment runs deeper than an ephemeral fancy for furry animals; and secondly, that the 'jobs or flowers' choice is no longer sufficient as a standard political rebutal to the environmental pressure groups.[11]

The most telling effect of pro-environmental public opinion has been upon people's voting intentions. In March 1987, before an official announcement of a general election date, Friends of the Earth in conjunction with the World Wildlife Fund commissioned a Mori opinion poll centred upon public attitudes to environmental issues.[12] Some 70 per cent of respondents said they would take party attitudes to the environment into account when they voted, whilst 81 per cent of respondents indicated that government should give a much higher priority to protecting the environment.

Opinion polls have been found to influence the voting intention, of the public, but in an inconsistent and partial way.[13] There is little evidence to suggest that party attitudes to the environment did sway voters in the 1987 General Election. The fact that the public continues to say it would switch party allegiances because of party positions on environmental issues tells us that pro-environmental support remains high; however, it is still unlikely that party attitudes to the environment will have anything other than a minor influence on voting behaviour at a general election. Public opinion would seem to have a more direct effect upon party strategies leading up to a general election.[14] Indeed, many politicians in the major parties believe strongly in the power of public opinion to change policy and ultimately party beliefs.[15]

The opposition parties are particularly anxious to illustrate their awareness of the public mood regarding the environment. The Labour Party's 'Labour Listens Campaign' was designed precisely to

D

demonstrate that, in the widest sense, it was concerned with what people wanted. Similarly, Labour's 1987 election campaign strategy slogan – 'Labour Putting People First' – could also be said to have a responsive ring about it. The Alliance parties in their election campaign had emphasised that 'governments should learn to listen to the people to whom they are accountable'.[16] As an ideal, this is difficult to challenge, but the leap from the listening process, actual or symbolic, to that of policy making is a major one – one that the Labour Party and the Alliance did not make prior to the 1987 General Election.

Before the 1987 General Election, the Labour Party, suffering an erosion of its working-class base and its regional representation, searched for new policies to attract a relatively new electorate. Public opinion was not, however, a direct contributor to Labour's environmental policy at the time of the election. As one of the Labour Party's Regional Whips observed: 'Labour Party policy on the environment has grown with public perception of the issues and this is exhibited by the polls that now appear regularly in the quality press.'[17] This admits that the public opinion polls were being monitored, but rather than actually shaping policy, public opinion was used to legitimise policy positions already established. Environmental activists in the Alliance parties, eager to test their value politics with the voters, also saw public opinion as being of strategic importance prior to the 1987 General Election, not to identify areas of environmental concern and the depth of concern before policies were assembled, but to emphasise environmental policies already worked out. As a member of the Liberal Energy Policy Panel stated prior to the General Election: 'a look at the weekend opinion polls on the nuclear question tells us that we have got it [party energy policy] right.'[18]

Have the opinion polls had any influence upon Conservative attitudes to the environment? Governments clearly wish to identify themselves as possessing and exercising the responsibility allocated to them via the ballot box; but the idea of responsibility is coloured by political objectives, party ideology and allegiances to key interest groups. For instance, despite a consistent number of opinion polls indicating the strength of the anti-nuclear power lobby, the Conservatives have not weakened in their commitment to develop the industry as stated in their 1983 general election manifesto.[19] Instead, they have consistently adjusted the rationale behind their pro-nuclear policy in order to deflect public feeling. Initially, economic reasons seemed to lie behind the development of a nuclear energy programme; nuclear power, it was argued, would emerge as the cheapest energy option for the UK. Following the 1984 miners' strike, the importance of developing the nuclear power industry was buttressed by strategic arguments relating to the importance of maintaining a diversity of energy supply. With continued questioning of the economic viability of nuclear power, particularly in the wake of Sir Frank Layfield's report of the Sizewell B public inquiry, the government found that against a background of public concern for issues such as acid rain and global warming, their nuclear power policy could now be justified for environmental reasons. This ironic switch in policy rationale did not entail any capitulation of government energy policy goals in the face of public opinion. Indeed, it seems to indicate the government's deep-seated commitment to a prestigious technology, and the benefits it is recognised to bring in terms of overseas investment.

Taking account of public opinion regarding nuclear power has not been a priority for a party with such a large and powerful majority. With such power, the government can be afford to be selective in the way it responds to certain issues the public express concern over – or dismiss it altogether. Public concern about the nuclear industry has been high for many years (although more recently the emphasis has moved to the problems of radioactive waste disposal), yet this has had little influence on a party which, according to one Tory back bencher, is 'out to prove the public wrong about an industry which promises to be good yet is persistently naughty'.[20]

Where pro-environment public opinion has influenced the Conservatives, it is where that opinion has been concentrated amongst existing Tory voters and potential defectors to the Liberal Democrats. In the lead-up to the 1987 General Election, for example, several Tory MPs including the Chief Whip, were acutely aware that increased environmental concern expressed by their own constituents on issues ranging from straw burning to low-level radioactive waste disposal could lose them votes. Adept political manoeuvring ensured that such a situation did not arise either because policies were dropped, or because emphasis was switched to wider election issues. Where policy programmes were dropped, as in the case of exploration for low-level radioactive waste sites, MPs were able to turn potential political humiliation into a victory for the representative processs.

Public support for the environment continues to remain high and seems unlikely to diminish in the foreseeable future. As such, politicians of all parties find it increasingly difficult to ignore: a point recognised by the environmental pressure groups which we now consider.

Pressure group pressure

As outlined in chapter 2, the UK environmental movement is centred upon core pressure groups whose membership has dramatically increased throughout the 1980s. Furthermore, the resources of the environmental pressure groups have substantially increased. Taken as a whole, environmental groups employ over 1,000 permanent staff and work with an annual budget of approximately £150 million.[21] The increase in membership has heightened the stature of the environmental pressure groups in the eyes of politicians. Moreover, whatever the accuracy of Lowe and Goyder's 1983 estimate that three million people belong to environmental pressure groups, the figure has undoubtedly made a considerable impact upon the politicians, who have constantly bandied it around in their rhetorical exchanges on the environment.[22]

Membership size aside, the parties have increasingly recognised the skills and commitment of the promotional pressure groups. Their ability to attract media attention and thus influence public opinion on specific environmental issues has certainly strengthened their hand. Where perhaps this mobilisation of public support had been related to some single issue or some single pressure group, environmental issues have increasingly become the concern of a range of groups. The 1982 CLEAR campaign for a ban on lead in petrol, for instance, attracted the support of some twenty-five other pressure groups. Groups such as the CPRE and FoE now recognise that collaboration with other groups with mutual interests enables them to increase their level of political influence.[23] Thus, pressures for the environmental cause have intensified as a network of groups, all of which recognise the same aims, has evolved.

Opportunities for environmental pressure groups to influence the workings of government directly have also increased, particularly since the 1979 reform of the Select Committee system in the House of Commons. As the process of environmental policy making in the UK has developed, technicalities have increasingly become important at the formulation and execution stages. Furthermore, the public are ever more attuned to the details of policy and their consequences. This has made it easier for the more specialised pressure groups to achieve 'insider' status by providing quality background information and details of likely policy implications. Environmental groups such as the CPRE, Transport 2000 and FoE have developed degrees of credibility which mean they are now in a position to participate in what Richardson and Jordan have termed 'policy communities'.[24] Such groups have been called upon to give evidence and advice to Departmental Committees and House of Commons and House of Lords Select Committees. As their expertise comes to be respected in such quarters, so their credibility becomes strengthened in the eyes of the parties.

The impact of the environmental pressure groups upon each of the major parties in terms of rhetoric, policy and ideological change varies considerably with their differing political needs, their differing styles and the strategies adopted by the groups themselves. The majority of environmental groups are non party political. However, during three consecutive terms of Conservative government, alliances between the groups and the opposition parties have formed, and information and ideas have been exchanged. Theoretically, such relationships may only last while a party is in opposition, but given three consecutive Conservative administrations, relationships have had longer than usual to develop.

In terms of being able to shape environmental policies of the major parties, the influence of groups such as FoE, CPRE and Greenpeace is carefully contrived to be indirect, lest it offend the established rubric of party procedures or wound the independence of the groups themselves. Relationships between the parties and pressure groups are clumsy and uneasy. The general view of members of the main parties would seem to be that although the pressure groups have their hearts in the right place, they have little idea regarding the complexities of day to day politics.[25] As a senior Labour Party MP commented: 'We owe a great deal to the likes of Friends of the Earth. I see them as playing an important role in bringing issues to our attention. It is now up to us to find political solutions to what are essentially political problems; something pressure groups know little about.'[26] Similarly, a former Liberal Party Chairman observed, prior to the 1987 general election: 'The pressure groups have succeeded in shaping up a green agenda but it remains to be seen whether or not issues such as acid rain and ozone depletion can be handled on a party political stage.'[27]

Although perhaps aimed at the more radical pressure groups rather than the established lobbyists, comments such as those above highlight the sacred functional boundary between the elected and the unelected: those who are empowered to make decisions and those who are not. Pressure groups may thus be congratulated for raising awareness and providing information, yet their ability to influence party decision making is something to be denied.

For environmental activists within the Labour Party and the Liberal Democrats, environmental groups act as a useful source of technical information. The task of accumulating material with which to attack the Conservative Government's environmental policy is made that much easier if material produced by Friends of the Earth or Greenpeace is available. Facts uncovered by environmental groups quickly find their way into MPs' speeches and party publications, and in this way, the slow, often imperceptible process of permeating party ideologies can begin.

Where exisiting or proposed government policy is the common enemy, the opposition parties may be more responsive to ideas put forward by the environmental groups, particularly if they have no policy position of their own. However, just because alliances may be formed against the government from time to time, the environmental policies (or lack of them) of the opposition parties are not immune from attack.

In 1986, for instance, Frank Cook MP organised a Shadow Cabinet meeting between Labour leaders to discuss the party's energy programme in the wake of Chernobyl. Aside from Neil Kinnock, John Cunningham and Stan Orme, the meeting also included SERA, Greenpeace and FoE. Contributions from the represented pressure groups were acknowledged as being of immense value (although the issue was fudged). As a result of this consultation, the NEC statement to the 1986 party conference (No. 63) was constructed and subsequently approved by a two-thirds majority. However, whereas the principle of phasing out the nuclear power programme under a future Labour administration was readily accepted by the three groups, the indecision regarding the time-scale of such a move was not. Did this indicate a lack of environmental concern on the part of the Labour Party, or a lack of political understanding on the part of the pressure groups? The answer would seem to lie somewhere between the two suggested positions, although the pressure groups' do not have to worry about answering to the electorate.

Within the Conservative Party, attitudes to the environmental pressure groups vary considerably. Back bench MPs possess a healthy respect for environmental pressure groups and their role, albeit indirect, in policy making.[28] Reformist groups such as the Royal Society for the Protection of Birds, the Civic Trust and National Trust – groups which have sizeable Conservative membership – have been the more successful in terms of influencing the thinking of Conservative Party members. The CPRE in particular has achieved considerable success in exploiting the inate Conservative concern for the countryside. Focusing primarily upon conservation issues, the CPRE closely monitors the government environmental policy proposals and this watchful eye is both noticed and respected by ministers.

Persistent and intense lobbying by the CPRE was rewarded when a new clause was introduced into the 1985 Agriculture Bill (Act 1986) obliging the Ministry of Agriculture to strike a 'reasonable balance' between the interests of agriculture and the conservation of the countryside. Similarly, the Bill provided for the designation of Environmentally Sensitive Areas: something the CPRE had lobbied for some two years earlier. What was essentially a policy adjustment under CPRE pressure has since been cited by the government as being a policy initiative. There appears to be an air of inevitability regarding the awareness-raising role of groups like the CPRE amongst 'wet' Tory MPs and a welcoming attitude regarding their role as 'environmental policemen'. Indeed, some on the left of the Parliamentary Conservative Party have linked this with the evolutionary character of environmental concern and the slow but certain integration of their ideas into Conservative thought – for them, the most natural repository available. However, those same MPs also saw the null impact of environmental groups on the policy makers within the party as inevitable. As one Tory MP put it: 'Common sense and popular demands mean little to a party machinery which seems to run on autopilot.'[29]

Conservative attitudes to the more radical pressure groups remain relatively hostile, particularly amongst the policy makers. While some groups are seen as merely 'slighty nutty', others are seen as

having 'a subversive influence on the democratic process'.[30] Within
Conservative Central Office, the opinion was that single-minded
environmental groups may ultimately be pushing for the right outcomes, but were pushing the wrong way and far too quickly. Further
up the hierarchy, a senior adviser on environmental policy within
Mrs Thatcher's Policy Unit had remarked that, whilst the environmental pressure groups may have succeeded in creating a wider
awareness of green issues amongst the public, it was the 'creativity
and conviction' of the Conservative Government that was the over-
riding driving force. Moreover, with regard to what the pressure
groups had to offer, the message was that 'the government is not
overly concerned with pressure groups nor overly concerned with
the unions'.[31]

Amongst the left of the Conservative Party, attitudes toward the
environmental groups are positive and bode well for the future.
Certainly the pressure groups themselves are working hard to
improve their credibility. However, within the decision-making
executive, attitudes seem to indicate not merely a passive denial of
influence of the radical environmental pressure groups, but rather a
worrying attempt to resist influence.

Out of all the environmental pressure groups, perhaps the most
successful in terms of shaping a 'green agenda' for the major parties
during the 1980s has been the Green Alliance. Established in 1978,
its cross-party activities and low-profile lobbying has made its mark
on the environmental thinking of the major parties. Through its
formal and informal 'bridge-building' meetings between ministers,
party officials and leading environmentalists the Green Alliance has
gained considerable credibility. With a staff of only four in 1988 and
a relatively small but prestigious membership (approximately 450 in
1988) of key environmentalists and personalities, the Green Alliance
has cultivated insider status within the major parties. It advises a
number of MPs on environmental issues, arranges for the placing of
parliamentary questions, prepares briefings for environmental
debates and publishes a Parliamentary Newsletter. Its aims to 'promote an ecological perspective' within each party, to improve co-
operation and co-ordination of other environmental groups and to
develop 'green ideas' into policies are pursued with reticence and a
sound understanding of the intricacies of party politics. As the
Director of the Green Alliance puts it: 'Rather than simply threaten
politicians with the dire consequences which might follow if they

mishandle an issue, the secret of successful lobbying is to offer them messages which they can use.'[32] The subtlety of such pressure politics seems to have found favour with the politicians, who appreciate the sensitivity and political understanding shown. According to senior Liberal and SDP activists at the time, the Green Alliance was seen as instrumental in ensuring that all the parties included detailed statements on the environment in their manifestos, leading up to the 1987 election.[33]

The effect of the Green Alliance on the environmental thinking of the major parties individually is overshadowed by its effect on the overall political agenda, largely dictated by the government. Good connections with the Tory Government have proved valuable despite ideological crossfire from the Greens and the left. At times when conviction politics threatened to marginalise the high-profile environmental groups, the Green Alliance has managed to penetrate at least some of the Conservative anti-environment armour.

The relationship between the Green Alliance and the Conservatives has not always been as cosy as a lunch with Mrs Thatcher when Prime Minister would at first suggest.[34] In the early 1980s, for instance, the Green Alliance was quick to attack the government for neglecting the countryside and the rural communities of Britain.[35] However, the respectable, constructive, and creative lobbying of the Green Alliance has found favour amongst important elements of the government. In 1987, for instance, at the suggestion of the Green Alliance, Mrs Thatcher's environmental policy adviser held a seminar at No. 10 to address key aspects of agricultural policy. This was attended by both MAFF and DOE officials, as well as key environmentalists, and went some way to reducing policy differences between the two government departments.

The continuing success of the Green Alliance's pressure upon the main parties is due to its ability to play upon the inherent competitiveness of British party politics, a phenomenon we shall return to later. Morever, success is linked to a willingness to tackle the interface between environment and economy and to open up the environmental debate to industrialists. Mainstream politicians would seem eager to respond to environmental questions phrased in pragmatic economic terms: the language they understand.

From a pluralist perspective of the British constitution, it would seem reasonable to argue that the well-developed network of environmental pressure groups provides the greatest pressures for party 'greening'. Certainly such groups have secured a significant degree of political recognition and an unprecedented level of credibility. They can also claim to have exerted considerable influence on the environmental policy processes at both government and party level. Their influence is often a product of protracted, disparate, often underestimated campaigns, rather than immediate confrontations; it revolves not only around changing policy, but maintaining it as it stands where applicable. However, many campaigns of the environmental groups remain issue-specific, tending to fade away in true 'issue-attention' style. Despite growing memberships, many groups still lack adequate resources to pursue and co-ordinate the campaigns they would like. Furthermore, however well researched and articulated group contributions may be, the major parties and government can readily dismiss such pressures when it suits them.[36]

The trade unions as environmental pressure groups

The network of environmental groups has widened to include those sectional pressure groups which were not previously recognised as specifically concerned with environmental issues. Contacts between the trade unions and promotional groups such as Greenpeace and Transport 2000 have been particularly notable. Although we will return to the role of the trade unions as a constraining factor in the 'greening' of the parties, here we look at their role as a positive environmental influence.

Many of the trade unions, undergoing a period of untidy introspection in the face of a declining membership and a long time without any significant political influence under a Conservative Government, have been only too ready to seek support from the environmental movement. Symbiotic relationships have been established, providing the unions with a public profile which would be otherwise reduced or at least marred by a hostile press and by environmental groups with opportunities to swell their ranks and increase their credibility.[37]

There certainly seems to be an element of opportunism in the way the trade unions have united with environmental groups. However, over a period of time the trade unions, along with the rest of society, have gradually succumbed to the pressures of the environmentalists and have recognised an increasing degree of overlap in interests regarding the problems posed by rapid socio-economic and technological change.

In terms of exerting positive pressures on the major parties with regard to environmental policy, the trade unions as sectional groups have, as one would expect, had little impact on the Conservative Party or the Liberal Democrats, the obvious focus for trade union pressure still being the Labour Party. Labour's rightward shift, particularly since 1987, may have loosened the bonds between the party and the unions, but the traditional and intimate relationship between the two still remains.[38]

The unions have carefully embraced many of the ideas of the environmentalists, and even with a reduced role in Labour's policy-making machinery, they have still been able to make significant inroads into party thinking. Indeed, environmental ideas as compared to the more traditional concerns of the unions have perhaps secured the easiest ride within a party anxious to play down the 'beer and sandwiches' image. A well placed NUPE-sponsored Labour MP offered the following plausible explanation:

I have no doubt that if we had a 100 plus majority in the Commons, then calls to re-introduce secondary picketing would be received more readily within the Party. But since we are still in opposition it is important that we address the question of what is relevant to the public and it is important that the unions do the same. If they start to address wider issues affecting all of society rather than just what matters to their own membership, then the Labour Party will respond positively.[39]

Through the Labour Party NEC, several unions which have supported environmental actions and policy changes are represented. Unions such as the NUM, NUR, NUPE, TGWU and GMB have a played a major role in shaping Labour Party policy; it would seem that unions which have already adopted their own environmental policies, or which have a particular interest in doing so and which share informal alliances with the environmental pressure groups, should be able to push the environmental cause within the party.

Environmental concern within the trade union movement has a proud history. Indeed, the unions had embraced some key 'green' ideas long before the formation of an environmental movement. Nuclear disarmament, women's rights, internationalism, social justice, as well as a basic concern for the health and safety of workers, can now be recognised as pertinent parts of the environmental matrix and not merely a function of the employer–employee relationship. However, environmental concerns have always been seen as peripheral to the unions: sideline issues to health, safety and democracy. Concern has widened, labels have changed, and the concerns of the working classes have become those of the middle classes and, in doing so, are becoming mainstream. Yet the link which could be forged between the demands of the unions and those of other environmental groups is still hindered by the sectionalisation inherent in the trade union movement.

For instance, an ASLEF policy document of 1976, 'Transport for the Nation', highlights the need for an integrated public transport system that reduces air and noise pollution levels, increases energy efficiency, serves the public, and eliminates conflict with regard to road-building in the countryside. This has all the hallmarks of environmental common sense.[40] Yet it is problematic to divorce these recommendations from the implicit need to protect the jobs and improve the working conditions of train drivers. Similarly, do we interpret NUPE's opposition to nuclear power (since 1980) as a self-interested move to protect their own members who would be in the forefront of the danger should a Chernobyl-like accident occur in the UK; or was it prompted by a genuine concern for public safety, the threat of radiation leakage and the burden of nuclear waste disposal?

The failure to separate the seemingly narrow interests of the trade unions from the public environmental good remains as intractable as ever. After a long period of Conservative government, the trade unions found it difficult to convey their concern for environmental issues, even to some members of the Labour Party. Moreover, the unions still have to overcome the inherent cultural prejudice which views environmental issues as conservation and countryside issues and, as such, wholly separate from the problems faced by the vast majority of the UK's urban population. Within the Labour Party it would seem that the apparent self-interests of the unions are actually fusing together under the environmental label. Motivations for union positions are becoming subsumed beneath a slow disintegration of territories. If environmentalists realise that work – its purpose, operation, location and its products – are central to the future of the planet, then trade unions should be better received as a positive environmental pressure groups within the Labour Party.

The competitive edge

The combined activities of an increasingly aware public and politically active environmental pressure groups penetrate through to individual politicians. They can be considered the initial recipients of such pressures, but they may not be in positions to take policy decisions themselves or initiate changes. The positions they hold vary from party to party and range from government ministers and MPs to civil servants and local party activists. As individuals or by working in groups the politicians can then exert pressures through a variety of existing forums, specific to each party, in order to influence the decision makers.

Individual politicians responding to the demands and ideas of the environmental movement may be divided into two main types. Firstly, there are those who respond to environmentalist pressures purely as a function of their position. Members of Parliament, as elected officials have a duty to represent the interests of their constituents and to deal with their problems and grievances. An MP may pursue an interest publicly through questions to the appropriate minister or direct to the Prime Minister, through debates within the House of Commons or inconspicuously 'behind the scenes'. They may ally themselves to other MPs or bodies concerned with the same issue in order to strengthen their level of influence. Particularly for back bench MPs in the parties, strength would seem to lie in numbers, and through informal groups greater pressures can be brought to bear on party decision makers. In this way, environmental issues emanating from constituents or pressure groups are handled in exactly the same way as those from the myriad of other groups advancing their interests.

However, politicians rarely respond to events and issues blindly. This introduces a second category of politicians who respond to and take up environmental pressures as a function of their own interests and not just because they 'have to' in the progress of their duty. Of course there is much overlap between the two types of motivation, which vary with the pressures themselves in time and intensity. In the context of the pressure–response interpretation of the 'greening' of party politics, it is the former mechanistic form of reaction which is important, where politicians engage in the process of pressurising for changes to environmental policy in just the same way as they would for any other policy field. As time progresses and pressure from lobbying groups continues, what begins as routine representation of an environmental cause or group may well develop into a personal interest. The intensity of interest and commitment is of course tempered by party position, party policy and more practical considerations regarding other duties. The degree of self-motivated interest in environmental issues within the politicians will be explored more fully in the next chapter, but at this stage we can assume that such personal concern for an environmental issue will act to intensify the greening process in the arenas of party power.

Peer pressure acts between the parties as well as within them. The inherent 'tit for tat' style of British party politics ensures that the parties are continually competing on a majority of issues including the promotion of a green image. It is this competition that the Green Alliance has sought to harness. Politicians are ever conscious of what other politicians in the other parties are up to, particularly with regard to relatively new political fields such as the environment. New ways of conquering public opinion and deflecting criticisms with regard to the more sensitive issues are always being sought after. Although more a function of human psychology than political science, the process of 'looking over one's shoulder' is at the heart of many party policy decisions and is nothing more than shrewd political manoeuvring.

The emergence of the Liberal/SDP Alliance before the 1987 election as the anticipated third political force highlighted this process. A political centre with strong green claims already in the Liberals and the Social Democrats eager to develop an identity increased the competitive edge. Getting out in front in the opinion polls on as many issues as possible prior to an election, particularly in the southern marginal seats, became increasingly important and maintained the momentum of party 'greening'.

The parties without the responsibility of government are perhaps more ready to take the initiative on environmental policy. Without the duties of government, the opposition parties are able to pursue links with pressure groups more freely and respond to a range of issues in a less constrained way. Their incentive in doing so is to achieve political power, whereas the Conservatives since 1979 have been chiefly motivated by the need to maintain power. Both motivations are strong, but in the case of the party already holding office there is considerable advantage in being able ultimately to control the agenda.

The competitive edge in relation to the environment also acts at an international level, when the British Government experiences peer pressure from other nations. Britain's tag as the 'dirty man of Europe' may be constantly shrugged off by government ministers; privately, however, the criticisms are taken note of. A Conservative MEP noted shortly after the 1987 General Election:

I am always ready to refute the criticisms about our performance in environmental matters compared with the other EC nations. I know what goes on in the other nations. Most of the EC members are in trouble with Brussels over drinking water rules. But the idea that we are the dirty man of Europe sticks in the minds of the public and of course provides good ammunition for the opposition. This is taken seriously by ministers. It doesn't look good and perhaps we need to be less defensive.[41]

Whatever the facts, rhetorical exchanges about Britain's standing in some sort of mythical league of European environmental policy serve to keep Conservatives on their toes. Pressure within the party comes not only from those who see the intrinsic virtue of adopting a more proactive approach to environmental policy, but also emanates from longstanding Tory Europhiles who would like to see the party more committed to Europe. Within the executive, however, it would seem that Britain's environmental record within the EC is beyond challenge, indicating that the pressure to compete does not influence government policy. Mrs Thatcher regularly declared (and by all accounts believed) that Britain had an environmental record 'second to none', suggesting that she felt no need to take notice of the competition.

Although the opposition parties are keen to point out how far the government may be lagging behind other nations' approaches to the environment, they are clearly less affected by peer pressure from abroad, in the official sense of having to respond to the relevant regulations, directives and decisions issued by the EC. They do, however, take note of what is happening in Europe. Sweden's approach to environmental policy under a socialist government, for instance, is cited by environmentalists within the Labour Party as being a worthy model for the party to adopt. Norway's energy policy and even conservative Switzerland's integrated transport policies have been proffered by Labour Party activists as potential development models for a future Labour government. Behind these suggestions lies the idea that within the Labour Party, environmental policy should not always be based upon eternal protestations and innate socialist reaction to Conservative policies, but should take account of what is happening elsewhere.

The pressure of events

Evolutionary pressures are constantly fed by a range of developments which we can take to be largely coincidental, although when analysed in retrospect, the actual occurrence of such events – often the culmination of smaller incidents – may not have been totally unexpected. Their occurrence nevertheless contains enough of the elements of drama and surprise to have a seemingly more significant impact upon the public and the politicians than slowly evolving issues. Such chance factors can create new pressures and new pressure groups, but in the main they are used to bolster the political leverage of existing groups within the environmental movement.

Central to a pressure–response model of party 'greening' is the actual occurrence of problems in the environment. Once picked up by the media, these focus the attention of the public and the politicians on to three things. Firstly, the immediate results of the event are considered in terms of its effect upon the surrounding environment and population. The precise impact of an event upon an area or activity may not at first be known and therefore monitoring may be required. Secondly, explanations are sought for the event's occurrence, frequently with the expectation of attaching blame to an individual or organisation. Thirdly, existing policies are considered in the light of the event, and future policy changes become a matter of debate.

Environmental disasters occurring at home tend to have the most impact upon the public and hence our politicians. In terms of attracting the attention of the government, the social and economic costs associated with such events need to be taken into account. An oil spillage may kill thousands of sea birds, but it also costs money to clean up and involves possible loss in tourist revenue. The first major super-tanker disaster involving the *Torrey Canyon* in 1967 still sticks in many minds. At the time this produced a number of responses from the Wilson government, chiefly the establishment of an *ad hoc* coastal pollution committee which was to eventually lead to the creation of the standing Royal Commission on Environmental Pollution in 1970.

Small-scale environmental disasters at the local level, such as the pollution of water courses from pesticide run-off or the contamination of land sites by toxic waste, may seem remote from government and the policy-making machines of the major parties. Invariably, local MPs become involved, are faced with getting to know the facts of the episode and are made aware of the strength of sentiment surrounding environmental incidents. The frequency and geographical distribution of local environmental incidents may not be enough to focus attention on the policy framework to which those incidents relate. In an area of the UK with a substantial Labour parliamentary majority, a fish kill caused by farm silage discharge, for instance, would no doubt add weight to criticisms of Conservative agricultural policy and the control of water pollution, but probably not to a great extent. But in a Conservative constituency, protestations about the same event would be more worrying, particularly if it had managed to attract national media attention.

Environmental events with visible effects are of particular importance in contributing to changing the attitudes of politicians toward the environment and increasing the pressures for policy changes. The all-party members of the House of Commons Select Committee on the Environment on Acid Rain acknowledged that their trips to see the lifeless lakes of Sweden, the dead trees in the Black Forest and the damage caused to the stonework of Lincoln Cathedral, had significantly influenced the final recommendations of their report, essentially to join the '30 per cent club'.[42]

The importance of an event producing a visible effect which can be measured in terms of damage and disturbance to an ecosystem cannot be overstressed. The more catastrophic events tend to produce a more direct political response in terms of remedial action rather than those events that which have being building up for a long time. This emphasises the idea of the politician acting as the ultimate sceptic, dealing only in the world of tangible facts, where the economic, social and political consequences are expressed through public opinion and the affected interest groups and can be readily assessed.[43] Whereas this is an all too easily accepted view, it is helpful in explaining why environmental issues which have temporally staggered and piecemeal effects, such as hedgerow removal or the addition of nitrates to water courses, do not make the agendas of government until visible effects manifest themselves.

The opposition parties need not wait for environmental events to occur before responding with remedial policies. However, given that the policy agendas of the parties tend to be full and largely under the influence of the party in government, a much more characteristic reaction is to use the rhetoric of 'we told you so' when an event takes place.

Environmental events occurring elsewhere in the world have a less pressing effect upon the parties, given that the effects are not experienced by voters directly. However, events abroad do show up in public opinion polls and comparisions between nations are made, although they can soon be forgotten in the light of domestic issues. More than ever, events abroad provide evidence of the trans-nationality of environmental problems and invoke the feeling of 'it can happen here'. The accident at the Chernobyl nuclear reactor in April 1986 and the effects of radioactive fallout experienced directly by the hill farmers of North Wales and Cumbria, whose sheep stocks were contaminated, perhaps provides the best example, with anti-nuclear-power opinion polls showing significant increases in public support immediately after the event. Yet the effect of the Chernobyl disaster on the energy policies of the major parties and on the wider environmental context of these policies, was not so straightforward.

The response of the Conservative Government to Chernobyl was both defiant and predictable. With almost patriotic fervour, a government long established as the champion of the nuclear industry portrayed the Chernobyl accident as a purely Soviet experience based upon inferior design, engineering and management – a position supported by Lord Marshall and the CEGB and the Prime Minister. Speaking to the Bow Group in 1986 on nuclear safety, Waldegrave carefully turned the events of Chernobyl to his party's advantage.[44] As well as providing him with the opportunity to highlight the inadequate standard of life of Soviet society, its secret and authoritarian regime, it also provided a platform from which to launch an offensive against the oil and coal industries. In a swift move, to an audience far from being converted, he extolled the safety record of the British nuclear industry, and through a castigation of coal-fired power stations on the grounds of their contributions to acid rain and global warming, he justified Sizewell B and the entire Conservative energy policy.

While the Chernobyl disaster may have reinforced fears within the anti-nuclear lobby, for a government so resolutely committed to the nuclear industry, ideologically, institutionally and economically, the passage of events had little effect amongst those of influence within

the Conservative Government. Having said this, the Chernobyl inci-
dent did have an effect on some Conservative Party members remote
from the locus of power. For such individuals, although there is little
chance of their effecting changes in party policy directly, the event
raised questions in their own minds, which we can assume would
otherwise not have had the chance to germinate. A former front
bench Conservative minister, now enjoying the 'freedom' of the back
benches, reflected on the government's handling of the Chernobyl
event:

I can understand why we have not been panicked by what has happened in
the Soviet Union [a reference to Mrs Thatcher's written parliamentary reply
to Sir Trevor Skeet regarding the lack of need for evacuation plans given a
nuclear accident on the French or Belgian coasts], but I am afraid that there
exists a lack of sensitivity regarding how people feel about what has happened. In my view we are making the mistake of not being seen to listen
people's fears whether we consider them irrational or not.[45]

This view highlights an issue distinct from whether the government
pursues a policy of nuclear expansion or not. It cuts through to the
government's handling of environmental events, the public perception of risk and the lack of responsiveness by the Conservatives to
public unease. In one sense Chernobyl presented the Conservatives
with an opportunity to adopt a more cautious and sensitive
approach to its energy policy (without changing it) at a time not too
distant from a general election. However, the power of conviction
politics and the confidence of a parliamentary majority meant that
for Conservatives, Chernobyl became nothing more than an
inconvenient distraction.

The effect of the Chernobyl disaster on the 'greening' of the
Labour Party manifested itself in two ways. Firstly, in conjunction
with the pressures of public and environmental group opinion, it
provided a well-timed impetus to pushing through the anti-nuclear
votes at TUC and party conferences. It is likely that, even without the
stimulus of Chernobyl, a non-nuclear policy would have been
adopted, and that the event acted as a catalyst rather than a creator
of policy, particularly with regard to the trade union vote. Intensive
lobbying by the anti-nuclear unions and the Socialist Environment
and Resources Association (SERA) had already laid the ground for a
policy change, but the Chernobyl tragedy certainly helped. Tom
Sawyer of NUPE made the link between public service workers and
the nuclear industry: 'Our objections to nuclear power on grounds of

safety have been tragically confirmed by the Chernobyl disaster. Many of the people who have died of radiation were emergency rescue workers. If an accident on this scale occurs in Britain, NUPE members would be at the forefront of the Danger.[46] It also arrested the indecision of the Labour leadership on nuclear power, leading Neil Kinnock in a *New Socialist* article to say for the first time: 'I therefore give this clear and unequivocal guarantee that the next Labour Government will not sanction the ordering of another nuclear power station.'

International events such as Bhopal, Seveso, *Exxon Valdez* and the Sandoz chemical spill on the Rhine, as well as the daily tragedies in the UK industry, appeal directly to the very nature of the Labour and trade union movement.[47] They lend themselves well to a socialist analysis and show that, in terms of influencing policy, the type of environmental event or perceived hazard is important. This is certainly illustrated by the way in which the Labour Party in comparision with the other major parties gave such a high profile to the issue of asbestos in its environment proposals for the 1987 General Election. Asbestos is an issue the trade unions have pushed for strongly in the Labour Party because it has long dominated their health and safety agendas due to the deaths of several workers and proposals to expand the asbestos industry.

Often, there need only be knowledge of a potential environmental event or a possible hazard to stimulate a growth in public and political pressure. Rumours of land release in the green belts, planning applications for open-cast coal extraction or new road proposals may be enough to influence government and party policy decisions. The mobilisation of interest groups in response to environmental threats may lead to policy reassessment or even a climb-down given strong enough opposition, although the overall effect is more to limit the damage of anti-environmental policies rather than encourage the formulation of positive ones. The attempts by the Nuclear Industry Radioactive Waste Executive (NIREX) in 1985–7 to assess areas such as Billingham for the disposal of intermediate level waste and Bradwell, Fulbeck, South Killingholme and Elstow as possible sites for the disposal of low-level radioactive waste triggered off immediate and intense public opposition to government policy (or lack of it). Clearly, no disaster took place, and yet the visibility of public pressure regarding an issue too hot to handle forced the government to drop its investigations. Although NIREX's decision to pull out of the investigations were said to be based upon revised estimated costs of disposal, the potential hazards perceived to be associated with a policy seeking low-level waste disposal sites proved too much in areas where four Tory MPs, including the Chief Whip, were in danger of losing their seats.

The pressure of revelations

Environmental events themselves are seldom enough to promote a significant response from sceptical politicians. Concern regarding the implications of an event may be discussed in rhetorical terms, but changing policy, particularly if it would seem to break with a party's wider ideological programme and appeal, requires a more scientific basis than the emotions which may be high at the time.

Working in tandem with the pressure of events are key environmental findings. Investigations into environmental disasters, problems or proposed developments may be many years in their compilation, but it is the release of the findings which provide the main impact. Information, often restricted to a group of experts, regarding an environmental issue is dispersed amongst the public, pressure groups and the politicians. Such information can provide the proof sought by the non-expert political parties, and on the basis of this proof, policy positions may be reinforced or altered; at the very least, highlighted information may provide an opportunity (or an excuse) for further investigations.

Revelations regarding the state of the environment takes several forms, provisionally called informal, semi-formal and formal. Popular books and environmental journals publicise contemporary issues and ideas in an informal way and influence public opinion.[48] But having moved away from the melodramatic, 'doomsday' styles of the classics of the early 1970s, such publications are taken increasingly seriously by the politicians. With the maturing of the environmental movement, a new generation of literature has emerged which deals with key issues in a well researched and politically accessible way, although the emotional element usually remains as an extra cutting edge.[49]

From their own particular ideological corners, but also from a personal point of view, leading party politicians also contribute to the diffusion of environmental awareness by writing books and articles on their own particular environmental interests.[50] Rarely do

such contributions reveal anything new about environmental problems and seldom are they constructed in anything other than standard party political rhetoric; however, their importance lies in the
fact that they attract the attention of other politicians and party
activists.

Revelations, allegations and new evidence regarding environmental issues are conveyed via a variety of television programmes.
Specialist programmes such as BBC 2's 'Nature' provide analysis on
the full range of environmental issues, whilst the investigative television journalism of programmes such as 'Panorama', 'World in
Action' and 'First Tuesday' has increasingly been used to 'expose'
national and international environmental problems such as waste
disposal, rainforest destruction, pesticide pollution and the threats
to the UK's green belts.

Following the broadcast of such programmes, MPs can find themselves under pressure from an enquiring public with regard to issues
they had previously given little consideration. The effect of allegations made via television can be quite dramatic in forcing political
action. For instance, only two days after a documentary broadcast
by Yorkshire Television in 1983 – 'Windscale, Nuclear Laundry' –
had alleged that discharges from normal operations at Sellafield were
at levels high enough to increase the statistical incidence of radiation-
induced cancer amongst the local population, and despite counter-
claims braodcast by BNFL, the Social Services Secretary had
appointed Sir Douglas Black to examine the evidence. Such examples
reaffirm the power of the media in being able to challenge, if not
change, policy; as a senior back bench Tory MP put it: 'You just
cannot afford to not to watch television any more. If your constituents are queuing up to see you about why the farmers are pouring
silage into the streams you have to know what they are talking
about.'[51]

Semi-formal environmental findings include reports and recommendations issued by pressure groups and aimed at government.
These may be delivered as part of a wider consultation exercise,
where government or Parliament requests groups to provide evidence to the Royal Commission for Environmental Pollution, or a
relevant departmental or select committee. In such cases the extent of
the evidence put forward is not decided by the groups themselves,
but is balanced against evidence from other bodies. As environmental groups expand their staff and level of organisation, they are

able to produce reports and findings of their own without the formality imposed on them by government or parliamentary procedure. Well-informed studies can influence the government directly. For example, in 1985, Friends of the Earth produced a report on 'Tree Dieback' in the UK.[52] It claimed that 69 per cent of beech and 78 per cent of yew in Britain's forests showed signs of damage caused by acidic air pollution similar to that thought to have caused the decimation of the Black Forest in Germany, and also that trees weakened by acid rain would be increasingly susceptible to other diseases and periods of drought. These conclusions flew in the face of a report produced by the Forestry Commission earlier in the year which had stated that no evidence of new forms of tree damage had been found. In the light of the FoE report, William Waldegrave, then Environment Minister, announced to the Commons that the Forestry Commission was to carry out a new study of the nation's trees along similar lines to that taken by FoE.

Formal environmental revelations are the commissioned reports produced by the relevant parliamentary select committees, the standing Royal Commission on Environmental Pollution (RCEP) and reports produced by international organisations with an environmental brief. Reports by the Royal Commission and the parliamentary select committees may well include evidence given by environmental pressure groups, but the recommendations of the reports are intended to be a balanced consideration of all the facts gathered in their preparation. The government is obliged to respond to the findings of reports produced by a select committee or a Royal Commission, while in the case of a report produced by an environmental group it has no such obligation.

Reports released by the relevant parliamentary select committees and by RCEP have produced mixed responses from government. On the one hand, following the publication of the Commission's Ninth Report on 'Lead in the Environment' (1983), the government agreed to seek a ban on lead in petrol.[53] The effect of the report in this instance was closely linked to the previous work of the CLEAR pressure group, and acted more as a final straw than a dramatic revelation in its own right. On the other hand, the Tenth Report on state-of-the-art methods of pollution control, 'Tackling Pollution – Experience and Prospects' (1984), brought a characteristic government response of caution and procrastination.[54]

The importance of formal reports resides in the authority of their compilers, a point which the opposition parties are quick to high-light. Government cannot dismiss the recommendations of such an eminent body as RCEP lightly, particularly if a study has been commissioned by the government in the first place. However, whilst government is obliged to respond to reports that may be highly critical of its activities, it is not obliged to accept the recommendations put forward. Rather than be seen to reject the results of a carefully constructed study outright, the government may employ a range of tactics by which it can deliver its decision, including delaying its response until an issue has 'cooled off' in the public eye, and making minor concessions in existing policy without any dramatic shifts in direction.[55]

Reports that take an international perspective on environmental matters put the government's commitment to the well-being of the international environment to the test. Several powerful reports were produced during the 1980s which attempted to put over the key concept of global inter-dependence in ecological and economic terms to the governments of the world and stimulate co-ordinated dialogue and action.[56] In the case of the World Conservation Strategy, and to some extent the Brandt reports of 1980 and 1983, the pressures acting on the Conservative Government were framed in moral terms rather than in any political or economic way. Consequently, what little response there was took the form of rhetorical posturing rather than of any policy innovation. It can be argued that any other form of response at the time would have been unimaginable, given the island mentality of UK politics generally, the inate nationalism of the Tory Government, and the tendency for these reports to be written in a politically neutral style.[57]

The Conservative Government's response to the 1980 World Conservation Strategy did not, in fact, emerge until 1986! Entitled 'Conservation and Development – The British Approach', a glossy publication provided little evidence of the government's commitment to an international approach to environmental policy.[58] Instead it presented a rosy picture of Britain's green and pleasant land, and extolled the virtues of previous Conservative environmental legislation, British science and the British voluntary sector. 'Conservation and Development' was the major environmental policy statement of the Conservative Government during the 1980s, but it contained little in the way of the creativity and commitment that was shown in the 1983 'Conservation and Development Programme for the UK', put together by a number of conservation bodies – also a response to the World Conservation Strategy.[59]

The most innovative report to deal with the complexities of the international environment to date is the 1987 Brundtland Report, 'Our Common Future', the report of the UN World Commission on Environment and Development.[60] The major theme of the report is its call for 'sustainable development' and the need to see economic and environmental concerns as complementary. Indeed, breaking with the 'doomsday' messages of previous reports, a new era of sustained economic growth is advocated as the way to tackle world environmental problems. Underlying the report was a political analysis that provided more direct and positive pressures for political action than any previous publication.

At the time of its publication, the Brundtland Report appealed most strongly to the opposition parties each seeking a new radicalism with regard to the environment. The ideas on economy and internationalism contained in the report were warmly welcomed at the time by the Labour Party and the SDP/Liberal Alliance. Labour in particular welcomed the interventionist theme of Brundtland because it supported the party's idea for a separate Ministry of Environmental Protection by its call to give 'central economic and sectoral ministries responsibility for the quality of those parts of the environment affected by their decisions'. The radicalism of Brundtland implied that it would need to be preached in an evangelical way; as a Labour MEP put it: 'The report is tailor made for Kinnock. I can't think of any other leader who could put such a radical message across.'[61]

The radicalism of Brundtland made little impression on the Conservative Government in 1987, and Mrs Gro Harlem Brundtland made no secret of her feelings toward Mrs Thatcher's non-contribution to the environmental debate. However, what was radical then is now mainstream. The 1990 White Paper, 'This Common Inheritance' echoes much of Brundtland's thinking, particularly with regard to sustainable development.[62] However, while the concept is now established in the rhetoric, it may be that the real radicalism of Brundtland has still to make its mark on the major British political parties, none of which have shown serious commitment to long-term environmental thinking or of working in a situation of global co-operation.

The pressures of legislation

Government and the major parties may respond to the pressures outlined above by legislation. If this is sufficient to remedy environmental problems, then pressure may subside, although public satisfaction with legislation is harder to measure than dissatisfaction. Political pressures may continue or resurface if the legislation is inadequate to deal effectively with the problems at hand, or if the problems themselves persist and outgrow the provisions laid down.[63]

Loopholes within existing environmental legislation provide targets for the pressure groups and the opposition parties. Until Dr David Clark MP, for instance, successfully piloted an Amendment Act through Parliament in 1985, the 1981 Wildlife and Countryside Act was attacked by conservation groups because of its 'three-month loophole'.[64] Similarly, the eleven-year delay in the complete implementation of the 1974 Control of Pollution Act consistently presented environmental groups and the opposition parties with opportunities for attacking government over the deterioration of water quality. As long as environmental policies fail to deal with actual environmental problems either by overlooking key elements, or by relying upon the UK's voluntary style of practice, they focus attention on the search for better legislation.

Proposed legislation also provides opportunities for the mobilisation of pressure on government. In February 1986, the Conservative Government published proposals for the privatisation of the water industry in which it was suggested that all the regulatory functions of the water authorities were sold off with the rest of the industry. The proposals provoked a storm of protest from the environmental pressure groups, the trade unions and the CBI. Their combined lobbying, and an unprecedented published legal opinion by the CPRE, aided by the Institute for European Environmental Policy, forced the government to withdraw the idea of legislating to sell the industry as a whole. At the time of the general election in June 1987, the government further responded to the environmentalists by announcing the creation of a National Rivers Authority (NRA) through which environmental quality would be managed by a public body in compliance with EC law. However, as a result of further pressures by the water authorities in 1987 Lord Belstead, then Minister of State for the Environment, announced that the NRA would be a 'relatively slim-line operation' likely to be tendered out to the water authorities themselves.

The single most important source of legislative pressure on the British Government and to a lesser extent the opposition parties, emanates from the EC.[65] Environmental directives are of particular importance and serve to standardise environmental quality objectives throughout the European Community. They are always on the agenda and whenever a minister visits Brussels he is confronted by them. However, in general, Community agreements and policy directives, in principle binding on the UK, have been consistently blocked and delayed by governments.

Whilst the Conservative Government has continued to oppose calls for legislation from the EC, the quality of the environment has continued to decline and the resolve of the environmental groups has strengthened rather than weakened, and pressures for policy changes have increased. Several reasons why the Conservative government has consistently resisted environmental initiatives from the EC can be put forward. The first relates to the nature of EC directives and centres upon the cost of implementing measures. Unlike the majority of European states who aim for strict quality controls in order to stimulate overall investment in developing abatement technologies, the British Government prefer to see environmental controls as being as cost-effective as possible and this inevitably entails waiting until monies are available. The desire to be cost-effective is also influenced by the Conservatives' desire to be as non-interventionist as possible in terms of industry, and a tradition which prefers flexible objectives rather than legally binding standards.

A second reason is the apparent geographical insularity of the UK from the rest of Europe. The fact that the UK does not share any national boundaries other than Eire, is surrounded by water and is influenced by westerly winds, has cultivated the idea of immunity from environmental pollution. Linked to this is a certain ideological arrogance that Britain should not have to meet high costs to achieve standards which are perhaps desirable for continental Europe but are adequate for Britain. This was a point put across by Nicholas Ridley when, as Secretary of State for the Environment in July 1989, he criticised EC standards for tap water as being 'ridiculous, extravagant and unnecessary'. Moreover, an understanding of the transnationality of pollution has still not permeated a party which, according to one leftward Conservative Prospective Parliamentary

Candidate (PPC), 'was more concerned with the effects of acidification on Scotland than on the Black Forest because that's
where the best fishing is'.[66]

A third reason for Conservative resistance to EC legislative
pressures had been reluctance to adopt the 'precautionary principle'
with respect to pollution control measures and an insistence that EC
laws be based upon 'sound scientific evidence' rather than emotion.[67] The argument for establishing unequivocal scientific evidence before policy decisions were taken was very much a trait of
Mrs Thatcher. In the early 1980s Mrs Thatcher, backed by Lord
Marshall of the then CEGB, had refused to accept that emissions
from British coal-fired power stations were responsible for Scan-
dinavia's acid rain. Despite pressure from Dr Martin Holdgate,
Chief Scientist at the DOE, pollution control measures were held
back until the Prime Minister and Lord Marshall were proved
wrong. But even before Mrs Thatcher's departure, there were
pressures within the party, particularly amongst MEPs and some
cabinet 'wets', that the UK could not afford to ignore the precautionary principle, partly as a function of wider pressures for
European integration, and ultimately because it is likely to be more
cost effective.

The Labour Party's response to an environmental policy climate
increasingly dominated by EC legislation has been mixed. Whilst any
sign of procrastination by the Conservatives presents an opportunity
for attack, Labour has been cautious of its own ambivalence toward
the EC, and the party has consequently been slow to capitalise on the
pressures acting upon the government. With attitudes toward
Europe still spilt within the party, the question of whether a future
Labour government would respond to environmental directives any
differently from the Conservatives remains open. In comparision,
the Europhilia exhibited by the Liberal Democrats has meant a keen
welcome for European transnational legislation. It may even be
argued that Liberal Democrat environmental policy has evolved
specifically to suit an institutional framework that the EC can be seen
to provide.[68] Clearly, the Liberal Democrats are not in a position to
react to the pressures of EC legislation, yet they have welcomed it
from the political sidelines in such a way that indicates a positive
effect on party environmental policy. As a leading activist in the
Liberal Ecology Group put it: 'To be Liberal is to be European. This
means we recognise the interdependence of nations. In environ-

mental terms, as with other areas, we must work with this in mind.'[69]

The combined pressures for change

The interdependence of the pressures acting on government and the opposition parties makes it difficult to single out any one force responsible for party 'greening'. Moreover, although long-term trends may be identified with the benefit of hindsight, there is a strong element of coincidence regarding which pressures act upon the parties at any one time. There is no way of knowing when or where an environmental disaster will take place, and as the processes of environmental degradation continue, as pollution levels increase, as resources become stretched and the resistivity of environments is eroded, the 'environmental time-bomb' syndrome continues to manifest itself to the public and politicians alike. It is the understanding of environmental risk which pervades the build-up of public and institutional pressures on the major parties. Environmental problems will continue to dominate people's lives, despite Mrs Thatcher's remarkable statement to the contrary that: 'In the next five years we will have got rid of most of our problems.'[70]

Pressure for positive action on the environment continues to grow, and the main parties are increasingly aware that protest, criticism and lobbying are no longer the preserve of a few environmental pressure groups; traditionalists have become radicals over issues which previously were of little interest. From the Women's Institute's protestations about pollution, the *Daily Telegraph*'s concern for the future of the British countryside, to Prince Charles's persuasive intervention in the North Sea Summit of 1987, the pressures for a cleaner and greener world are becoming stronger, better organised and more articulate. The Conservative Government is the sitting target for the majority of pressures, yet Labour and the Liberal Democrats continue to feel the effects of an environmental push, particularly from their constituency roots.

It is the job of the politician within party and government to offer the public and the various representative bodies serious responses to an ever-changing world, dominated by matters environmental. These responses range from total indifference and well-reasoned deferrals, rousing rhetoric and empty promises, to shifts in policy and concrete changes in legislation. But as we have pointed out, party policy and party style is not only a function of what the electorate wants, it is also based upon what the party itself wants in ideological terms and in terms of members' interests. These factors dominate and shape the type and intensity of the responses given.

The problem with the pressure–response interpretation of party 'greening' is that it views 'greening' as a product, automatically produced out of numerous interactive pressures, and takes no account of the conflicts which inevitably arise at the various stages of the policy process. Ideally, the pressure–response model assumes that when evolutionary and/or coincidental environmental pressures are applied, the parties respond favourably, making them somehow measurably 'greener' than before. However, outcomes are difficult to measure with any clarity and positive responses are far from guaranteed, as indicated, for instance, by the Conservative Government's rejection of the recommendations put by the 1984 Select Committee on the Environment's fourth report on acid rain.

Further examples, such as the Labour Party's policy on nuclear power, would seem to indicate that the parties enter into protracted struggles with environmental pressures. The anti-nuclear pressures of the non-party-aligned environmental groups such as FoE, and those aligned with the party such as SERA, produced no immediate or clear-cut response when they were first applied to the Labour Party. Rather, the process of policy change within the Labour Party has been switch back-like. After a long period of attrition by the various pressures, a 1986 Labour Conference decision, accelerated by the Chernobyl event, consolidated existing 1985 anti-nuclear power policy, although uncertainty remained with regard to the time-scale for the phasing out of nuclear power. During the 1987 General Election this uncertainty increased, and under the influence of the electricity privatisation agenda set by the government and the decline in salience of the nuclear power issue in the public mind, the Labour Party's present commitment to a non-nuclear energy policy is challengeable.

The responsive account of party 'greening' helps explain some of the successes of the environmental movement, yet fails to take account of the basic conflicts that arise between environmentalists and the parties, and the internal ideological tensions which reside in the parties with regard to environmental issues. The constraints which operate will be examined in a later chapter, but these aside, the pressure–response model does not explain the unprecedented momentum of party 'greening' during the 1980s. Commentators have suggested that the rise of the Green Movement in Europe as a major political force triggered a process of environmental intro-spection amongst the UK parties.[71] However, politicians of the leading parties are too well aware of the dominance of the UK constitution and the weaknesses of the Green Party challenge to have been significantly influenced by activities in Europe. Moreover, pro-environmental public opinion and pressure groups which have held prominence for nearly two decades have been ignored by each of the major parties at various times, and environmental events, scientific evidence and existing legislation have also been side-stepped. We can conclude, therefore, that other factors have contributed to the 'greening' phenomenon within the political parties – factors which relate to the internal dynamics of the parties and the system they operate in. These are discussed in the following chapter.

Notes and references

1   See for instance: Solesbury, W. 1976. 'The Environmental Agenda.' *Public Administration*, 54. Winter. 379–97.

2   An understanding of the history of environmentalism leads one to suggest that society has always contained an element pushing for environmental improvement.

3   Downs, A. 1972. 'Up and Down with Ecology – the Issue-attention Cycle.' *The Public Interest*, 28. 38–50; note 1, *op. cit.*

4   Forman, F. N. 1985. *Mastering British Politics*. London: Macmillan.

5   For an indication of the long established levels of environmental concern amongst EEC nations see: Watkins, L./Worcester, R. M. 1986. *Private Opinions – Public Polls*, Chap. 10. London: Thames and Hudson.

6   The issue of acid rain gained extensive media coverage through the publication of the House of Commons Environment Select Committee Report which was published in July 1984.

7   See: Wilson, D. (Ed.) 1984. *The Environmental Crisis: A Handbook for All Friends of the Earth*. London: Heinemann Educational Books.

8   Nimbyism is a prominent feature of public environmental concern and a difficult problem for policy makers to overcome, particulary with regard to sensitive issues such as the disposal of low- and intermediate-level nuclear waste.

9   See: Elcock, H. 1976. *Political Behaviour*. London: Methuen and Co. Ltd.

10   See: Jowell, R. /Witherspoon, S. (Eds.) 1985. *British Social Attitudes Report*. Gower. 1985 *et seq.*

11   The classic case of such a conflict, although somewhat dated, is given by Gregory, R. 1971. *The Price of Amenity: Five Studies in Conservation and Government*. London: Macmillan, London: St Martins Press.

12 Mori. *Environmental Policies: Influence on Voting Intention*. March 1987.

13 See: Anthony, R. 1982. 'Polls, Pollution and Politics: Trends in Public Opinion on the Environment.' *Environment*, 24, No. 4. May. 14–20, 33–4; Dunlap, R. E. 1987. 'Polls Pollution and Politics Revisited: Public Opinion on the Environment in the Reagan Era.' *Environment*, 29. July/Aug. 6–11, 32–7.

14 See: Harrop, M./Miller, W. L. 1987. *Elections and Voters: A Comparative Introduction*. London: Macmillan Education. The point is also made by Tyler, R. 1987. *Campaign! The Selling of the Prime Minister*. London: Grafton Books.

15 Robinson, M. D. 1990. 'The Greening of British Party Politics – The Superficiality and the Substance'. Unpublished PhD Thesis. University of East Anglia.

16 SDP/Liberal Alliance. 1987. *Britain United – The Time has Come*. Hebden Bridge: Hebden Royd.

17 Personal Communication.

18 Personal Communication.

19 Conservative Party, 1983. *The Challenge of our Times*. Manifesto. The Conservative Party.

20 Personal Communication.

21 Burke, T. 1987. 'The Effectiveness of Green Groups.' Speech, Institution of Environmental Sciences, 1 December.

22 Lowe, P./Goyder, J. 1983. *Environmental Groups in Politics*. Resource Management Series. London: Allen and Unwin.

23 See for instance: CPRE Annual Reports 1984–1987; Perrin, J. 1988. 'Friends in Need.' *Environment Now*, Feb./March. 14–17.

24 Richardson, J. J./Jordan, A. G. 1982. *Governing under Pressure: The Policy Process in a Post-Parliamentary Democracy*. Oxford: Martin Robertson.

25 Note 15, *op. cit.*

26 Personal Communication.

27 Personal Communication.

28 Note 15, *op. cit.*

29 Personal Communication.

30 Personal Communication.

31 Personal Communication.

32 Burke, T. 1985. 'A Welcome Growth of Greenery.' *The Times*. 19.8.85.

33 Personal Communications.

34 The Green Alliance was instrumental in organising a meeting between six leading UK environmentalists and Mrs Thatcher in 1985 – the first formal discussion of its kind with the then Prime Minister.

35 See: Waller, R. 1982. *The Agricultural Balance Sheet*. Chertsey: The Conservation Society.

36 See for instance: Department of Environment. 1984. *Acid Rain: The Government's reply to the Fourth Report from the Environment Committee*. (December) Cmnd 9397. HMSO.

37 Key examples of symbiotic relationships during the 1980s have been the use of TUC support by CLEAR in their campaign to ban lead in petrol and NUS support for Greenpeace's campaign to ban the sea dumping of radioactive waste in 1983.

38 See: Punnett, R. M. 1987. *British Government and Politics* Aldershot:. Gower.

39 Personal Communication.

40 ASLEF, 1976. *Transport for the Nation*. ASLEF's reply to the Transport Policy Consultation Document.

41 Personal Communication.

42 See: Rossi, H. 1986. 'Towards the Next Century: Developing a Long-Term Political Strategy for Sustainable Development.' From Sustainable *Development in an Industrial Economy*. Proceedings of conference held at Queen's College Cambridge, 23–25 June 1985. UK CEED. The '30 per cent club' consisted of those nations which were committed to reducing SO_2 emissions (based on 1980 levels) by 30 per cent by 1995, as laid down by the European Convention on Long-Range Trans-Boundary Air Polution.

43 Note 1, *op. cit.*

44 Waldegrave, W. 1985. 'Nuclear Safety', Talk to the Bow Group, 21 July.

45 Personal Communication.

46 Sawyer, T. 1987 Speech, Conference at South Bank Polytechnic, London. 28 April.

47 Bryson, N. 1988. 'Trade Unions and Environment.' *New Ground*, No. 17, Spring. 6–7.

48 Amongst the classics that caught the imagination of the public and are reference points in the history of the modern environmental movement are: Carson, R. 1962. *Silent Spring*. Boston: Houghton-Mifflin; Ehrlich, P. 1968. *The Population Bomb*. London: Pan/Ballantine; Meadows, D. H./ Meadows, D. L./Randers, J./Behrens III, W. W. 1973. *The Limits to Growth*. London and Sydney: Pan Books.

49 Macrory, R. 1986. *Environmental Policy in Britain: Reaffirmation or Reform?* International Institute for Environment and Society. IIUG. dp 86–4. Berlin. Macrory argues for instance, that Marion Shoard's scathing polemic against the damages inflicted upon the countryside by modern agricultural practices helped to fuel demands for the 1981 Wildlife and Countryside Act. See: Shoard, M. *The Theft of the Countryside*. London: Temple Smith.

50 See for instance: Body, R. 1984. *Farming in the Clouds*. London: Maurice, Temple, Smith; Carlisle, K. 1984. 'Conserving the Countryside: A Tory View.' Conservative Political Centre; Hain, P. 1983. *The Democratic Alternative*. Harmondsworth: Penguin Books; Owen, D. 1984. *A Future That Will Work*. Harmondsworth: Penguin Books; Patten, C. 1984. *The Tory Case*. London: Longmans; Williams, S. 1985. *A Job To Live: The Impact of Tomorrow's Technology on Work and Society*. Harmondsworth: Penguin Books.

51 Personal Communication.

52 Friends of the Earth. 1985. *Final Report: Tree Dieback Survey*.

E

Friends of the Earth.
53 Royal Commission on Environmental Pollution. 1983. *Lead in the Environment.* 9th Report. Cmnd 8852. London: HMSO.
54 Royal Commission on Environmental Pollution. 1984. *Tackling Pollution: Experience and Prospects. 10th Report. Cmnd 9149. London: HMSO.*
55 Drewry, G. 1985. 'Select Committees and Back-bench Power.' In Jowell, J./Oliver, D. (Eds.) *The Changing Constitution.* Publisher not known. 127–48. Drewry indicates with reference to select committee reports in particular, and the reports of other appointed bodies in general, that although the recommendations may be initially dismissed out of hand, they may lodge in the minds of decision makers only to resurface at a later date apparently as a minister's own idea.
56 International Union for the Conservation of Nature. 1980. *World Conservation Strategy.* Geneva: IUCN; Brandt Commission. 1980. *North–South: A Programme for Survival.* London: Pan; Brandt Commission. 1983. *Common Crisis – North–South: Co-operation for World Recovery.* London: Pan.
57 See: Redclift, M. 1984. *Development and the Environmental Crisis.* London: Methuen; Sandbrook, R. 1986. 'Towards a Global Environmental Strategy.' In Park, C. (Ed.) *Environmental Policies: An International Review.* London: Croom Helm. 289–302.
58 Department of Environment. 1986. *Conservation and Development – The British Approach. The United Kingdom's Government Response to the World Conservation Strategy.* London: HMSO.
59 World Wildlife Fund *et al.* 1983. *The Conservation and Development Programme for the UK – A response to the World Conservation Strategy.* London: Kogan Page.
60 Brundtland Commission. 1987. *Our Common Future.* Oxford: Oxford University Press.
61 Personal Communication.
62 Department of Environment. 1990. *This Common Inheritance.* London: HMSO.
63 See: Hogwood, B. W. 1987. *From Crisis to Complacency? Shaping Public Policy in Britain.* Oxford: Oxford University Press.
64 Through this, sites could be destroyed within a period of 'consultation'. An estimated 156 SSSIs were damaged or destroyed in this way between April 1983 and March 1984 (Nature Conservancy Council, Evidence to House of Commons Select Committee on Environment, 1985).
65 Haigh, N. 1986. 'Devolved Responsibility and Centralisation: Effects of EEC Environmental Policy'. *Royal Institute of Public Administration,* 64, Summer. 197–207.
66 Personal Communication.
67 The West Germans have been the leaders in the adoption of the precautionary principle – the 'Vorsorgeprinzip'. See: Royal Commission on Environmental Pollution, 1988. *Best Practicable Option.* 12th Report CM 310. London: HMSO.
68 David Steel, when leader of the Liberal Party, and Simon Hughes as

Liberal Environment Spokesman made this point during speeches.

    69   Personal Communication.
    70   Television interview with Michael Buerk, 'Nature', 2.3.89.
    71   See for instance: Paterson, T. 1984. *Conservation and the Conservatives*. London: Bow Publications Ltd; Paterson, T. 1984. 'Why True Blues Must Go Green.' *The Times*, 6 October; Porritt, J. 1984. *Seeing Green: The Politics of Ecology Explained*. Oxford: Basil Blackwell.

5

Volunteers, values and votes

Public opinion, pressure politics and newsworthy disasters have always been concerns of the environmental movement. They also appeal to party politicians who pride themselves on their responsiveness to various outside influences. But there is more to party politics and party policy making than soulless, calculated reactions, dressed in rhetoric. The 'greening' process runs deep, and cannot be explained away simply as a reaction to environmental pressures; a strong sense of deliberation now pervades thinking in some sections of the parties.

This chapter examines these reasons for party greening, reasons which are intrinsic to the parties' ideological development. Whilst not denying the range and effect of exogenous pressures acting to 'green' parties and government, the model put forward discusses a complementary set of endogenous factors which are often overlooked. Essentially, it turns the pressure–response model on its head by locating the initiatives for greening *inside* the party as well as outside.

A particular notion underlies the pressure–response model of 'greening': that politicians of all parties are isolated from the motivations and aspirations of the environmental movement. This notion assumes that they only act when prodded, or when given a large enough incentive. Pressure groups and environmentalists actively promote this notion; it helps to legitimise the environmental movement's political status and boosts its members' morale. It also plays upon public ignorance of the political process and the sense of alienation that the public feel toward politicians of all parties.[1]

An interpretation of party 'greening' as a voluntary, deliberate process relying upon internal initiatives rather than external pressures has two main foundations which are particularly difficult to separate in practice. Figure 5 shows the central features of an intentional model of party greening. The model deliberately excludes external inputs and the lines of contact extend only within the boundaries of party, to emphasise how a party can 'green' itself.

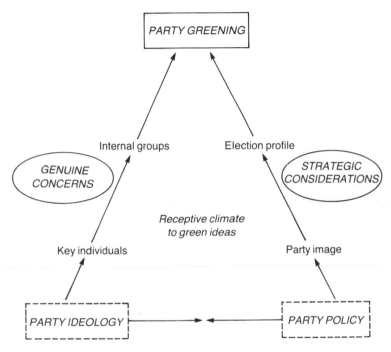

Fig. 5 The 'intentional' model of party greening

The model complements the reactive account given in chapter 4 and encapsulates a central tension between a party's calculated desire to absorb and integrate environmental considerations and ideas into party policy for short-term political gain, and a genuine desire to incorporate environmental thinking into party ideology. The two motivations are not mutually exclusive as party ideology informs policy positions, and in the course of policy formulation party beliefs may be open to adjustment or reinterpretation. The model assumes that parties can develop a greener posture for strategic reasons alone and can adapt or alter specific policies without questioning fundamental party beliefs. It also assumes that specific groups and individuals within the main parties may attempt to redefine the parameters of party ideology in order to reflect the wider changes in society. The two motivations meet to produce a greening effect, creating a climate within each party which is more receptive to external environmental influences.

Genuine concerns

There are individuals within each party who are genuinely concerned with the promotion of environmental issues and green ways of thinking. For despite the responsibilities politicians carry and the ideological positions they hold, they are still members of a wider society and thus subject to its influences and pressures. They are thereby exposed to the many developing dimensions of environmentalism already touched upon: the increased media coverage, growth in pressure group numbers, grassroots constituency interest, and new projects with environmental implications. Of course, for the same reasons that some individuals are not environmentally concerned, some politicians may just not be interested. However, politicians have more reason to listen to and act upon the protestations and activities of environmental groups in local communities than the general public.

A major problem arises in distinguishing between a politician's genuine interest and concern for environmental issues and calculated political manoeuvres. The various motivations are widely spread throughout the parties and operate at different times and under varying circumstances. What is presented as heart-felt concern for an issue at the time, may later come to light as a shrewd career move or a planned distraction from a more unwelcome issue. Similarly, environmental interest suspiciously viewed at the time as being out of character, may turn out to be perfectly genuine after events have unfolded. However, previous activities and statements can provide evidence that a Member of Parliament is genuinely environmentally aware and concerned. The wider public and the environmental movement are more likely to give an MP credence if he or she has previously spoken on environmental issues in the House of Commons, tabled parliamentary questions regarding the environment, debated the issues in public, contributed to the environmental literature, held an environmentally related position within the party, or is a member of an environmental organisation in his or her personal capacity.

However, some members 'awaken' to environmental issues relatively swiftly and, despite the lack of a track record, are no less concerned. Other party members can claim concern for purely tactical reasons, despite a background of commitment to an environmental cause. There are no cast-iron guarantees. Generally though, some measure of genuine understanding and feeling for environmental matters can be related to a party member's political and personal background.

Key individuals within Parliament

Politics is about politicians, and it is the individuals within politics who contribute to its uncertainty and its 'mystery'.[2] The growth in public awareness of, interest in and concern for the environment has been well documented via public opinion polls and analysis of media coverage. However, there has been very little analysis of the role of individual politicians, of how they are influenced by the environmental movement and of how they in turn influence the environmental thinking of their own parties. The recent birth of the environment as a party political issue, the constant fluctuations in attention between it and other issues and the difficulty in delineating it as a separate issue are reasons for the lack of research in this field.

Within Parliament, the visible political forum, there has been a steadily growing interest in environmental matters. Since 1985, *Dod's Parliamentary Companion* has listed the political and social interests of MPs. These lists have been supplied to Dod by the MPs themselves and would therefore seem to provide a fair guide to the level of interest.[3] Table 3 illustrates a slow but steady growth in the number of MPs who list conservation and the environment as special interests.[4]

The ranking position of interest in environmental issues is, of course, influenced by the circumstances at the time of compilation. Elections alter the complexion and party distribution of the MPs themselves. The total number of interests has increased, but the interest expressed in the environment and conservation sectors has maintained its position. The top-ranked interest is consistently foreign affairs, usually followed in various orders by defence, trade and industry, education and health. In 1987 (before the election), marginally more MPs expressed an interest in the environment and conservation than they did for the long-established fields of health and education.

Although in 1988 the number of MPs expressing an interest in environmental issues represented some 15 per cent of the total 650 elected, this may be an underestimate. The environment/ conservation headings cover a wide range of specific topics such as inner-city regeneration, wildlife, ancient monuments, green belt issues and nuclear waste disposal. Other headings may conceal more specific environmental interests, for example agriculture, rural affairs, heritage, animal welfare, energy and transport. Furthermore, MPs known to have an environmental interest, such as William Waldegrave, former Under Secretary at the DOE, are not listed in *Dod's Parliamentary Companions* up to 1988.

Table 3 *Environmental/conservation interests of Members of Parliament, 1985–1988*

	1985	1986	1987	1988
No. of interests listed	112	114	149	163
Rank of environment & conservation	6th*	5th	4th	5th
No. of MPs listing environment & conservation	75	92	98	100
% Conservative	49	59	63	55
% Labour	22	27	30	37
% Liberal	2	3	3	3
% Social Democratic Party	1	1	1	1
% Official Unionist Party	1	1	1	1

* Indicates joint position with another interest (health care).
Source: Derived from *Dod's Parliamentary Companions*, 1985–8.

Levels of interest expressed by the MPs are relative to the number of parliamentary seats the parties hold. In 1988, the fifty-five Conservative MPs with environmental interests was out of a total of 376. In other words there were 321 Conservative MPs who did not express an interest in conservation and the environment, and those that did also had a variety of other interests. Members of Parliament have to deal with day-to-day matters (environmental or not) of the party, the House and their constituencies. The pressures of time allocation for any issue is high, particularly for high-profile front bench politicians, and to some extent the environment can be given more time by back benchers.

For the Liberal Democrats with relatively few MPs, allocating time to the environment above the most pressing of issues is problematic. With portfolios spread thinly, MPs have to be flexible and briefed to speak on whatever questions arise. It is therefore difficult for even the most committed MP to specialise in environmental policy. For example Simon Hughes, arguably one the 'greenest' MPs in the House of Commons, has a limited amount of time he can devote to environmental issues. Before the 1987 General Election this was particularly frustrating for Liberal environmental activists, particularly those on the Environment Policy Panel who tended to use Simon Hughes as their direct link into the parliamentary party.[5]

As MPs have increasingly been expected to fulfil a more professional and specialist role, the pressures on their time has grown.[6] This has led to a corresponding increase in the use of paid and voluntary staff to carry out research relevant to an MP's position and interests.[7] The influence of research assistants is significant, as some MPs come to rely on them increasingly. A research assistant for a leading SDP MP spoke of his 'marked degree of influence' regarding whom his employer meets and what he says.[8] Whereas the general pattern of influence would seem to work from MP to researcher, the latter becoming interested in the environmental work of the former, a MP may develop and deepen his or her interests through the less constrained, often enthusiastic help of a research assistant.

Although the role of the House of Lords within the British polity is constantly open to debate, it is similar to the House of Commons in that it does contain a number of members with environmental interests, spread throughout the parties. No equivalent of Dod's listings exist, for the House of Lords. However, certain members stand out as being environmentally active. Lord Peter Melchett, a Labour peer and former Labour minister, has campaigned for many years for access to the countryside via his post as president of the Ramblers' Association; in 1986 he became chairman of Greenpeace. Within the Liberal Democrats, Baroness Robson, spokeswoman on health and the environment, has long campaigned on environmental issues. Baroness Robson was perhaps the prime mover in stimulating Liberal Party interest in the environment in the early seventies, when she organised a seminar on population and the environment. Others of note are Baroness Seear, a former Social Democrat who has been particularly active in organising meetings with many environmental groups, and the Earl of Cranbrook, a Conservative peer, who has campaigned for wildlife protection and the preservation of the rain forest. Indeed, since the 1987 General Election, two peers succesively held the posts of Minister for the Environment, Countryside and Water: Lord Belstead and the Earl of Caithness.

The reports produced by the relevant House of Lords select subcommittees have been thorough and enjoyed some success in influencing the finer points of government policy.[9] Furthermore, the quality of environmental debates is high within the upper chamber where there is more time available for such debates than in the Commons. However, the number of interested, let alone active, 'green' peers is relatively slight. The peers may be less constrained in terms of workload than their Commons counterparts, but the breadth of their interests is far more diverse, possibly causing more competition for their Lordships' attention. Although Mrs Thatcher used two members of the upper house as environment ministers, and both Labour and Liberal parties have environmental spokesmen within the House of Lords, formal contact between peers and the decision-making bodies of their respective parties is negligible, their influence tending to be party- and issue-specific, informal, and spasmodic. Their ability to influence their parties in a 'green' direction is thus limited.

Key individuals outside the parliamentary parties

Outside Parliament, the number of 'environmentally informed and aware' individuals has grown within the policy-making, research and administrative institutions of the main parties. Unlike MPs, such people are difficult to group together, given the variation in formal and informal party structures and the overlap in party functions that may occur. They range from local party activists to those involved in the centralised party bases. We can suggest that there is generally a two-way interchange and influence between party members at local constituency and national levels. Environmental initiatives may be taken up by a party at local council level, and their success or otherwise may be brought to the attention of the local MP or to a member represented at a policy-making forum of the party. Senior members of environmental non-governmental organisations may be members of a particular political party in a personal capacity even if the bodies they represent are non-party-political. Green activists may also be found within internally organised party groups or organisations directly affiliated to a particular party.

Under Mrs Thatcher and her self-appointed Policy Unit based at No. 10 Downing Street, the role of Conservative Party Central Office in policy formulation decreased and its role was restricted chiefly to providing information. Before the 1987 General Election, an environmental desk, provided a political briefing service to ministers and advisers and offered political critiques of other parties' environmental policies. The very existence of such a service specialising in environmental issues indicated demand for it from both parliamentary and constituency members. The other mechanism that Conservative Central Office can use in relation to spreading the environmental word through the party is to use the weekly bulletin *Politics Today*. This publication states various aspects of 'official' party policy and attacks the policies of other parties.[10]

Elsewhere within the Conservative Party organised groups have both facilitated, and to some extent supported, publications on the environment by key individuals.[11] In 1985, for instance, the irreproachably Thatcherite Centre for Policy Studies, published a paper by Andrew Sullivan, a former lead writer with the *Daily Telegraph*, entitled 'Greening the Tories – New Policies on the Environment'. Although shallow on policy innovations, Sullivan succeeded in illustrating that environmentalism was merely an extension of Conservative Party philosophy. Teasing environmental concerns from the writings of Burke, Wordsworth, Disraeli, through to Baldwin, Churchill and Betjeman, Sullivan argued that conservation and Conservatism were inseparable. His style of writing was unashamedly romantic and wholly English in a deliberate attempt to seek the sympathies of the Thatcherites. In fact, the arguments he put forward found favour in all denominations of the party. In terms of changing party policy, 'Greening the Tories' did little more than support what was already being done. The real influence of Sullivan's efforts lay in the subtlety of his approach. As one Conservative 'wet' pointed out with regard to Sullivan's work: 'There's just no point in becoming all socialist about the environment, not in this Party. This is the stuff we will all buy.'[12]

Through the leftish Bow Group, the so-called 'licensed dissenters' of the Tory Party, three excellent and, in their own way, radical, papers have been published by its Parliamentary Liaison Officer, Tony Paterson. Each paper was critical of aspects of the government's environmental policy or lack of it. In June 1984, 'A Role for Britain in the Acid Rainstorm' urged that the nation's power stations should be fitted with de-sulphurisation equipment. When Waldegrave in his 1986 conference speech announced the government's intention to pursue such a programme, he acknowledged the influence of Paterson's arguments.

In October 1984, the Bow Group published Paterson's 'Conservation and the Conservatives' which set out an environmental agenda that the Tories could take into the 1987 election. Welcomed by Waldegrave as being 'helpful', and generally well received amongst the majority of the Bow Group's 107 MPs, this publication contained such ideas as having a specialist Conservation Minister in the Cabinet, leasing the rainforests and lessening the UK's dependence on nuclear power. These ideas were too radical for the majority of the party and the influence of the paper was less direct, doing more to reinforce the attitudes of those Conservatives already active in promoting environmental awareness than producing any converts.

In 1989 Paterson published 'The Green Conservative' through the Bow Group. This paper was largely a re-emphasis of his earlier ideas, shaped by subsequent developments, but still radical. He proposed programmes of energy efficiency, the recycling of waste, improved freedom of information for public bodies, and taxing nuclear energy to generate capital for alternative sources. The underlying critique was that established Tory (as opposed to Thatcherite) principles such as order, tradition, patriotism and individual responsibility should guide government environmental policy. Paterson criticised the intransigence of the government, and warned that the strength of the green vote in the 1990s would be decisive. Despite the radical ideas put forward, it is likely that 'The Green Conservative' will find a wider and perhaps more responsive audience than previous publications, given the developments of the last five years.

Green activists outside Labour's Parliamentary Party are to be found within the trade unions. Mention has already been made of the important role of the trade unions acting as effective environmental pressure groups to influence Labour Party policy and thinking, though the unions tend to pursue those issues that are closest to the hearts of their own members. Increasingly there are individuals with important voices in the Labour Party – on the NEC and within the Labour Co-ordinating Group (the largest left-wing pressure group within the party) – whose thinking goes beyond this. Key figures such as Tom Sawyer, Deputy General Secretary of NUPE and a former Chair of the NEC Working Party on the Environment (a leading light behind Labour's radical Environment Statement in 1986) and John Edmonds, General Secretary of the General, Municipal, Boiler Makers' and Allied Trade Unions (GMBATU) and a Kinnockite, are now striving to re-emphasise the links between environmental concern and socialism. Differences between the unions on the nuclear power industry are being tackled by attempting to integrate workers' concerns with environmental issues. In a speech at a fringe meeting organised by FoE, Greenpeace and SERA at the 1986 Labour Party Conference 1986, Tom Sawyer announced that: 'Our policies for the environment are informed by our view of society as a whole. You can't tackle the environment without policies for the economy, for industry. You can't protect the environment for some, unless you recognise the need for jobs for all.'[13] These ideas are being put forward at a time when the relationship between the unions and the Labour Party is being redefined and when there is a reaction against the 'New Realism' of Eric Hammond, the leader of the Electricians' Union (EETPU). For a party seeking to play down memories of the winter of discontent on the one hand and yet improve relations with the unions on the other, influential individuals who understand the interdependence of the environment, the economy, women's rights and the peace movement are able to make considerable headway.

There has been a dramatic increase in the number of green activists within the constituency Labour Parties in recent years. The strong environmental emphasis adopted by many Labour local authorities, together with local membership trends toward younger more active members eager to campaign on issues they identify with and keen to work with local environmental groups, has encouraged proactivity amongst CLPs. Moreover, environmental programmes carried out by Labour authorities such as Haringey, Lambeth, Sheffield and, up to 1985, the GLC, have influenced thinking at the centre of the Labour Party. Ken Livingstone MP and David Blunkett MP, for instance (representing Brent East and Sheffield Brightside respectively), have previously been directly involved with high-profile local authority environmental programmes for their areas. This has

encouraged them to respond positively to environmental developments within the Labour Party at national level. Indeed, their
involvement in local environmental politics has involved reaching
out beyond specific issues to an environmental 'attitude' which
encompasses a concern for a grassroots approach to the environment
rather than the paternalistic 'top-down' approach reminiscent of
municipal socialism.

Grassroots activism on environmental issues is also a strong
feature of the Liberal Democratic Party. The former Liberal Party
had long recognised that local politicians had a particularly strong
role to play in party policy making, with individual party members
able to bring 'green' ideas up to national level, based upon
experiences from all parts of the country. It was local activists which
tended to make up Liberal Party committees and the twenty-three
policy panels which were operating up to merger with the SDP. The
policy panels of the Liberal Party addressed many aspects of the
environment – energy, agriculture, transport and planning – and
contained party members eager to put across the environmental
message to the party leadership, Party Council and the Annual
Assembly as the supreme policy-making body. The Liberal Environment Panel was active in supporting local activists by the production
of 'Green Briefing' documents, designed to help them campaign on
environmental issues in their own areas.[14] This back-up work, which
also included giving out environmental press releases to regional
parties, was aimed at building up the green activists within the party
at local level. As the chair of one policy panel put it shortly before the
General Election in 1987:

> This party runs on good will and enthusiasm. If we are going to convince
> the electorate of our green credentials we need people to knock on doors and
> tell the public about how the government is doing zilch about pesticide
> run-off and nitrate build up in our soil and water and what we would do
> instead. Its all very well being able to ask Parliamentary questions on the
> environment but our strength lies at local level.[15]

The Liberal Environmental Co-ordinating Group was the prime
mover in co-ordinating the enthusiasm of those individuals within
the policy panels and was responsible for the 1986 policy document
'Survival: The Liberal Way to an Environment for the Future'.[16] This
contained a comprehensive set of environmental policies, produced
with minimal consultation with the Social Democratic Party. Its
most notable idea was that the government should establish a

department for environmental protection, to be as central to decision-making as the Treasury is now.

In its albeit short political life, the SDP made a significant contribution to the 'greening' of British party politics. Unlike the Liberals, the number of environmental activists outside the small Parliamentary Party of the Social Democrats was small. However, the party did contain a number of important and well established environmental strategists who were prepared to lead from the top. Many of the key actors responsible for SDP environmental thinking already had long-standing involvement with respected environmental groups; these included Tom Burke, Director of the Green Alliance, an SDP PPC for Surbiton in the 1987 General Election and a significant catalyst in the greening of all the major parties, David Astor of the CPRE and Nigel Haigh of the Institute of European Environmental Policy (IEEP).

These 'high-level' environmental activists formed the basis of an Environment Working Party which was to be the power house for SDP environmental thinking up to the 1987 election. In January 1985, this working group under the chairmanship of Bill Rodgers produced a Green Paper 'Policy on the Environment'. With relatively few amendments the Green Paper became a White Paper in July 1985 entitled 'Conservation and Change'.[17] It was well received by a press still unsure of the environment/party politics mix, although the paper was seriously dismembered by the then Ecology Party.[18] The document mirrored much of the accommodatory approaches to the environment practised by its creators. Its focus upon the concept of 'green growth' was dismissed by Porritt as 'a tawdry, dishonest little trick', but the integration of environment and industry, and a Euro-centric approach was essentially a brave attempt to fuse innovative ideas being developed independently by the environmentalists with a party philosophy which did not exist.[19]

Because many of the green activists within the Liberal Democrats are community-based, it is perhaps difficult for outsiders to really appreciate the commitment they have to the process of 'greening' their party. The impression that comes over is of a party of escapist green cranks, well versed in radicalism cultivated because they have been an opposition party for so long. However, this image masks an organisational miracle which allows green activists at local level to influence party thinking at national level.

Crusaders and opportunists

Two ideal-types can be used to identify key individuals within the major parties. They can be defined as 'crusaders' or 'opportunists', depending upon the motivation behind their interests and involvement in environmental concerns.

The interests and concerns politicians pursue are to a large extent dictated by the kind of external events and pressures examined in chapter 4. However, their response to these events is dependent upon a complex mixture of ever-changing elements including personal commitment, age, ambition, party profile, the particular environmental issue and adherence to party ideologies.

Through interviews with party members and analysis of their actions, it becomes apparent that commitment to, and understanding of, environmental issues exists. Some politicians take environmental issues more seriously than others. Their responses to the warnings of the pressure groups differ. Their understanding of the science underlying environmental issues and its implications for the long rather than the short term also varies. Moreover, the environmental concern a politician exhibits varies in time and extent during his/her career. Although it is not possible to pigeon-hole party members with absolute certainty, it is useful to identify the levels of environmental concern present and the sort of motivations lying at the root of such concerns.

Environment is the classic 'apple pie' issue which everyone likes and it would be a foolish politician who openly admitted to not caring about the environment. In rhetorical terms alone, all politicians are environmental crusaders. 'Crusaders' is an appropriate term for those individual party members who spend the majority of their time seeking to improve the environmental credentials of their own party. The spirit of party competition can take hold and thereby move environmental concern higher up the political agenda.

The distribution and commitment of crusaders varies in government and party structures. The pressures of work on those playing a leading role in their parties means that to draw comparisons in terms of commitment with those working at constituency level would be unfair. Opportunities to influence party policy are reduced outside government or parliamentary ranks and it can be argued that it is only those individuals who hold positions of power in their respective parties who are *de facto* crusaders. However, it does not necessarily follow that the Secretary of State for the Environment and attendant ministers are champions of the environmentalist's cause. Although they may have an interest in some of the responsibilities of the post, it is far more likely that they will be selected for the post on the basis of political competence. Political advisers (civil servants appointed by ministers) can brief ministers regarding the 'environmental facts', but this does not take into account the depth of understanding or concern a minister may bring to a post.

It was only when Chris Patten had been appointed Environment Secretary that the Conservatives could lay any real claim to having an environmental crusader in the cabinet. This is no reflection on the work carried out by Michael Heseltine, Patrick Jenkin, Kenneth Baker or even Nicholas Ridley. They all possessed political strengths not founded in the environmental sphere and all became preoccupied with other aspects of the DOE's work. During the mid-1980s, the most able Tory crusader, William Waldegrave, gained both respect and some sympathy from environmental pressure groups, the Greens and members of the opposition. His promotion in September 1985 from Under Secretary of State for the Environment to Minister of State for the Environment, Countryside and Local Government was taken to be a symbolic indication of the Conservatives' commitment to a 'greener' outlook.

Classification as a crusader depends upon a number of factors. John Cunningham, as Shadow Environment Secretary from 1983 until his move to party campaign manager in 1989, seemed by virtue of his long-standing position to be a 'natural' champion of the environmental cause. Cunningham combined his scientific background and a great deal of political acumen with an extensive understanding of the environmental movement. However, his deep commitment to a host of green issues was negated by his pro-nuclear-power stance – a point he has never been allowed to forget by environmentalists inside and outside the Labour Party.

In contrast to Cunningham, David Clark, Labour's former spokesman on Environmental Protection, showed all the signs of an environmental crusader *par excellence*. In July 1970 he made his maiden speech in the House of Commons in a pollution debate: 'I suppose I am regarded as one of the younger generation. I think that we can perhaps forgive our elders for their political mistakes, but I do not think we shall forgive the elder members of the community if they do not help us get rid of the scars of pollution.'[20] Throughout his political career, David Clark's commitment to the environment has been evident, from pressing for the banning of heavy lorries from minor roads in 1972 and trying to make returnable bottles compulsory in 1980, to his successful Wildlife and Countryside Amendment Act of 1985. His election to the Shadow Cabinet as spokesman on environmental protection in November 1986 was an innovative move, given that he was not shadowing anyone in the government. This was done in the belief that a future Labour government would have a separate ministry of environmental protection. When moved to Agriculture and Rural Affairs in a post-election reshuffle, David Clark was reported to be upset about the change. Seen by some as Kinnock's way of diffusing possibly embarrassing conflicts between Clark and Cunningham regarding nuclear power and as reinforcing Kinnock's support of Cunningham as his leading 'manifesto man', green activists within the party mourned the move as short-sighted. As a well-placed observer put it shortly after David Clark's move: 'Jack understands the issues, but David feels passionately about them and passion in the Labour Party seems to be on the way out at the moment.'[21]

Perhaps David Clark's most important success within his party was to begin to point out the interrelationship between environmental protection and job creation. For a party which arguably had long relied upon a programme which sought to protect and create jobs in manufacturing industries, seemingly at the expense the environment, the idea that a concern for the environment could actually create jobs was a novel one. The perceived threat to jobs had always been a major impediment to the political parties' uptake of green ideas, particularly during periods of economic stagnation, and especially in the Labour Party, whose main appeal was still to blue-collar workers. Following an introductory Labour Party report on 'Jobs and the Environment' in October 1986 which examined the changing attitudes of economists to the environment, David Clark employed a researcher to produce a further report which examined the job-creating potential of the party's environmental policies.[22] The second report in January 1987 gave the number of jobs that could be created in the various sectors of environmental protection as 200,000. Not only was this report a reflection of David Clark's own confidence in the importance of the environment to the party, it was also a smart political serenade to the trade unions. In the lead-up to the 1987 election, the 200,000 figure began to appear in the rhetoric of the trade union leaders, indicating an important change of attitude which still persists today.

However deep an activist's commitment to 'green' issues, it is only rarely that one person can find the time to explore environmental issues laterally, unless given the environment portfolio. It is more common for individuals to crusade for specific issues. Peter Hardy (MP for Wentworth), for instance, has long been recognised as the leading specialist wildlife conservationist inside the Labour Party. Similarly, Sir Richard Body MP, as a farmer and Chair of the House of Commons Select Committee on Agriculture, is recognised as the leading campaigner for environmentally-friendly farming within the Conservative Party.

Specialisation can strengthen a party as a whole and can lead to a process by which links between issues begin to reveal themselves. The interdependence of issues is difficult to convey, and it is only when individuals begin to examine issues in depth that they become aware of the lateral links and environmental implications. Frank Cook's (Labour MP for Stockton North) interest in alternative forms of energy, for instance, was stimulated by his role in the opposition to the NIREX explorations for an intermediate-level radioactive-waste dumping site in his constituency in 1985. Whenever he can he seeks to provoke discussion in the party about renewable energy sources and recognises that his involvement in energy issues led to the realisation that it is difficult to fix any boundaries in environmental debates.

An interest in the environment can be introduced into a party and maintained there by an individual's outside involvement with a specialist environmental organisation. Many of the MPs listing conservation and the environment as a special interest are in some way connected with environmental groups and societies. Some are party-based groups, but many are non-political pressure groups and charities, associated organisations such as consumer and peace groups, and related professions such as planning and architecture. Such affiliations, although primarily extra-parliamentary, nevertheless filter through to relevant parliamentary debates. For instance David Clark, whilst Chairman of the Open Spaces Society, has on a number of occasions attempted to introduce a 'right of access' Bill into Parliament. Active interest in, or patronage of, pressure groups and environmental organisations leads to cross-fertilisation between pressure group and party members and across party boundaries.

An individual's past experiences can be relevant to and stimulate interest in environmental matters. Kenneth Carlisle MP found the inspiration for his 1984 party paper 'Conserving the Countryside' – endorsed by Waldegrave as a 'notable contribution' to party thinking – in the changes that he had witnessed on his arable farm in East Anglia.[23] Likewise Sydney Chapman MP, an ardent member of the House of Commons Environment Select Committee and the only qualified Town and Country Planner in the Parliamentary Conservative Party, brought with him a keen interest in Green Belt matters, architectural heritage and inner-city regeneration.

From an environmentalist point of view, it is common to find contradictions in the stance of politicians. It is not uncommon for Tory MPs to be members of the RSPB, campaigning for the preservation of birds, and yet also to be ardent supporters of the game-shooting lobby. This does not negate their claims of being environmentally sound. Contradictions are commonplace in politics, where motivation is a mixture of ideology, self-interest and party responsibility. Those who take specific environmental issues to heart are nonetheless crusaders who can *en masse* instigate wider changes of attitudes in their parties.

Some consider all politicians to be opportunists, particularly within the higher ranks of the parties where profile and image are all the more important. The environment is a political issue and as such can be used for political point-scoring. The steady growth in MPs displaying an interest in environmental issues can be interpreted as blatant opportunism. However, there comes a point where motivations become less important than the actions they produce. Opportunists are those party members who would seem to be engaging in environmental rhetoric and posturing solely for political reward, rather than because of any deep understanding of or commitment to the environment. In the words of Jack Cunningham, they 'flit in and out of the scene from time to time, if they think something is politically sexy or controversial'.[24]

Individuals do not openly admit that they are motivated by opportunism, and amongst all the major parties real opportunists are difficult to identify. However, the environmental opportunist possesses a limited history of involvement with environmental ideas or, more usually, no such involvement. Further evidence is provided if an individual who appears sympathetic has a background which includes episodes where he or she demonstrated hostility to 'green' issues and the environmental movement. But if party leopards can change their spots, what makes them do so? To fulfil individual ambition would seem to provide an obvious answer, yet even with its dramatically increased political prominence, the environment is hardly the route that successful politicians follow. Political reward for the party in office still revolves around high-profile jobs in the Home Office, Transport, Defence and the Foreign Office. For the committed green activist within the government, the rewards in terms of improving one's position and maintaining one's interest in the environment would hardly seem to be satisfied, even as Secretary of State for the Environment, under the present structure. Without a career structure within the parties for green activists, political success will continue to lie elsewhere, and most party members do seek political success.

Personal ambition is constrained by party needs and strategic thinking amongst party leadership, as was shown by David Clark's move to Agriculture and Rural Affairs. Individuals usually have little or no say about where they wish to work, and decisions take into account general political experience rather than subject expertise. To some extent career moves can be interesting opportunities to assess an individual's commitment to the environment. Waldegrave's departmental sidestep to Minister of Housing after the 1987 General Election was closely observed by those environmental groups with which he had previously had dealings. His concerns for protecting the countryside, and particulary the green belt, from over-development were carried over from his previous post to an extent. He emphasised that he was not in favour of building large numbers of houses, but was concerned to see that those that were built were well sited and designed to last.[25] However, Waldegrave surprised many of his previous environmentalist allies when, at a local government conference on housing in December 1987, he supported 'out-of-town' shopping development in the interests of the legitimate forces of competition.

It is, however, unfair to use these sorts of comparisons to assess the depth of environmental concern of an individual. Personal interests have to take second place to the demands of the post. In Waldegrave's subsequent positions of Foreign Minister and Secretary of State for Health, he has had little opportunity to publicly illustrate his private environmental convictions.

There are some individuals who, as true politicians, seize opportunities and jump on bandwagons whatever they may be. They may
recognise that they can use the environment as a vehicle to attack the
opposition or to attack individuals in their own party. They attend
environment meetings not because of their commitment to the issues,
although they may have a genuine concern for the environment, but
because it provides an opportunity to 'have a go' at key figures or
leaders. This is a situation that John Cunningham frequently found
himself in as Shadow Environment Secretary.

It is important not to give the question of motivation undue
weight. All politicians recognise that environmental problems have
both political explanations and political solutions. Opportunists can
act as useful allies to party crusaders. Indeed, opportunism may be
an important means of getting environmental ideas diffused through
the political parties, since all politicians can usually recognise a 'good
bet'.

Ideological drives

An important driving force behind the work of individual green
activists in the major parties is an understanding and use of party
ideology in relation to environmental questions. As outlined in
chapter 3, party ideologies act in various ways which relate to the
process of party greening. For key activists within each of the major
parties there are elements of each party's philosophies which drive,
legitimise and shape environmental concern. As we shall see later,
elements of the same ideologies also act as impediments to party
greening.

The idea that a 'green thread has always run through the blue
fabric of the Conservative Party' is a relatively new claim,[26] although
discussion and debate about environmental questions has always
taken place in the Conservative Party, whether in the 1870s or the
1970s. However, to argue that there has always been an intrinsic
ideological link between the principles of Conservatism and the
principles of conservation implies that environmental concern is
something much more fundamental than a series of political issues.
Sullivan sums up the values upon which he argues Green Conservatism is based as a concern for property and the responsibility
that goes with it, an understanding of community, a sense of history
and tradition, and a feeling for beauty:[27] concepts that could have

been picked straight from Waldegrave's own exploration of Conservative thought in his closely-argued book, *The Binding of Leviathan*.[28]

The notion of private property being essential to a 'free' and well-ordered society has been used to justify the Conservative programme of council house sales. Waldegrave saw this as part of the Conservative environmental quest and a way of breaking into an area of policy which was not usually seen to be a strong point of the party. The destruction of the council house estates and the decline of inner-city areas are said to be a consequence of people not being allowed to have a stake in their own communities. Waldegrave powerfully put over his belief that 'man and his community are inseparable' in his 1985 party conference speech:

Many of the old houses which went could easily have been renovated; but they were old and out of fashion. So they went and often with them went the whole fabric of a community that had built up naturally over the decades, even centuries – the local family and friends, the corner shops and pubs, local workplaces, everything that makes life livable in big towns. And often responsibility was abolished – as it often is – with property.[29]

It is the countryside with which Conservatives 'have always had a natural affinity' and where they have also had strong support.[30] Waldegrave's belief that society is 'something infinitely complex whose interactions we do not understand and which we can kill more easily than we can create' underlies his intellectually influential speech to the Oxford Farming Conference in January 1986: 'Neither the farming lobby nor the environmental lobby alone – let alone in conflict with each other – has the power to look after the countryside properly. That, I believe, is the reality of the opportunity offered to farmers by environmental politics, and to environmentalists by the farming interests.'[31] The speech emphasised the virtue of evolutionary and cautious attitudes which underpin the so-called 'voluntary approach' to conservation in the countryside, and its value lay in its attempt to cement the middle ground that was only just emerging between the farmers and the environmental lobby.

Just as tradition and the realities of the past are important ideological texts in the gospels of Tory Party environmental missionaries, so is the concept of continuity. Burke's concept of society and the role of government as 'a partnership not only between those living, but between those who are living, those who are dead and those who are to be born', would not appear to fit easily in the mind of any party politician whose main concern tends to be self-survival in the short term.[32] It evokes the idea of stewardship and comes very close to the Greens' position of having obligations to future generations. Key green activists within the Conservatives have used what in some ways is a radical philosophical strand as a lever for environmental concern. Chris Patten demonstrated his depth of understanding for the environment as well as Burkean Toryism, when he wrote in 1984:

We do not have freeholders' rights to the land we live in which allow us to do whatever we want with it. We are its trustees, obliged to pass what we inherited from the last generation to the next. The sympathies of the Conservatives should therefore be tilted firmly in the direction of those who wish to conserve the best of our environment and to improve the worst of it.[33]

The government readily cites actions which support this philosophical tenet: the amount spent on cleaning up polluted rivers and air and the increases in the budgets of bodies such as the Countryside Commission and the Nature Conservancy Council. Besides the expected opposition cries of 'not enough' and 'too late', contradictions are evident, and crusaders such as Waldegrave have been placed in uncomfortable positions. Waldegrave, for instance, had expressed his concern for a nuclear power programme in terms of the legacy of radioactive waste: 'To land this responsibility on succeeding generations is to make assumptions about future stability for which history offers no precedents.'[34] However, at the 1985 party conference Waldegrave declared: 'as an environmentalist, I can tell you that if we were starting from scratch we would quite likely choose nuclear power as the energy source most likely overall to protect our quality of life.'[35] Had Burke's influence worn off? It is unlikely. As Environment Minister, Waldegrave always had difficulty not only in accepting that nuclear power was to be maintained, but that so many of his colleagues wanted to see an expanded programme. As one party sympathiser explained the apparent incongruity: 'What a Minister says and what a Minister thinks need not be the one and the same. My guess is that it was in the Minister's wider interests that he did not rock the boat . . . let's face it, Party Conference is not the place to be anything other than politically Right.'[36]

The ideological base of the Labour Party is less cohesive than that of the Conservative Party, reflecting not only the shorter political history of the party, but also the variety of principles it encompasses.

Labour's constrained socialism, constrained both by the party's constitution of 1918 and the fact that the party operates in a capitalist economy, together with a plethora of amorphous socialist ideas and influences, do, however, go a long way in explaining green activism within the party.

Although there is much literature on the relationship between socialism and environmentalism, there has been little on the links between Labour Party philosophy and environmentalism.[37] The Party Objects of Clause IV of the party's constitution are couched in terms which are hardly likely to stimulate the environmentalist. The reference points of industrial toil and economic emancipation have lost much of their relevance over the past seventy years. However, many of the socialist values at the base of the Labour Party's constitution, values that preceded the formation of the party itself, are now being drawn on to develop the party's environmental thinking.[38]

Unlike the Conservative's preoccupation with the individual, Labour's concern is with society as a whole. It seeks to change the structure of society by moving it toward a socialist, egalitarian political economy, although it can be argued that the main concern of the Labour Party so far has been to minimise the effects of capitalism rather than instigate any major moves to remove the causes of inequality. It is the injustice of the inequality of wealth and the consequent inequality within society which is at the heart of Labour's position on the environment. In 1973, the Labour Party Green Paper 'The Politics of the Environment', strongly influenced by Anthony Crosland MP and Denis Howell MP, put over this concern:

The pit owner never lived in the shadow of the slag heap. The soot from the factory chimney did not fall on the bonnet of the owner's wife. Those who spoiled the environment of the workplaces which produced their profit could buy themselves out of those surroundings. But the people whose labour created wealth for others were left with the noise, the dirt, the ugliness, the stench and congestion at every growing point of capitalist enterprise. This is still basically true.[39]

Conditions since 1973 have changed, more through industrial decline than anything else, yet the underlying concern to redress the inequalities in society remains at the base of green activism in the Labour Party. Indeed, in some respects it has increased as the party has witnessed the growth of Mrs Thatcher's free-market enterprise economy. Labour's 1986 'Environment Statement' – the basis of its 1987 General Election manifesto commitments – went deeper and further than ever before, in terms of defining environmental problems and putting forward radical solutions.[40] The central ideological premise remained very similar to that put forward in 1973. As Tom Sawyer put over with passion at an evening environment debate at the 1986 Labour Party Conference:

This is no misty-eyed programme. It is a hard-biting socialist programme to tackle urban decay, for we know that for many, certainly the poor and the disadvantaged, environmenatl decay crushes their development, damages the quality of their lives and limits their horizons. Our programme is for those with no play space trapped in high rise flats, no decent lifts, no hope. Its for those with paper-thin walls reluctantly listening to their next door neighbour's television. It's for those who dread winter because fuel costs mean a constant choice betwen cold and hunger.[41]

The majority of Labour environmentalists start with an analysis of capitalism to explain the existence of environmental problems which is essentially Marxist, but proposed solutions derive from a peculiarly British style of socialism.[42] Labour has always found Marxism to be an uncomfortable ideology and has therefore adopted the gradualism of the Fabian socialists, seeking largely to maintain the political institutions of Britain. Reformism is the order of the day, which is a process rooted in a commitment to democracy and participation, ideas which marry well with green ideals.

David Clark's attitude to the environment draws strongly on the principle of social equality. Equal access to education, welfare services and the 'full fruits of industry' is extended to the environment. 'Everyone has a right to a clean and pleasant environment in which to live and work, whether they be rich or poor, black or white, urban or country dweller.'[43] Those in the less favourable areas and the unemployed are entitled to pleasant and healthy surroundings. The same argument can be applied, however, to those people employed (the vast majority of the electorate) and living in areas with strong local economies. Higher environmental standards are in demand as part of the quest for a better quality of life.

Side by side with Labour's concern for a redistribution of wealth and social equality is an ideological commitment to public or social ownership and the planned use of resources. All of the Labour Party's policy statements on the environment have these mechanisms at their centre as the means of achieving social justice, rather than a reliance on voluntarism.[44] The socialist principle of intervention by the state in order to manage and regulate the environment is widely accepted by Labour activists, although there is some disagreement on the amount of intervention that is required, mirroring the wider debate between the left and right wings of the party.[45]

David Clark MP, Chris Smith MP, Robin Cook MP, Ken Collins MEP and Tom Sawyer, Deputy General Secretary of NUPE are amongst those who have pointed not to a sudden discovery of environmental concern in the Labour Party, but rather a revival of concern which can be traced back to Robert Owen, William Morris, John Ruskin, Edward Carpenter and Robert Blatchford's Clarion Movement. These are the ideologues of today's Labour Party crusaders. As one trade union leader put it: 'We don't need Porritt with such a rich ancestry of environmentalists in the Party.'[46] The visions of the ethical socialists were built around not only beauty and craftsmanship – ideas often rejected as apolitical utopian escapism – but also values which run through socialist and trade union thought, such as community, dignity, co-operation and democracy. Robin Cook, MP and President of SERA, believes that the utopian vision of the early socialists should not be denied in Labour's approach to the environment. He admitted in 1988: 'I tend to share the wild view that a map of socialism that does not have Utopia on it is a map not worth looking at.'[47]

The ideological motivations for environmental activists within the Liberal Democrats have largely been inherited from the former Liberal Party. Principles of liberty and egalitarianism, and concepts such as diversity, community and interdependence, link liberalism intimately with ideas at the root of environmentalism. Indeed, the 'future generations' strand of thinking is enshrined within the preamble to the Liberal Democrat constitution which states: 'We believe that each generation is responsible for the fate of our planet and by safeguarding the balance of nature and the environment, for the long term continuity of life in all its forms.'[48] These links between Liberal philosophy and environmental concern are increasingly being teased out by party activists in order to entrench the legitimacy of 'green' thinking within the party. The 1990 document 'What Price our Planet?' coherently argues that an understanding of liberalism and its commitment to long-term concern for future generations and a global society ultimately leads to a desire to develop a sustainable society.[49]

The importance of the individual within Liberal ideology is echoed in an approach to politics which emphasises the role of local communities rather than the centralised state and seeks to protect people rather than institutions. It is an approach which manifests itself in the work of the key green activists in the party, and in Liberal Democrat policies for the devolution and decentralisation of power, together with increased public participation. The importance of community is central, not only in the sense of UK politics but also in relation to international politics. In the words of Richard Holme, a former president of the Liberal Party and long-standing party strategist and environmentalist:

We should put the politics of place alongside the politics of community as the microcosmic learning experience through which people can potentially understand the macrocosm of a small shared planet with finite physical resources, albeit with enormous human potential. A generation which understood that the residents of Shipshape Street could combine together to stop a local factory emitting its fumes across their washing, could also potentially grasp the need for local authorities to combine to resist a governmental threat to the Green Belt or the need for the countries of Europe to co-operate to stop acid rain.[50]

More than any other party, the Liberal Democrats espouse an ideological commitment to work within the EC and the wider international community. Stemming from the free-traders of the nineteenth century, internationalism is an important drive for environmentalists in the Liberal Democrats. There is a genuine belief in the interdependence of local and global communities and the need to tackle environmental problems through the most appropriate mechanisms. In contrast to the fears expressed in some sections of the Labour Party of a lack of parliamentary control and the nationalism held by influencial members of the Conservative Party, the Liberal Democrats are dedicated Europeans. As Simon Hughes puts it: 'Only if the European Community is the premise, can much environmental progress be made, because by its very nature it needs to be trans-national and therefore needs the sort of institutional framework the European Community can provide.'[51]

The Liberal Democrats have developed a pragmatic attitude to politics which would seem to be more appropriate to tackling environmental questions than that of any other party. This pragmatism includes a willingness to engage in ideological 'trade-offs' in its politics. Influenced by a long time out of government, and with their ideological position mid-way between the two premier parties, Liberal Democrats have the capacity to adapt their principles whilst not losing them. Trade-offs must be an essential part of the relationship between environmentalism and politics, for what is perfect in the environmental sense may not be perfect in a social, economic or political sense.

For activists within the major parties, environmental concern arises out of party ideology and not vice versa. Conservatism, socialism, liberalism come before environmentalism. They guide, shape and stimulate interest, action and commitment to matters green, and mark out party approaches to environmental policy. As will be explored in the next chapter, party ideology also contributes to ambiguity toward the environment. For some key individuals there is always some doubt as to how far a party's ideology can be pushed in the name of the environment. For example, Robert Hutchinson, a former Chairman of the Liberal Ecology Group, in his paper 'A Sustainable Society' critically examined the relationship between the ecological crisis and what the then Liberal Party could do.[52] While he accepted that the party had the appropriate ideological grounding for tackling the symptoms of environmental problems, he remained uncertain of his party's ability to tackle the causes. Crusaders in the other parties share this worry that a party's ideology may ultimately be incompatible with the measures required to tackle environmental problems. However, there is also a belief that ideologies are accommodatory by nature and that, although they may seem anachronistic now, they can and will change.

Group influence

If environmentally concerned individuals join forces, they can thrust environmental issues on to the agenda of those holding high office in parties and in government. Such collective endeavours take two basic forms, the formal and the informal. Formal environmental groups, as distinct from environmental policy committees and working groups (although membership may overlap), operate in each of the major parties and have definite organisational arrangements. These pressure groups were specifically formed to heighten environmental awareness and to infuse environmental ideas into their respective parties' policies. The method of influence of these groups is usually in the form of a product: a publication, statement, conference resolution or some other identifiable form of representation.

Although the Conservative Party did establish a Conservative Environment Forum in 1986, which Waldegrave chaired, and the SDP contained a low-profile, loose amalgamation of interested members entitled 'SDP Greens' during the mid-1980s, neither had any strong established group that could begin to influence party thinking in any significant way. The Labour Party on the other hand had the Socialist Environment and Resources Association, and the Liberals, the Liberal Ecology Group.

By far the most successful of these party groups has been SERA and its offshoot, the Socialist Countryside Group, with over 85 per cent of its membership in the Labour Party. SERA was established in October 1973, spurred on by the heady environmental rhetoric of the time and the desire to spread this message throughout the Labour Movement. From some 700 members in 1983, SERA's membership has expanded to thousands, and the group now enjoys consultative status within the Labour Party. Through its links with the trade unions, the CLPs and a range of green groups, SERA has set out to push the Labour Party towards adopting a comprehensive set of environmental policies, including positions which link in with the peace movement and the women's movement.

By organising fringe meetings at party and TUC conferences, and debates with other environmental groups, by putting forward conference resolutions, articles in its own journal *New Ground* and also in *Tribune* and *Chartist*, and via low-key 'corridor' lobbying of the PLP, SERA has had its share of success. The CLPs and union branches have tabled environmental resolutions at Labour and trades unions' annual conferences, which can be traced back to the campaigning of SERA. Moreover, SERA played a key role in drawing up Labour's environment policy statements of 1978 and 1986; SERA's vice-president, Chris Smith MP, was a member of the Environment Working Party responsible for the 1986 statement.

The increase in SERA's overall influence on the party has been aided by a dramatic increase in SERA's impact within the PLP where it now has thirty-two members, including Neil Kinnock and current SERA president, Robin Cook, (in 1983 only fourteen MPs were members of SERA). Information from Parliament is continually fed to the group via their parliamentary adviser and previous president, Nigel Spearing MP.

Throughout its life, SERA has had to battle against an attitude, once endemic in the Labour Party, that environmentalists were nothing more than middle-class discontents. As the group put it back in 1982: 'What SERA is attempting, more than anything else perhaps, is to reclaim the term "environment" and to demonstrate its importance, in socialist terms, to the Labour Movement.'[53] Arguably this has been the greatest success for the group. They have persuaded some of the trade unionists and party supporters that the environment is not a middle-class issue, but that it is the working class and the poor of society that are most affected by and at risk from environmental problems. The arguments have been backed up by an increasingly long catalogue of disasters such as Ethiopia, Bhophal and Chernobyl. SERA was the only pressure group to give evidence at the Windscale Inquiry on trade union rights in the nuclear power industry.

Despite its successes, SERA has still to tussle with a tradition in the Labour Party which is cautious where the economy and employment is concerned. Its monitoring of the Labour Party Policy Review process on the environment was testimony to its concern to see that a green future will come from a socialism which is rooted more in the ideas of Morris than those of Morrison. In SERA's own words: 'Our claim is to be a link between the visionary tradition in British socialism and the practical politics of getting things done. We think it is essential to maintain that connection if socialists are to offer real hope for real change.'[54]

For much of the 1980s, until the establishment of the Green Democrats working within the Liberal Democrats, the Liberal Ecology Group worked to 'green' the Liberal Party. Established in 1977, the LEG sought to encourage the adoption of policies based on sound ecological principles. It had a relatively small but intellectually influential membership, and although never having 'official' status in the party, the LEG was nevertheless instrumental in stirring up the green debate, mainly via fringe meetings at party Assembly, resolutions for Assembly and informal discussions with party members.

Representing the view of former Chairman Adrian Watts, that 'if you scratch any Liberal you'll find a Green underneath', LEG was purely a product of famed Liberal radicalism. It drew closely on Green Party thinking but naturally rejected the view that the interests of the environment are best served through a separate political party. In 1979, LEG published the first edition of its 'Manifesto' which set out the ways it wished to see Liberal Party policy proceed, following its symbolic resolution passed at Margate in 1974 which placed economic growth in the context of ecological constraints. In 1985, spurred on by the emergence of the Alliance and at the same time worried by its development, a second edition of the 'Manifesto' was produced.[55] This philosophically sound statement was an attempt to remind Liberals of their green roots in the face of possible compromises with Social Democrats. For although the LEG was aware of the environmental tradition in the party, it acknowledged that 'the extent to which the Party's policy is based on ecological principles is still limited' (LEG Manifesto, 1985).

Informal groups whose influence is less easy to trace and thus more difficult to analyse with accuracy do exist in all the parties, although no definite or lasting form can be ascribed to them. Essentially these consist of the crusaders and opportunists, but also include their allies who sympathise with the idea of deepening environmental concern in their parties, but are unlikely to take many initiatives. These activists may initially find themselves bumping in to one another at green fringe meetings at the annual conference, they may belong the party's environmental group and sit upon the environmental policy panels. Party friendships may be struck, centred upon common interests in the environment ideas and contacts maybe exchanged; the same names tend to appear on committee lists and meetings may increase in frequency. What emerges is a network of politicians within the parties and government all with a genuine interest in green matters, upon which each can usually rely for support. Allegiances may be dictated by the issues involved, by whether or not support will bring an individual political gain or loss, or even by whether a politician is available to attend a meeting or vote on an issue. At a parliamentary level, MPs may become recognised for holding their particular interests through the way they vote, the questions they raise and the committees they attend. Furthermore, on some environmental questions and before the party Whips get going, these networks may cross party lines, as witnessed by the work carried out by the Commons Select Committee for the Environment and the signing of Early Day Motions.

The number of individuals within these 'green networks' is constantly changing. Interests wax and wane relative to wider political and personal developments. As party portfolios are moved around and ambitions are pursued, network members may be forced to devote less time to its purpose. On the whole, however, there would seem to be an overall expansion of the networks as environmental issues pursue their way up the party agendas and new party members seek new and socially relevant avenues of interest. Furthermore, although party members may have to pursue different tasks, it is unlikely that genuine concern will suddenly fade away.

Strategic considerations

Lying somewhere between the genuine interest and concern that party members may show for the environment and the crude, cynical idea that parties only respond when pushed, is the dimension of party strategy. This too accepts the premise that politicians, as part of a wider society, may have very deep levels of concern for and understanding of environmental issues. However, it also acknowledges an essential element of the party political process, the desire to achieve enough electoral support through the ballot box to form a government. In between elections much energy may be directed to 'keeping afloat on an even keel', since the notion of political success for a party tends to be relative to its position at any particular time. The momentum of party politics ensures that a significant degree of effort is directed toward party gain and, in some cases, party survival. This would seem to contradict the view outlined above that there are genuinely concerned and enlightened politicians. Yet we have never attempted to mask the reality of party politics. What we have done is to move away from the purely negative and simplistic view that politicians and parties are solely motivated by devious and self-centred interests.

Just as we may not be able to distinguish the genuine environmental concerns of individual politicians, we also face problems in labelling party actions as being shrewd, strategic moves. In the first place the interests and activities of individual politicians may bear no relation to the overall intentions of their respective parties. Secondly, the idea of strategy implies some well-organised and long-term plan for the party, whereas it is more likely to evolve piecemeal amongst surrounding environmental and political developments between general elections. It also implies the existence of party strategists. They are certainly present within each party, though no title exists to denote their role. However, the strategists themselves do not work to some unchanging master plan, but to short-term programmes as they arise. Furthermore, it may well be that strategic political moves are quite compatible with a deep understanding and commitment to environmental issues. This latter point is central to the argument of the 'intentional' model, that interaction between a growing environmental movement and the generally intransigent and preoccupied political parties would have produced more conflict if there had not been some degree of compatibility. Indeed, this may lead us to suggest that there has been a certain inevitability about the greening of the British political parties.

Projecting a green image

Just as politicians are conscious of the images they project to their electorate, so too are the parties as a whole. On a general level, the main parties are eager to portray a wholesome picture of British democracy at work and to counter any ideas which might suggest a decline in political legitimacy. Of course the level of complacency about constitutional defects varies, and each party holds different views on how the constitution should function. However, in the main all the parties like to present an image of being representative (at least amongst their members), of being 'in tune' with the needs and desires of a constantly changing society, and of being responsive to these needs. In essence, as politicians and parties, they like to be seen to be doing their jobs well.

The parties have begun to assimilate elements of the environmental movement in order to uphold their responsible images. The extensive, diverse and persistent support for environmentalism, like that for any other issue, has grown to a point where it cannot be ignored, refuted or played down by any of the major parties contending for or holding power. The process of political accommodation hopes to serve two complementary and strategic purposes for the parties. Firstly, it seeks to end the perceived competition for public support, between the parties and the environmental movement. Secondly, it strengthens the parties' democratic credibility with the wider electorate. The parties are seen to be in touch with the environmentalists' cause and consequently concerned and approachable. The overall impression is that it is primarily the parties that are making all the running by absorbing the goals and demands of the movement. However, were it not for the presence and pressure of the environmental movement in the first place, party accommodation of the sort we are witnessing would not be taking place at all.

Taking up the ideas and suggestions advocated by the environmental movement is therefore perceived to be good for a party's image on two counts. More accurately perhaps, it may not be a case of positively cultivating a green outlook, but rather about taking those party members and groups who are already promoting green ideas more seriously and not attempting to block the pressures acting from outside the parties. The extent and importance accorded to possessing a green image is dependent upon a mixture of ideological drives and the desire to be elected to power. Broadly speaking, the opposition parties may find it easier formulating an environmental image without the responsibility of government.

Specifically, each party tends to specialise in issues which are commensurate with its ideology and interests. These issues provide the party with an image. Sometimes the image is built upon words such as 'tough', 'fair', 'strong' and 'weak'. Yet a balance needs to be struck between party image and the wider social pressures. For instance, the Conservatives cast an image which is one of being generally more concerned than Labour about the well-being of the countryside and changes in agriculture/farming practices.[56] In normal circumstances the Conservative Party would seek to maintain this image in order to secure the support of the farming and land-owning fraternity. By strategically choosing to deal with environmental issues that relate to the countryside, the Conservatives can seek to balance their image and the pressures for environmental concern. To an extent, the 'greening' of the Ministry of Agriculture and former Secretary of State, Michael Jobling's conversion to the idea of Environmentally Sensitive Areas can be seen in this light; the Minister of Agriculture undertakes an environmental initiative (albeit following long-standing pressure from environmental groups and the DOE), farmers gain, environmentalists are pacified, and the Conservatives' image as the party of the countryside is protected.

Catching votes

Intimately linked to the idea that parties are going 'green' to improve their public image is the notion that they are also seeking to increase the number of votes they receive at general elections.[57] It offers a seemingly simple explanation as to why party 'greening' may be taking place and was widely cited by commentators in the years leading to the 1987 General Election.[58] The prospect of a general election has the effect of forcing voters to make choices regarding which party they want to govern them. But elections also have the effect of influencing party strategies at the three stages before, after and during an election.[59]

Before an election, parties may choose their policies and often their candidates for their 'electoral appeal'. This assumes that parties know what is appealing (and conversely what is not appealing) to the voters. Indeed, it is near the time of an election when public opinion polls are taken most seriously by the parties. Generally, parties attempt to avoid particular policies which are not popular and adopt particular policies which are, although the former process seems to be rather easier in practice than the latter. During an election campaign, the parties enthusiastically focus upon their policy positions and are careful to be seen to be pleasing all sections of the electorate, at the level of rhetoric at least. It is at this time when an issue may rapidly rise in prominence as it becomes party political. After an election, the convention is that parties should take note of the lessons of the ballot box. But this is only partially true with reference to the party achieving election victory. Where an election defeat may encourage introspection and changes in party policy, organisation and leadership, victory can lead to complacency.

The end of one general election campaign is the beginning of a slow wind-up to another, and the proximity of an election is not in itself a reason for the high level of attention given by the political parties to environmentalist pressures. There is a strong incentive to gain electoral support by responding to, or being seen to respond to, the wishes of the mass environmental movement, particularly when environmental concerns have become prominent on the political agenda. Nevertheless, parties tend to respond to as many issues and groups as possible in order to gain votes, and within this context it is easy to see the sudden rise of 'green' concerns as an example of vote catching.

This election, orientated explanation of party greening rests upon the unproven assumption that there exists an as yet uncaptured 'floating' green vote. It implies that an identifiable membership of environmental groups are politically uncommitted and have been waiting for the party with the best environmental policies to come along before they vote at all. Although issues and policies are now recognised to have some relevance to voting behaviour under given conditions, they still have to be compared with longer term influences such as political inheritance, self-interest and past party/ government records.[60] It is unlikely, therefore, that substantial votes will be gained on the basis of party promises on environmental issues. Environmental policies form only a part of the spectrum of policies that influence voters. Those who are soley committed to environmental policies are probably already spoken for by the Green Party.

Prior to the 1987 General Election, key green activists in the main parties did believe in the existence of the green vote. This was not a belief in the notion that voters would make major defections to the Green Party if there were no major environmental advancements, though there was a serious worry in the highest ranks of the Liberal Party that potential Liberal votes could be lost to the Green Party.[61] Rather, Conservative Party managers and strategists warned of possible discontent amongst the farming vote and of close electoral encounters between the parties in marginal seats. This was particularly true in key seats in the cheese and wine belt of the south and south-east of the country where the emergence of the Alliance had increased party competition and directed attention to a range of developments with environmental implications – loss of green belt, road construction, amenity loss. In such cases it was perhaps understandable that the parties seemed prepared to become 'clients' for any uncertain voting element present. As votes have been hunted, the status of environmental issues on the party agendas has grown, providing the environmental movement with new opportunities to advance its position.

To some extent, green activists within the main parties deliberately overstated the importance of the green vote in a tactical move designed to encourage environmental debate. As a Conservative back bencher reflected prior to the 1987 election:

I'm not sure there is a green vote out there. There are a lot of environmentally concerned people but come a general election their minds will turn to other things, as will ours. If we are serious about a third term, fourth term, who knows, it is useful to pretend there is a green vote, it keeps us all on our toes and helps get things done now rather than when it may be too late.[62]

Before the 1987 General Election, all of the major parties laid their environmental cards on the table. Having strengthened their hand with the concession of a new combined pollution control agency in Her Majesty's Inspectorate of Pollution (HMIP), the Conservatives set out what they had been able to achieve in government in their manifesto. The range of policies was integrated more than ever before, and most sought to continue existing work rather than promise much that was new. As a voice from Conservative Central Office commented, albeit after the election: 'The public know we are the Party of the environment. We don't have to tell them, merely point out the fallacies and fibs behind the positions taken by the other parties.'[63]

The Labour Party's comprehensive and radical environment statement adopted at the party conference in 1986 was very much watered down in the 1987 General Election manifesto. The party had consulted over 100 groups in the course of putting together their environment statement, and yet throughout the election campaign little reference was made to its content. The Liberal/SDP Alliance too paid scant attention to the environment in their manifesto and during the election campaign generally. Athough environmental policy was one of the cracks that David Owen later suggested had been 'papered over', the low profile it was given was quite unexpected, particularly in the light of the earlier policy documents produced by both parties. If any party needed to make a populist appeal to the electorate, it was the Alliance. Instead, it inevitably found itself trapped in the two-party system it strove to break down.

Why were such seemingly popular policies so dramatically ditched by the major parties? Few party politicians took the existence of a green vote seriously, despite the earlier warnings of party strategists. Inevitably the momentum of the General Election took over, and green issues became overtaken by the traditional issues – defence, the economy, the future of the health service. Despite the influences of green activists and despite private polls commissioned by the parties which had suggested substantial voter sympathy for a high environmental profile, there was a strong sense of uncertainty amongst the parties about highlighting environmental issues during an election campaign. Why venture into the unknown, when they could continue with the comfort of the known? Moreover, speech writers, manifesto writers and media advisers were just not ready for an environmental election.

A further reason for the low profile of environmental concern amongst the main parties was the unexpected degree of consensus that existed between them on a range of environmental issues. A line-by-line examination of the environmental policies of the parties, particularly those of the Alliance and the Labour Party, revealed broad patterns of similarity. Both Labour and the Alliance were advocating new 'Ministries of Environmental Protection', a more sustainable approach to economic growth via government intervention, the development and enforcement of new codes of practice, performance monitoring via environmental audits, greater access to the countryside, and the need for a re-evaluation of the nation's agriculture and its dependence upon chemicals. Yet although there was consensus on many issues, consensus is an alien concept to British party politics, particularly at election time. The domination of the two party system and the confrontational approach ensures that parties emphasise the smaller percentage of issues where they differ, rather than the larger percentage that they do agree on. A green activist within the then Liberal Party ruefully commented:

What hope is there for green issues in our politics when Tweedle Dee and Tweedle Dum just have to disagree about them. You would think the best outcome of an argument – and we all like an argument – would be that both parties come away in agreement. Obviously not. Being in constant disagreement seems to keep politicians happy.

In the period of wound-licking after the 1987 General Election, the question of the green vote was brought up again. It was not an issue in the Conservative Party. Green Tory activists seemed happy with the amount of attention given to the environment in the manifesto and the election campaign, and were content that their commitment to the environment had been borne out by another election victory. In the Labour Party, however, questions were raised regarding the significance of environmental issues during the election and the prominence party policy was given. Some believed that the party would have captured important votes if environmental issues had been given a higher profile during the election campaign. In the heartfelt words of one Labour MP: 'We did bugger all about it.'[64] Yet although environmental activists, including some senior party members, were unhappy with the lack of attention given to the environment, they did not consider that an inordinate number of extra votes could have been secured had more time been given over to the environment. Jack Cunningham was convinced that environmental issues did not play a significant part in the general election. Although not happy about this himself, he did recognise that many of the issues the party had devoted much blood, sweat and tears to, including civil nuclear power, were not seen as matters of salience by the electorate. This analysis was borne out by the findings of polls commissioned by the Labour Party. Certainly, for all those party members involved with environmental matters it seemed as if the real task was to create a green vote and not assume that one existed already.

The Alliance parties also, emerged out of the general election wondering where the green vote, that many had pinned their hopes on, had gone. Some Liberals laid the blame on the SDP. They felt that the joint environment policy had compromised them, particularly on the issue of the future of the nuclear power industry. SDP members were also disappointed that their pragmatic approach to the environment and the economy had failed to attract support. In the slow disarray of merger talks, some Liberals, notably Simon Hughes MP and Felix Dodds (a former chair of the National League of Young Liberals), flirted with the idea of aligning themselves with the Green Party, such was their dissatisfaction with the SDP position on the environment.[65] These moves did not go unnoticed amongst Liberal Party strategists, and if anything, the feeling was strengthened that if the environment was given a higher profile in the future, votes would follow.

Despite the air of cynicism often associated with the parties' rush for votes, the ballot box is the basis of electoral party politics. Public support is shown in votes. Principles, however important they may be to a party, mean little without them. It would therefore seem inevitable that at such sensitive times as general elections, party agendas will be influenced, created or strengthened by the perceived threat of losing or the opportunity of gaining the environmentalist vote. However, the chase for what is a relatively small number of environmentalist votes cannot account for the depth of party 'greening'. In the short term the election factor only acts as a catalyst to stimulate party responses to issues that have already emerged. Environmental issues take their place with a host of other issues, and the 1987 General Election was no different to any other. A programme of policy alteration and adjustment, and in some cases a calculated dose of rhetoric, may be sufficient to encourage an undecided environmentalist punter – although, in terms of changing policy, the effect of elections is often over-estimated.[66] The main impetus comes from the party organisation itself, not from the voters for a few weeks before an election.

Internal drives: an assessment

As with the pressure-response model of party greening, there is a strong evolutionary dimension to an intentional interpretation. The networks of 'green' groups and individuals, and their interests in and knowledge of environmental issues, has developed over some twenty years. Within each party, awareness is heightened as points of contact between the environmental movement and the parties emerge. Punctuating this evolutionary process are the more reactive and short-term considerations regarding the interrelated goals of constructing an acceptable party image and achieving success in general elections. The line between the central motivations of genuine concern and pure electoral gain is blurred; it is difficult to separate the two, or locate the point in time when the former is used for the purpose of the latter. However, the net effect is the creation of a more receptive political climate for 'greening' to take place.

In some sections of the major parties there has been a natural progression from an attitude of responsiveness to an awareness of the fact that pressures can actually be turned to political advantage as new 'selling points', directed to the electorate as a whole. For some of the mainstream parties and party members this has required the re-evaluation, reinterpretation or new expressions of core party beliefs. For instance the Labour Party, in the review of environment policy which followed its election defeat, saw the need to develop a core philosophy about the environment. Of course this drew upon the basic beliefs of socialism, but it sought to knit them together into a framework of parameters which, when dealing with environmental issues, would not be negotiable. This was a historic move, marking the end of the party seeing environment merely as an aglomeration of various socialist ideas and disparate campaigns.

It is unlikely that the 'greening' of the British political parties represents a concerted effort to erode the social movement status of environmentalism. The environmental movement does not represent some form of strong, articulate or subversive threat which has to be defused. There are those who have argued that the more radical environmentalists have the will and capacity to de-stabilise the present social system, but they remain in a minority.[67] However, there does seem to be an element of indignant territorial encounter stimulated by the challenges that the environmentalists have thrown up. It is partly a case of the major parties acting to protect the ideals of representative democracy against the dissent shown by the environmental movement, and partly a case of defending their own specific ideological remits and political interests.

Because of the tradition and nature of the British party political system and the reformist way it operates, it also may be considered inevitable that the environmental movement is undergoing a process of almost unconscious absorption by the parties. Certainly Britain has no real background of political expression through the forum of social movements, and the politics of integration and accommodation are strong. To a large extent the peace movement, so strong in other Western European democracies, has been absorbed by the trade unions and the British Labour Party. Recently, the anti-nuclear-energy movement, often considered a cornerstone of the environmental movement, seems to be have been swept into the Labour Party's fold.[68] Of course, as any analysis of Labour conference votes on these issues shows, this process of integration is far from being neat and tidy. Tensions still endure and party battles still erupt, in part explained by the wider constituency held by a social movement which, unlike its party counterpart, is not so concerned with electoral advance.[69] However, on the sides of both party and movement, there seem to be incentives for some form of integration. This implies a level of compatibility between the aims of a party and those of a social movement. In the case of the environmental movement with its extensive aims and broad constituency, it may well be that in the process of its accommodation, the parties are presented with a such a variety of issues and positions that they can afford to be selective. How selective they are is discussed in the next chapter.

Notes and references

1   Rush, M. 1986. (2nd ed.) *Parliament and the Public*. London: Longman. Political Realities Series.

2   See: Forbes, I. 1983. 'Politics and Human Nature'. In Politics and Human Nature, Chap. 5. (Eds.) Forbes, I. / Smith, S. London: Francis Pinter.

3   *Dod's Parliamentary Companions* 1985–8.

4   In 1987 'ecology' was introduced as an interest by one MP and 'green issues' was a new interest heading introduced in 1988. MPs' interests were not recorded prior to 1985 but indications from long-serving MPs suggest that only a handful of members in each of the parties had an interest in environment/conservation.

5   Robinson, M. D. 1990. 'The Greening of British Party Politics: – The Superficiality and the Substance'. Unpublished PhD Thesis. University of East Anglia.
6   Vallance, E. 1988. 'The Job of the Backbencher.' *Contemporary Record*, Autumn. 10–12.
7   See for instance: Englefield, D. 1985. *Whitehall and Westminster Government informs Parliament: The Changing Scene*. Harlow: Longman: Radice, L./Vallance, E./Wills, V. 1987. *Member of Parliament: The Job of a Backbencher*. London: Macmillan Press.
8   Personal Communication.
9   See for instance: House of Lords Select Committee on the European Communities. 1984. *Agriculture and the Environment*. HL Paper 247. London: HMSO. The Committee's report shed light on the split between MAFF and the DOE and the failure to integrate the policies of the two departments.
10   Conservative Central Office. 1986. 'Protecting the Environment.'. *Politics Today*, No. 17. 27 October.
11   Corporate views of such groups are seldom expressed.
12   Personal Communication.
13   Sawyer, T. 1986. Speech at fringe meeting at Labour Party Conference. (Meeting organised by FoE/Greenpeace/SERA.)
14   These were 'Campaign Notes' to help initiate environmental action at the community level.
15   Personal Communication.
16   This built upon a discussion paper of the same name produced in April 1986.
17   SDP. 1985. *Policy on the Environment*. Green Paper, No. 10. January. The Social Democratic Party; SDP. 1985. *Conservation and Change: Policy for the Environment*. July. The Social Democratic Party.
18   Porritt, J. 1985. 'Updating Industrialism.' *Resurgence*, No. 112. Sept./Oct. 36.
19   Although guided by key principles, the SDP as a new party could not be said to have developed a philosophy in the same way as Liberalism. Indeed, the party appeared to pride itself on being free from ideological baggage.
20   Clark, D. in Hansard, 21 July 1970. 'Environmental Pollution Debate.' 370–72.
21   Personal Communication.
22   Labour Party. 1987. *Jobs and Environment*. Second Interim Report, January. The Labour Party.
23   Carlisle, K. 1984. 'Conserving the Countryside: A Tory View.' Conservative Political Centre. May.
24   Personal Communication.
25   See information provided by Porritt, J./ Winner, D. 1988. *The Coming of the Greens*. London. Fontana.
26   Paterson, T. 1984. *Conservation and the Conservatives*. London: Bow Publications Ltd.
27   Sullivan, A. 1985. 'Greening the Tories: New Policies on the

Environment.' Policy Study, No. 72. Sept. 1985. Centre for Policy Studies.
28   Waldegrave, W. 1978. *The Binding of Leviathan*. London: Hamish Hamilton.
29   Waldegrave, W. 1985. Conservative Party Conference Speech.
30   Forman, N. 1987. 'Conservative Environmental Policy.' Conference Paper. British Association of Nature Conservationists. Conference entitled 'How Green is My Party?'.
31   Waldegrave, W. 1986. Speech to The Oxford Farming Conference, 7 January. Reprinted in *Policy Challenge*, August 1986. Centre for Policy Studies. 4–22.
32   Quoted in Paterson, note 26, *op. cit.*
33   Patten, C. 1984. *The Tory Case*. London: Longmans.
34   Note 28, *op. cit.*
35   Note 29, *op. cit.*
36   Personal Communication.
37   See for instance: Williams, R. 1980. *Socialism and Ecology*. SERA; Pepper, D. 1984. *The Roots of Modern Environmentalism*. London: Croom Helm; Ryle, M. 1988. *Ecology and Socialism*. London: Radius.
38   The process of introspection that followed the defeat of the Labour Party in the 1987 General Election included a reassessment of the party's constitution. The 1988 document 'Democratic Socialist Aims and Values' attempted to link party ideology with environmental concern and thus complement the review of environmental policy.
39   Labour Party. 1973. *Politics of the Environment*. The Labour Party.
40   Labour Party. 1986. *Environment Statement*. The Labour Party.
41   Note 13, *op. cit.*
42   See for instance: Cook, R. 1984. 'Let's Make the Red Flag Green.' *The Times*. 24.4.84. 12.
43   Clark, D. 1987. 'View from the 'Green' Bench . . . Labour.' *New Ground*, No. 14. 3.
44   Including: Labour Party. 1976. *Labour's Programme*. Statement to Annual Conference. The Labour Party; Labour Party. 1978. *Labour and the Environment*. Statements to Annual Conference by the National Executive Committee. The Labour Party; Labour Party. 1982. *Labour's Programme: The Environment*. The Labour Party. 163–5. Labour Party. 1985. *Labour's Charter for the Environment*. The Labour Party; Labour Party. 1990. *An Earthly Chance*. The Labour Party.
45   A point made by many including: Wainwright, H. 1988. Interview: 'Green Politics and Labour.' New Ground, No. 17. Spring. 16.
46   Personal Communication.
47   Cook, R. 1988. 'Needed: a Green Vision.' *New Ground*, No. 19. Autumn. 3.
48   The Liberal Democrats' constitution is heavily influenced by the long-standing commitment to the environment by the Liberal Party.
49   Liberal Democrats. 1990. *What Price our Planet? A Liberal Democrat Agenda for Environmental Action*. The Liberal Democrats.
50   Holme, R. 1985. 'Green Democracy.' In *Green Commitment*. The Liberal Party. 21–3.

51 Address given to a Green Alliance Meeting, 9 May 1984.
52 Hutchinson, R. 1985. 'A Sustainable Economy.' Conference Paper. Green Briefing Conference. Organised by Link and The Liberal Ecology Group. February, 1985.
53 Extract from a SERA letter to all CLPs in March 1982.
54 Extract from 'SERA – Ten Years On', a briefing document produced by SERA in 1983 to celebrate ten years of campaigning.
55 Liberal Ecology Group. 1985. *The Liberal Ecology Group Manifesto.* (2nd ed.). The Liberal Ecology Group.
56 See: Brotherton, D. I. 1986. 'Research Policy and Review 8: Party Political Approaches to Rural Conservation in Britain.' *Environment and Planning A*, 18. 151–60; Lowe, P./Flynn, A. 1986. 'The Problems of Analysing Party Politics: Labour and Conservative Approaches to Rural Conservation.' *Environment and Planning A*, 19. 409–14.
57 To an extent this also includes by-elections and local elections.
58 See for instance: *The Economist.* 1985. 'Green Power: Rising Sap.' Editorial. 24.8.85; Paterson, T. 1985. 'Environment – Does the Prime Minister Care?' Crossbow, Summer; Owens, S. 1986. 'Environmental Politics in Britain: New Paradigm or Placebo?' *Area*, 18 (3) September.
59 Harrop, M./Miller, W. L. 1987. *Elections and Voters: A Comparative Introduction.* London: Macmillan Education.
60 Note 59, *op. cit.*
61 Note 5, *op. cit.*
62 Personal Communication.
63 Personal Communication. Conservative Central Office employed a researcher to highlight the weaknesses of the other parties' environmental policy to MPs and Conservative Prospective Parliamentary Candidates in the month leading to the 1987 General Election.
64 Personal Communication.
65 See: Cooper, T. 1987. 'Across the Divides.' *Green Line*, No. 55. September. 10–11; Dodds, F. 1987. 'Across the Divides.' *Green Line*, No. 55. Sept. 10–11; Goodwin, S. 1987. 'The Green Party Conference.' *Independent.* 21.9.87.
66 Note 59, *op. cit.*
67 For a rightest reactionary view of the environmental movement and their political influence in Western Europe see: Pfaltzgraff Jnr, R. L./Holmes, K. R./Clemens, C./Kaltefleiter, W. 1983. *The Greens of West Germany: Origins, Strategies and Transatlantic Implications.* Special Report. Institute for Foreign Policy Analysis Inc: Cambridge, Massachusetts and Washington, D.C.
68 See: Lowe, P. D./Rudig, W. 1984. 'The Withered "Greening" of British Politics: A Study of the Ecology Party.' Paper presented at the UK Political Science Association Conference, Southampton, 3–5 April; Ward, H. 1983. 'The Antinuclear Lobby: an Unequal Struggle?' In Marsh, D. (Ed.) *Pressure Politics.* London: Junction Books. 182–211.
69 An important point made by Smith, G. 1976. 'Social Movements and Party Systems in Western Europe.' In Kolinsky, M./Paterson, W. E. (Eds.) *Social and Political Movements in Western Europe.* London: Croom Helm. 331–54.

6

Irresistible forces and immovable objects

Throughout the 1980s the combined effects of the pressures from outside and inside the main political parties stimulated the process of 'greening'. However, the process has not been straightforward. There are sets of constraints acting on each party which have limited the pace, extent and depth of the development of pro-environmental attitudes.

The constraints operate as a filter through which environmental policy proposals and 'green' ideas have to pass before they are sanctioned. This screening process can have three basic outcomes. The first, but uncommon, outcome is where environmental ideas and initiatives encounter no obstruction and are taken up by a party in an unaltered form. The second outcome is where ideas are put forward but come up against resolute and lasting obstacles and are consequently rejected by those holding power and influence: hence, 'green' individuals may be prevented from occupying positions of influence. The third, most likely, outcome occurs when environmentalist pressures come up against the range of constraints operating and are metamorphosed by them, making them acceptable in the parties' own terms.

The resilience and longevity of party constraints relates to both internal party matters and also to the depth and persistence of the environmental pressures and drives. Although the environmental movement often seeks swift changes, it is constantly restrained by the slow, deliberate pace at which the major political parties work. Figure 6 portrays the maze of interdependent factors which make up the complex party filters through which pressures for 'greening' pass. The constraints function at two connected levels; those specifically party-based, and those that relate to particular interest groups and lobbies allied to the parties.

The pressures for change confront a series of possible impediments: party members with conflicting party or personal interests or a lack of understanding of environmental issues may be unsympathetic; established procedures of government and the parties may cause delays and may block initiatives. Similarly, existing party policy commitments can run counter to environmental developments. Ultimately, the pressures for change have to confront the ideologies of the parties. A further source of resistance emanates not from the parties and their members direct, but from the economic and political interest groups which align themselves with the parties and which represent the social, political and business interests which can conflict with 'green' ideas.

There is no co-ordinated or conscious attempt by the parties to apply these constraints, nor any definite time-scale to the process. Some constraints may be the product of a particular individual whose views may not be wholly in keeping with the rest of the party, whilst others may be a function of party beliefs. Moreover, some constraints may operate temporarily, whilst others may last for many years.

The ease or difficulty by which environmental issues pass through this system of party checks and balances relates to their precise nature and timing. Certain issues may be more compatible to one party than another, or may be presented at a politically favourable time and thus may meet with less resistance. The vigour with which constraints are applied relates to the potential effects that 'greening' may have upon the parties. One would expect that environmental ideas which challenge party policy and ideology would be subject to a number of impediments. If an idea is not totally rejected, it is very likely moulded so as to 'fit' with prevailing party orthodoxy: 'greenness' wrought in a party's own image.

Party members as constraints

In principle, all politicians of the major parties seem to be in favour of improving the quality of the environment, even if they exhibit their concern in different ways according to party differences. However, each politician, even within the same party, has his or her own definitions regarding what 'the environment' is and what constitutes 'quality'; standards vary and perceptions of impacts differ. These

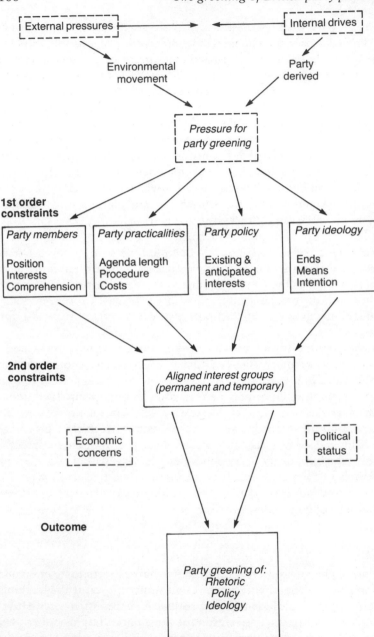

Fig. 6 Constraints upon the greening of the parties

obvious differences are reflected in the range of motivations which lie behind individual politicians who block the progress of 'green' ideas and the development of environmental policies. For some, resistance may be only passive, due to a genuine lack of interest in environmental matters. Despite the relatively recent increase in the number of MPs across the main parties showing an interest in environmental matters, there are still many who remain uninterested. They may be drawn into the environmental debate from time to time, but either because of age, background, suspicion of the environmental movement or mere apathy, they remain unbothered.

As a former trade union activist explained:

It's quite understandable that some colleagues who are well respected throughout the Labour and Trade Union Movement are just not turned on by the environment as an issue. They do their jobs to the best of their ability and attempt to get the best deal they can for their members. It's not because they don't understand the issues of acid rain and tropical de-forestation. Its just that they are not really interested in them. I can understand that. You have to remember that only ten years ago congress was all about pay bargaining and unemployment. For some, and they are now in the minority, trade unionism was not environmentalism.[1]

Few politicians would seem to be unaware of environmental issues, although the priority they are given varies according to the nature of the issue and what else occupies the political agenda. International issues such as global warming, ozone depletion, desertification and soil erosion may have to take a back seat for the MP or local councillor concerned with the imminent closure of a local industry or Mrs Smith's family income support claim, but even such seemingly distant issues are now being taken seriously by politicians of all parties. Indeed, in the lead-up to the 1987 General Election, one Conservative PPC actively campaigned in the run-down council estates of east London on the issues of rainforest destruction and the effects of acid rain.

The priority that the environment is accorded relates not only to the level of interest politicians have in it, but also to their other interests. Personal business or professional interests may conflict with supporting environmental concerns, although this is difficult to identify with any certainty. In the case of MPs, conflicts arise between the needs and interests of constituents and the environment. Constituency interests usually take second place to an MP's concern for wider aspects of party policy.[2] A notable exception of recent years to this general rule was Jack Cunningham. The stance he has taken on the issue of civil nuclear power has been widely publicised as an example of conflict between constituency interests and the development of environmentalism within the Labour Party. Amongst 'green' Labour MPs, CLP members and SERA members Jack Cunningham – or as he was known in some circles, 'Nuclear Jack' – was identified, in the words of Peter Hain, vice-chairman of the Labour Co-ordinating Committee, as 'a millstone around the Party's neck'. He was seen as responsible for 'tainting' Labour's otherwise radical position on the environment and as a major impediment blocking the further 'greening' of the Labour Party.[3] Shortly after the 1986 TUC General Council's statement recommended to call a halt to the UK nuclear power programme, it was believed by senior Shadow Cabinet ministers that Neil Kinnock would have to respond to pressures from within the party and remove the environment portfolio from Cunningham. Kinnock resisted, giving Cunningham total support, but the pressures for his removal remained until Cunningham was moved to the post of Campaign Co-ordinator in 1989.

On reflection, the view held by many green activists both inside and outside the Labour Party that Cunningham was an obstacle to party 'greening' was badly distorted for a number of reasons. Firstly, Jack Cunningham was caught up in a change of party mood. When he was returned MP for Whitehaven (now Copeland) in 1970, anti-nuclear-power pressures were virtually absent within the party, and environmental pressures were largely centred on pollution issues. The anti-nuclear-power lobby in the Labour Party was itself a mark of the success of the 'greening' process that was taking place, but it was only one aspect. On the majority of environmental issues discussed, Cunningham was very much in the forefront of party thinking. Secondly, as a party strategist, Cunningham recognised, as did pro-nuclear allies Dale Campbell-Savours MP and Tam Dayell MP, that if they themselves were seen to adopt the anti-nuclear position of the party, they could lose votes within their constituencies. Cunningham further suggested, prior to the 1987 General Election, that an anti-nuclear-power policy could lose votes in twenty marginal seats which had nuclear installations.[4] Thirdly, Cunningham took the pragmatic view that even with a policy that called a halt to nuclear power, the legacy of existing stations would remain and these would have to be managed and handled in an environmentally responsible way: a position that many senior colleagues, including David Clark MP, agreed with. Fourthly, Cunningham's support for the well-being of his constituents actually reflected deep criticisms of the nuclear industry. As far back as 1975 he had pressed for the prevention of discharges from Sellafield into the Irish Sea, and in Parliament, he raised the question of community health and nuclear installations.[5]

In the Conservative Party, too, there are individuals who have acted as obstacles to party 'greening', although well-disciplined party unity has perhaps prevented them from suffering the internal attacks that Dr Cunningham experienced in the Labour Party. However Nicholas Ridley, when Secretary of State for the Environment, seemed to achieve almost cult status as an impediment to party 'greening', certainly in the eyes of the environmentalists. As an ardent Thatcherite, Ridley was suspicious of any change that did not emerge from Mrs Thatcher's handbag. He rapidly seemed to adopt the view that Chancellor Kohl had held – that environmentalists, like tomatoes, start green and then proceed to turn a nasty shade of red. In a speech to the Conservative Graduates Association in December 1987, Ridley made his feelings toward the environmental pressure groups known, whilst offering his own distinctive monetarist brand of environmentalism:

I must declare my own view, which is that people are more important than concepts, particularly when those concepts are intellectually flawed and based on hysteria rather than logic. Times have changed. The time has come to take stock . . . The environmental factors have to be weighed against the other factors. Compromises have to be made between what is best in environmental terms and what is commercially viable and desirable.[6]

Such views, together with a well crafted lack of subtlety, hardly encouraged environmentalists either outside or inside the party. Yet despite Ridley's open hostility toward much environmental thinking, he achieved a marked degree of practical success:[7] the North Sea Conference in 1987, the establishment of HM Inspectorate of Pollution, the setting up of National Rivers Authority, and major clean-up programmes on drinking water and sewage discharges, Ridley's record, as compared with his predecessors, was very good. Yet these successes perhaps lay more in Ridley's political acumen rather than any proactive, positive beliefs in turning the Conservative Party 'green'.

Apart from the few inevitable exceptions, the Liberal Party and the

Social Democrats contained the lowest quota of members which could be considered as blocks to 'greening' – a position which has been largely transferred intact to the Liberal Democrats.[8] Arguably, the middle parties were never really large enough to contain significant constraints in the form of party members. Aside from odd tensions between Liberals and Social Democrats prior to merger, there were no major camps of difference based upon left and right ideologies and no internal interest groups. Furthermore, spurred on by the Liberals, the Alliance was seeking to acquire a policy angle to mark it out as a party truly original in its thinking and not merely a fence- sitting or opportunist party. The environment was seen as one area in which it had taken the lead, and there was every motivation to pursue it.

It's not what you know, it's where you are

The position, power and influence members hold within the main parties is central to their effectiveness or otherwise as a blocks to the 'greening' process. Extensive support for environmental measures amongst party activists at the grassroots, or amongst back benchers, may lead nowhere if no support is located in the central decision-making structures of the parties. Such support need only be passive rather than active, maybe taking the subtle form of 'turning a blind eye' to the development of green ideas and individuals. On the other hand, if there is opposition to green developments within a party from those that matter, this may be expressed just as subtly, perhaps by alteration of an individual's position and policy brief or by deliberatley mis-managing the amount of political time allotted to an environmental issue.

Potentially the most important sources of resistance within the major parties lies with the leadership. Conversely, support for the environment from party leaders and senior party management provides the most effective stimulus to party 'greening'. Access to party leaders and their advisers is important if any serious change in party thinking and strategy is desired. Where the party leaders themselves do not finally decide party policies, their influence on the policy-making processes is great, being fulcrums of party pressures from both the pro- and anti-environmental sides. Although the normative objective of a party leader is to achieve a balance between these pressures for the sake of party unity and strategy, the leaders as individuals have their own levels of interest and their own interpretations of the relationship between the environmental movement and their respective parties.

Throughout the 1980s the main party leaders have gradually awoken to the environmentalist pressures inside and outside their respective parties. However, each in their own way has exerted a constraining influence on the progress of environmental thinking. Realistically, given the demands put upon them, party leaders cannot be environmental crusaders. Yet having their commitment and support is an important symbolic gesture, and without it the process of party 'greening' is made that much more difficult. We can suggest that enthusiasm for going green amongst certain sections of the parties may have permeated to all sections had the respective leaderships, their allies and advisers been more responsive.

As leader of the Liberal Party, David Steel was perhaps the most receptive to environmental pressures from inside and outside the party, although this was probably due more to the close contact the Liberal leadership tends to have with the party, and with the influence of Steel's close advisers, rather than any personal preoccupation with the environmental cause. Steel's politics were founded upon co-operation, and he used the leadership more as a mouthpiece to put over the ideas of the party rather than to express his own ideas. Inevitably, the views of his close advisers, which included stalwarts of the environmental movement such as Des Wilson and Richard Holme, rubbed off on Steel. Fortunately, his own interests in Europe and in the freedom of information issue were compatible with environmental concern and were easily woven into those speeches he addressed to environmentalist audiences.[9]

The impression Steel gave green activists within the Liberals was one of flexibility. This worked both ways, and some doubted his commitment to the environment in the face of attempting to cement a long-term relationship with the SDP. As one Liberal PPC, prior to the 1987 General Election put it: 'Dr Owen is a charming man in the literal sense of the word and David Steel is easily charmed . . . we can only hope he does not compromise our radicalism for green issues.'[10] Yet Steel listened carefully to the grass-roots of his party and was wary of going against their enthusiasm. On the nuclear power issue in particular, Steel backed his party's position which was near-identical to the one adopted by the TUC Conference in 1986. In the context of the Alliance, this itself put Steel and Owen at odds.[11]

The first party leader during the 1980s to commit himself to a platform of environmental concern was David Owen of the Social Democrats. At a speech delivered to an audience of SDP members and invited leaders of environmental organisations at Bedford College in November 1983, Dr Owen announced that the SDP was the first political party in Britain to incorporate the British response to the World Conservation Strategy into its thinking. Dr Owen had earlier gone to the authors of this report published earlier in the same year and had asked to discuss its implications and how the SDP could play a part. The importance of Dr Owen's speech was to highlight the concept of what he termed 'green growth'. In his words:

Previous approaches to the environment have˙assumed that there is an inevitable antithesis between the environment and the economy, that the one can only thrive at the expense of the other. The SDP offers something wholly new in rejecting this assumption and with it the fake choice it poses between the further extension of bureaucratic controls or the unchecked assaults of the market place ... What we are proposing is the development of a thoughtful growth – a green growth that recognises the interdependence of economic and ecological priorities.'[12]

With this speech and other subsequent pronouncements, David Owen, guided by political adviser Alex De Mont and Tom Burke of the Green Alliance, laid claim to the title of environmental crusader. However, others within the SDP were conscious of his political guile and remained unconvinced of his passion for the environment. Certainly within the framework of the Liberal SDP Alliance, Liberals saw Dr Owen as a factor of resistance, not encouragement. Owen's preoccupation with economic growth, albeit 'green growth', was regarded with suspicion by a party who in 1974 had supported an Assembly resolution on economic growth which had challenged conventional assumptions behind its pursuit.[13] Moreover, green activists in the Liberal Party had been conscious of Owen's origins within the technocratic Labour Party of the 1970s and were particularly sceptical of his position on civil nuclear power and the importance of the UK nuclear deterrent.

Although aware of the problems in putting forward a joint policy programme for the Alliance in the 1987 General Election, the absence of a radical, hard-hitting position on the environment in the election manifesto seemed to confirm Owen's selectivity in 'green' matters and Steel's willingness to kowtow to him in true 'Spitting Image' fashion. The discontent that many Liberals felt with the

Alliance leadership in the post-mortem that followed the election flop of the third force in British politics was not to be forgotten by Paddy Ashdown.

In an interview with SERA's journal *New Ground*, shortly before being elected leader of the Labour Party in 1983, Neil Kinnock stated: 'I believe that environmental policies must take a higher place in Labour Party thinking. Ecological and environmental preservation is a major part of socialist practice and Labour must bring that achievement into the forefront of our image.'[14] In a later edition of *New Ground* Kinnock was taken to task for not matching up to his rhetoric. In 1985, Kinnock replied to this via a well-argued article shortly before the launch of the 'Charter for the Environment', declaring that 'Labour does have the necessary will, sense of urgency and determination' to tackle environmental problems.[15] But despite such statements, Kinnock has been cited as an important impediment to the development of environmental thinking in the party by SERA, some CLP members and some PLP members.[16]

Certainly the Labour leader had an important role to play. In the words of Dale Campbell-Savours: 'We need the Labour leader increasingly to use his access to the Despatch Box to hole the Thatcher green charade.'[17] How much an impediment to the 'greening' process Kinnock was depended very much on where you were standing. The perception of Kinnock being anti-environmental rested largely upon his loyal and enthusiastic support for Jack Cunningham and, by implication, support for the nuclear industry. But in terms of Kinnock's attitude to other environmental issues, there is little evidence to suggest that he was anything more than barely interested. Discontent with both Kinnock and Cunningham regarding environmental issues tended to mirror the tension between the leadership/Shadow Cabinet and the NEC. Broadly speaking, the environment became yet another issue on which the Kinnock/Hattersley ticket could be attacked by the alternative approach of Tony Benn and Eric Heffer. At the Socialist Conference, organised by the Socialist Society at Chesterfield in October 1987 as a forum for reaffirming socialism against the backdrop of a third election defeat, this analysis was borne out.[18] Although the conference did explore the increasing amount of common ground between reds and greens through a workshop entitled 'The Challenge of Green Politics' (organised by SERA and the Green Party), it largely focused upon old-style labourism and the inadequacies of the Labour leadership.

From the Labour Shadow Cabinet's point of view, and others in the PLP, it was the hard left who represented the major constraint on developing a greener approach for the party. As a member of the Shadow Cabinet declared:

I don't think that there are too many people on the Hard Left that take any significant or enduring interest in the environment at all frankly. Not in my experience . . . All the serious work is being done by the people who are willing to dedicate themselves to the necessary research, consideration and understanding which goes into producing a document like this [the 1986 environment statement].[19]

From this side of the Labour Party, Kinnock was seen, not as an impediment, but as increasingly aware of the importance of the need for environmental protection. Described by a close colleague as possessing a 'developing concern for the environment', Kinnock's concern did develop rapidly in the aftermath of the 1987 election defeat when it was suggested that the environment had not been given enough attention. In his speech to the party conference in 1987, Neil Kinnock for the first time, referred to the environment on two occasions, once in relation to Labour's commitment to safeguarding it and once in relation to the Conservatives, intransigence in failing to support international agreements. For some 'green' activists in the party, those two brief references represented a slow but important realisation by the Labour leader that the environment was of growing importance to the party.

Of course, the most important individual in British politics is the Prime Minister, and throughout the 1980s Mrs Thatcher's influence on the progress of environmental thinking in the Conservative Party and in British party politics was enormous. Back bench 'green' activists, sympathetic ministers, and the most scientifically authoritative of civil servants, may have made much noise, but in the Conservative administrations of the 1980s, they did not appear to make the decisions that counted. Mrs Thatcher's 'conviction politics' and 'no-nonsense' style of how the nation should be run meant that her attitude to environmental policy was crucial. But within her own party her concern and interest in environmental matters seemed to stretch no further than an obsessive irritation with the litter problem. Indeed, during the Falklands War, she is reported to have said: 'When you have spent half your political life dealing with humdrum issues like the environment, it is exciting to have a real crisis on your hands.'[20] Until September 1988, although long aware of environmental issues, Mrs Thatcher's interest in them was never high. Her understanding of them varied and her commitment to them was demonstrated chiefly through occasional rhetoric.[21] But despite a shabby record and constant finger-wagging from environmental groups, few Conservatives were publiclly willing to portray Mrs Thatcher as an impediment to the 'greening' of government and the party. Prior to the 1987 General Election, despite warnings from back benchers and green activists within the party regarding the vote-losing potential of key environmental issues, Mrs Thatcher seemed totally unconcerned.[22] This lack of concern was also shared by her senior environmental adviser in the No. 10 Policy Unit and by Cabinet colleagues, one of whom expressed the view in 1986 that he did not believe the public was concerned with the environment at all![23]

Mrs Thatcher's apparent resistance to environmental matters was locked up within her distinctive brand of Conservatism, loosely known as Thatcherism. Her perception of the environmental movement, the problems it addressed and the proposed solutions ran directly against her style and her political beliefs; the consensus politics of the environmental groups lost out to the politics of conviction; internationalism, so desperately needed to tackle the 'big' environmental issues, fell foul of nationalism; public spending, needed to tackle some environmental problems, gave way to a propensity to accumulate wealth privately; most apparent, the essential mechanisms of regulation and control were overtaken by a commitment to free-market economics.

Listeners were therefore taken by surprise when, in a speech to the Royal Society on 27 September 1988, Mrs Thatcher spoke about her 'own commitment to science and the environment' and that 'protecting this balance of nature is therefore one of the greatest challenges of the late Twentieth Century'. In the speech Mrs Thatcher cogently played to the gallery by establishing her scientific credentials and by extolling the virtues of science, making them relevant to global warming, the destruction of the ozone layer, acid deposition and water pollution.[24]

A short time later at the October Conservative Party Conference, Mrs Thatcher astounded the environmental movement and party members again when she announced in her address: 'It's we Conservatives who are not merely friends of the Earth – we are its guardians and trustees for generations to come . . . No generation has a freehold on this earth. All we have is a life tenancy – with a full repairing lease. This Government intends to meet the terms of that lease in full.'[25] Interestingly enough, Mrs Thatcher's pronouncements, important though they were, stood out at party conference against a very poor address by Nicholas Ridley, who in his reply to the environment debate focused almost exclusively upon green belt policy and the need for housing development in the most ambigous of ways.[26] Strongly influenced by Waldegrave and Patten and their adherence to the philosophy of Edmund Burke, Mrs Thatcher's speech pointed to a new proactive approach to the environment. This was endorsed by a television interview in March 1989 with Michael Buerk as part of BBC's 'Nature' series, where Mrs Thatcher again attempted to heighten her environmental profile.

The seemingly gestalt-like conversion of the then Prime Minister to greenery was very hard for environmentalists to believe. From being so openly a opponent in the environmental debate, the Prime Minister was now attempting to lead it on issues which had been been around for at least five years previously. Several reasons can be put forward to explain the turnaround. Firstly, for someone so concerned with scientific proof as the basis for decision-making, Mrs Thatcher could not resist the evidence any longer. Agreement amongst the international scientific community regarding ozone depletion in particular, and increasingly with regard to global warming, meant that politicians were left without excuses for inaction. Secondly, the international environmental questions on which Mrs Thatcher concentrated gave her opportunities to play the role of international stateswoman. The Bush presidential campaign coincided with her speech and was focusing on 'green' issues; it is highly likely that Mrs Thatcher was aware of this and the implications this may have had for future relations with Reagan's successor. Thirdly, in the wake of any notion that Thatcherism may have been running out of ideas in the early stages of a third term of office, the environment was perhaps an ideal issue on which to take a new political initiative. Events such as the deaths of North Sea seals in 1989, and the alarm regarding the *Karin B* toxic waste ship, perhaps spurred the rhetoric onward, but it did seem as if Conservative strategists had found an area of policy which they could

'Thatcherise'.

In policy terms, the effect of Mrs Thatcher's transformation was limited. It realised some extra cash for environmental spending, gave a new lease of life to the environmental protection element of the DOE, and assisted placing the issue of global environmental change on the agenda of the United Nations. Arguably, such outcomes would have come about anyway. But in political terms, the Thatcher speeches of 1988 and her high profile involvement in the International Ozone Conference in 1989 were to mark the end of a period of post-electoral quiescence. More importantly, they indicated that as Prime Minister, Mrs Thatcher had been the most significant impediment to the 'greening' of British politics until this time.

Political practicalities

British party politics operates within dynamic constitutional guidelines and in a style which has developed over many years. Social change is achieved through constitutional methods and wherever possible via consensus. In order for environmental ideas and policy initiatives to make political progress, they must conform to explicit and implicit conventions that have been adopted by the main parties. In doing so, they may be constrained by a number of practical problems arising from the 'rules' of the party political 'game'.

One problem relates to the language used to convey environmental concern. Whereas the environmental movement has often brought issues to the attention of the public via emotional appeals, politicians tend to seek hard scientific fact. According to a senior Conservative Party researcher, shortly after the 1987 General Election the emotional phrasing of some environmental problems and the fact that some environmental groups pushed their demands 'too hard' had resulted in a feeling of antagonism against the environmental movement. 'While some groups,' he said, 'attract admiration, there is growing hostility toward some single-minded groups who clearly do not appreciate that this government has to take a balanced view.'[27] However, many environmental groups have moved away from solely emotional protest and are now able to express issues in the clinical scientific language that some politicians wish to hear. In some cases, scientific jargon may not be the best way to stimulate the interest of politicians, a majority of whom use emotive language in their everyday exchanges. Environmental problems have emotional outcomes as well as scientific explanations, giving politicians some choice as to how they address them. Some issues, such as the death of the North Sea seals, are difficult to express in anything other than emotive terms. This is the language that the public understands and that politicians know that the public understands.

Environmental groups pushing for change in the political parties do suffer from an image problem, particularly amongst the Conservatives. The problem of credibility is recognised by many of the groups, and is seen partly as a problem of perception from those in the cosy club of Parliament, and partly as being self-inflicted. One Tory back bencher and self-confessed 'Heath-Man' summed up the prejudicial situation faced by the environmental groups thus: 'For unless and until environmentalists are seen as people who wear pin-stripe-grey suits, clean collars and regimental ties and wear clean shoes, or as long as they are seen as way-out wierdos, or as long as it is easy to dismiss them in this way, then that does damage to their image within the Tory Party.'[28] Prejudices such as this are not confined to the Conservatives, nor do they revolve solely around physical appearances. Amongst some members of the main parties, there exists an inate attitude of elitism toward the environmental movement; a feeling that those at the centre of party politics are somehow the only ones that can really understand the political processes and its practicalities; a feeling that politics is for elected politicians alone. A senior parliamentary adviser for the former SDP, speaking in 1986, exemplified this attitude saying that:

Unlike the environmental lobby, I'm not going to say that every time there comes a difficult choice of say, preserving the environment, preventing pollution or something else, that we're going to plum for the environmental option because there may be other imperatives which are more important . . . I don't think the environmentalists are in the position to make choices like this.[29]

In a party system based upon relatively short electoral horizons, environmental issues, the implications of which may be measured in decades and centuries, make strange bedfellows with economic questions such as interest rates and unemployment. For government and the major parties, policy making, strategic and financial planning is usually geared to one or two years and conventionally focuses upon the most certain and predictable outcomes possible. The uncertainty

attached to issues such as global warming makes those issues difficult
for the machinery of the parties to handle, and it is difficult for party
members to accept that thse issues can be sold to an electorate
perceived to be predominantly concerned with what happens toady
rather than tomorrow. This perception is outdated; the public's
concern for future generations is displayed in issues such as nuclear
and toxic waste disposal, while politicians of all parties genuinely
struggle to think of solutions to problems which have a time-span far
longer than their careers. It is not surprising that attempts to deal
with the storage of low- and intermediate-level nuclear waste have
been given a low profile by the government since they found how
politically 'hot' such issues can be. In the meantime, the time bomb
ticks away.

In order that environmental issues and proposals could be made
more appealing to the parties, they could be expressed in a timescale
more in keeping with budgetary and election planning. Whether this
can be achieved without losing the fundamental themes of such
issues is debatable, although given the gravity of some environmental problems, the narrow temporal perceptions of party politics
may have to widen sooner or later.

The long-term aspect of environmental issues entails that any
environmental action involves large capital outlay and long pay-
back periods. As Chris Patten was fond of reminding critics, having a
'full repairing lease' costs money. Of all the constraints acting upon
the major parties, it is the financial constraint which has tended to
underlie all the others. Environmental concern has infiltrated the
parties throughout times of economic decline as well as times of
economic growth, but only recently has there been a realisation that
there is no inevitable conflict between the two. Politicians have
usually viewed environmental protection and management as non-
profitable activities and a further drain upon already scarce
resources. For the opposition parties, free from the responsibility of
balancing the books, it is easier to theoretically allocate resources for
environmental programmes, although both the Labour Party and the
Liberal Democrats appear to recognise that environmental protection is expensive and that ulimately the public will have to bear
the costs. For the Conservatives, holding the responsibility of
government and thus holding the purse strings, it is not so easy. A
Conservative MEP summed up the position prior to the 1987 general
election, saying: 'Acid rain is an environmental issue of tremendous

importance – I believe it has tremendous political importance too – but for the government the price of electricity for the consumer is also an important environmental issue . . . The acid rain issue is not just a scientific or technical issue it has to be an economic issue as well.'[30] The overwhelming feeling amongst environmental activists within the Conservative Party, certainly before the 1987 election, was that in order to protect and improve the environment, wealth had to be created *a priori*, with little attention seemingly given to the relative value of departmental budgets.[31]

Whilst individuals within the opposition parties can fudge the issue of funding for huge public investment, the Conservative Government cannot. Nevertheless, all politicians tend to see the costs before the benefits.[32] There has been relatively little authoritative research regarding the economics of environmental concern. In 1986, David Clark MP commissioned an investigation into the relationship between environmental policy, employment creation and macro-economic policy.[33] At the time this was a bold move toward the removal of an important constraint on the Labour Party: environmental protection as a threat to union jobs.

In recent years there has been a sea change in the main parties' perceptions of the economics of environmental policy. Politicians are more willing to talk about the benefits of environmental concern, and the costs and discussions about funding for environmental programmes are not so readily side-stepped. There are three main reasons for this change. The first relates to the general rise of environmental issues on the political agenda of all parties. Given mounting national and international pressures for environmental action, the parties are being forced into including environmental spending in their budgetary calculations to an unprecedented degree. The second reason can be traced back to Mrs Thatcher's 'green' Royal Society speech in which, referring to environmental protection measures, she declared: 'Even though this kind of action may cost a lot, I believe it to be money well and necessarily spent because the health of the economy and the health of our environment are totally dependent upon each other.'[34] Leaving aside the contentious issue of how much constitutes 'a lot', this statement did open up the coffers to a limited extent and suggested that the 'precautionary principle', long since adopted in some EC nations, would be implemented in Britain. The speech implied that wealth need not be created first, but that in raising the priority of the environment, funding could be redirected from other areas.

The third reason for this new-found willingness to deal with the economics of the environment relates to the development of new and political acceptable mechanisms for doing so. 'Environmental economics', particularly the influential ideas of David Pearce and his *Blueprint for a Green Economy*, has emerged as a framework through which the parties can pursue policies of environmental concern without adopting politically dangerous 'either/or' positions regarding industry, business and jobs.[35]

Government and the major opposition parties work to a system which accords priorities to a myriad of different issues. Those with top priority make it on to 'the agenda' – a list of the most important matters to which political debate is directed, attention is being given and on which action is required.[36] However, agendas are finite, particularly at government level, but also at party level since the boundaries of party policy tend to be 'etched in' by government action or inaction. Environmental interests, put forward by outside pressure groups or inside party activists, have to compete with the fullest range of interests and issues. Amongst these are the 'traditional' concerns of party politics, health, education, the economy, unemployment and defence. As long as these issues remain salient, particularly at general elections, where they form the basis of party campaigns, the less time the parties have to devote to environmental problems and ideas.

This is a particularly significant constraint upon party 'greening', for it seems unlikely that 'top line' issues can ever be demoted. Moreover, the parties always seem to have less rather than more time to deal with them. However, the impediment of a limited agenda can be circumnavigated if an environmental element can be integrated into existing primary policy concerns.

As well as a normative inevitability about the fixed length of party agendas, there is also some degree of manipulation and control exercised regarding their content. Government can exclude or remove environmental problems from the political agenda by using various techniques of 'agenda management'.[37] 'Official' statistics can be used to play down a problem; comparisons with other nations can be made to highlight British standards; time-scales can be changed and levels of investment can be made to look greater than they are. Furthermore, environmental policies can be redefined so their salience is played down and their real focus can be side-stepped through the use of 'placebo policies' – introducing policies which remove the symptoms of a problem rather than its causes. This latter point applies to the majority of environmental issues.

Agenda management also takes place in the major parties regarding issues which are known to elicit party disagreements (perhaps based upon previous poor policy performance, divergent policy options or total lack of policy) and which may upset a party's image. Parties may therefore be selective in the way they handle the pressures for 'greening', seeking out issues to capitalise on in the face of party competition, or those which have some political neutrality.

Within government there is an underlying element of competition between those policies which are already on the agenda, as well as competition to get on to it. This competition is embodied in the departments of government and the shadow departments of the main opposition parties. In the most basic sense, it is competition for resources from the Treasury, the department that pervades all of government. Resources relate to the priorities of the time, although the key areas of defence, education, health, etc. more or less guarantee the lion's share. But it is also competition for power. Empires that have been built up are eagerly defended. Key personalities are influential in protecting their portfolios, securing the position of their departments on the political agenda, together with the subsequent budgetary rewards. Clearly, within the opposition parties actual budgets are not being fought over, though potential allocations are inferred by the importance given to policy areas.

An idea to establish a Ministry of Environmental Protection mooted in 1986, for instance, faced considerable 'behind the scenes' competition in the Labour Party and contributed to Neil Kinnock's indecision regarding whether it should be headed by minister of Cabinet rank. In the lead-up to the 1987 election, Brynmor John MP, John Home Robertson MP and Stuart Randall MP had put together a well-argued case for a Department of Rural Affairs that would supersede MAFF, and cases were also made for ministries for women, overseas development, urban affairs, regional affairs and sport, recreation and leisure, all with claims for a Cabinet-ranking minister.[38] Clearly, having a seat around the Cabinet table where the important decisions are taken is important, but the table is only so big.

An important constraint arises from the youth of the environmental idea in party politics and the inability of politics to draw tidy boundaries between the various environmental policy sectors and sub-sectors. The existing departmental structure has evolved to serve an approach to governing which was relatively simplistic in the manner in which policy areas were identified as discrete and manageable units. This legacy has caused serious problems in initially allocating responsibility, and responsibility for an area of environmental policy ultimately carries with it resource implications and implications in terms of public relations.

The most widely acknowledged departmental clashes in environmental responsibility have been those between the DOE and MAFF. For many years, each department was unclear about the other's actions, and non-communication was the norm. Grants and subsidies for hedgerow removal, field extensification and drainage until relatively recently flowed easily from MAFF in response to sets of economic triggers and interests which are not the concern of the conservationist arm of the DOE. Environmental groups and party activists, far from being satisfied with the work of the DOE and its own internal conflicts, have long recognised some of MAFF's activities as a constraint. Despite the formation of an internal Environment Co-ordination Unit and criticism by two House of Lords Select Committees in July 1984 regarding MAFF's display of insensitivity toward the public's concern about the environmental implications of agricultural policies, MAFF was long seen to be pulling in the opposite direction to the DOE.[39]

To some extent MAFF's role as an institutional impediment has been lessened, partly due to the work of William Waldegrave when Environment Minister and partly due to the Department's own realisation of the increasingly unified pressures for change, particularly from the EC. The introduction of the ESA system was perhaps a turning point, but there is still a long way to go before the drives of agricultural policy can be reconciled with those of the environment.

Policy positions

Linked closely with the institutional frameworks in which government and the parties operate are policy positions which may have taken considerable time to evolve. The parties never start with a clean sheet and simply take up new sets of policies. The pressures for 'greening' not only have to confront an agenda of existing policies, they may also have to deal with the expectations party members and interest groups have, in terms of the policies adopted by the parties.

Government policy on every issue has an impact upon the environmental drives and pressures acting within the Conservative Party. Even those areas of policy which do not seem at first glance to be relevant, such as defence, have 'knock-on' effects, influencing the amounts of time and resources that are available. However, there are long-standing government policies which clash with the promotion of environmental action. The 1987 Conservative manifesto commitment to a programme of major capital investment to build an extra 450 miles of motorway and trunk road by 1990, for instance, not only ate up resources that could have been used for environmental improvement and protection it also posed a threat to the environment in terms of landscape and habitat disturbance, encouragement for green belt development and ultimately atmospheric pollution. Road building no doubt relieved enormous pressures upon some communities and was therefore of environmental benefit. Moreover, government transport policy does include investment in British Rail services. But the main thrust of the policy can be seen as being against environmental groups wishing to see an ever-decreasing dependence upon the car and considerably more investment in public transport systems.

A source of conflict also arises between environmental concern and government energy policy. Whereas environmental gains are being made with the de-sulphurisation programme of coal-fired power stations, the commitment to developing nuclear power and the use of PWR reactors seems to run contrary to environmental interests. It is a policy that would be very hard to justify to the electorate on the grounds that the government would like to see further erosion of the position of the National Union of Mineworkers (NUM) or, in the light of the Sizewell inquiry, on economic grounds. In terms of the risks from radiation, the potential for catastrophes and the problems of nuclear waste storage, transport and disposal, the environmentalists seem to have a very sound case against such a policy. But the government too have legitimate environmental arguments that justify their policy – world resources of fossil fuels are more finite than uranium, the efficiency of the nuclear process is high, and there are no emissions of greenhouse gases. These arguments are difficult to disagree with, particularly given that environmentalists attach a lot to the risk factor rather than actual damage to the atmosphere that is now being identified.

Who are the true environmentalists in this case? There is no real answer; for whatever the rationale for or against Conservative pro-nuclear policy, in order to change or reverse it, the arguments against have to be considerably more powerful, or the government has to be defeated through the ballot box. Given the amount of attention given to global warming, including that given by the Tories themselves, it is likely that the arguments being put forward by the government will be the more influential. In the second instance, even if Britain's nuclear programme did soar to prominence in a future general election, it is unlikely to be the decisive issue which brings down the Conservatives. It can be argued that the policies of the major opposition parties are more easily broken down by environmentalist pressure because election success is not necessarily dependent upon this. Sound arguments and persistent lobbying at least have a chance to instigate changes in the policies of the Labour Party and the Liberal Democrats.

The lack of policy or an unclear policy in a party can be just as much an impediment to the 'greening' process as an opposing policy position. This has perhaps been illustrated in the Labour Party's ambivalent attitude toward Europe. When the issue was discussed in 1981, there was a strong feeling to withdraw from the EEC. Since then, party policy with regard to Europe has been side-stepped; Labour has avoided attacking the sluggish Conservative response to EC environmental directives, for fear of dragging up the party's anti-European past. In 1987, a Labour MEP estimated that no more than six Labour MPs actually understood the workings of the EC and that MEPs had not really enjoyed high status in Labour's headquarters or the PLP.[40] This ambiguity closed off an important channel of influence for 'green' activists in the party (given that many environmental gains have been through European pressures).

Party ideologies

In chapter 5 we drew attention to the role that ideology can play in the development of pro-environmental party thinking. However, the systems of beliefs at the heart of each party also form the most complicated but fundamental constraints affecting the 'greening' process.

If a party is to absorb the ideas of the environmental movement, the ideas have to be compatible with the principles by which the party functions. Broadly speaking, the goals of the environmentalists are by and large acceptable to the main parties, at least at the level of rhetoric. Each of the main parties have found it relatively easy to agree in principle that concern for the environment is important and warrants attention. However, the assumptions that define levels of concern, and the political values which inform the direction and intensity of environmental action, vary between party and movement and from party to party.

To be acceptable to the political parties, environmental beliefs invariably require modification. The degree of modification varies with the beliefs themselves (some being more ideologically acceptable than others to each party), the political circumstances in which beliefs are put forward, and the attitudes of key party recipients.

Though the main British political parties have each attempted to move away from consciously possessing 'an ideology' at different stages of their development, they are nevertheless recognised by them.[41] Party ideologies relate closely to individual party members, their political history, party status and influence. Their spread is therefore wide, and at different times and under various conditions, the functions of a party's ideology may shift or one aspect may be stressed instead of another.

The intrinsic variety in a party's ideology has mixed consequences for the challenge of environmental ideas. On the one hand, there are party members who experience few problems in reconciling 'green' thinking and environmental policy initiatives with existing beliefs, even if this does mean moving the ideological goalposts a little. On the other hand, there are hard-liners who see their beliefs as immutable and unable to accommodate any new 'green' emphasis. Between the two positions are those who attempt to avoid ideological conflict by seeking to handle environmental issues on a non-ideological level, concentrating upon pragmatic adjustments to policy. A senior Labour MP summed up this approach by reflecting: 'I am essentially a pragmatic politician and what I am concerned about is seeing positive changes [in the environment] brought about tomorrow or next year, rather than a philosophy which is capable of defence in a junior common room in a British university and which hasn't got a hope in hell of being accepted by the British electorate.'[42] Yet adjustments can only be made to a limited extent, partly because they involve a 'cover-up' of party beliefs and not their removal, and partly because an increasingly sizeable section of the environmental movement is dissatisfied with piecemeal tinkering of policy and is pressing for deep-seated changes in how the political parties deal with environmental issues.

Ideological diversity is present within the major parties to varying degrees. Within the Conservative Party, certain traits of Toryism can be seen as inherent blocks to the development of environmentalism: in particular, the importance placed upon the national interest and its protection. This recognisable Conservative principle helps to explain the Conservative Government's resistance to EC environmental directives. This may not be indicative of antagonism to environmental initiatives *per se*, but relates to the more general condition of Europhobia so strongly played on by Mrs Thatcher both in and out of office.

As mentioned earlier, there is much in Toryism and the intellectual tradition of Burke to stimulate Conservative interest in the environment.[43] However, the Conservative Party of the 1980s was dominated not by Tory ideology, but by Thatcherite neo-Liberal thinking: a doctrine held with a passion equal to that exhibited by the most radical of environmentalists. But to what extent have the ideas of Thatcherism acted as a constraint to the 'greening' of the Conservative Government?

The fundamental belief that the individual should be accorded as much freedom as possible presents the greatest challenge to a movement whose shibboleth has, since its earliest days, been control. The commitment to personal freedom and the operation of a free market economy run counter to the mechanisms of state planning and responsibility, regulation and public ownership – mechanisms close to the heart of the majority of environmental groups. These are not the only forms of action that are recommended, but they are central to the environmental movement. Calls for tighter planning in the countryside, public access to the land, the protection of the green belt and designated areas of countryside, tougher controls on factory emissions and the pollution of land, air and water, together with increased public spending, have been met with the ideas that the market will be responsive and regulate itself, voluntary action will succeed in the place of control, and the private sector will deal with environmental problems far more efficiently and cost-effectively.

In line with Mrs Thatcher's personal politics of conviction, the ideology of Thatcherism has not turned in response to growing pressures from the environmental movement. Indeed, the dismissive attitude of the Thatcherites toward the environmental movement has actually strengthened its resolve. Environmentalists are driven by a moral imperative which seeks to right a cumulative catalogue of wrongs prevalent within developed economies since the industrial revolution. The powerful yet transient ideas of a political party would seem only to make the environmentalists more determined.

To its followers, Thatcherism is seen as being compatible with environmental concern. Indeed, it can be argued that rather than a constraint, Thatcherism for some was seen as the ideal instrument for developing environmental concern within the party: the extension of property ownership has been viewed as a positive environmental development, giving the individual a material interest in his or her surroundings; the goals of economic and social mobility are cited as having positive environmental benefits, such as the restoration of old buildings and the release of under-used housing stock; the de-industrialisation of the UK, through the processes of refinement and rationalistaion via the transfer of ownership to the private sector equal environmental gain; the encouragement given to the replacement of a heavy industrial base by the new 'sunrise' industries has meant an end to localised pollution and contamination and has helped facilitate derelict land; and despite much opposition from the environmental lobby, the privatisation of the water industry and the creation of the National Rivers Authority was widely proclaimed by the government as an important mechanism for environmental protection and improvement.

But those areas of environmental policy which appeared to be compatible with Thatcherism have been mainly limited to development policy.[44] Market forces have been readily harnessed, for instance, in the creation of the Urban Development Corporations. Moreover, private development has been encouraged through the introduction of simplified planning zones, whilst planning controls, appeal procedures and local democratic processes have been effectively weakened. As Blowers puts it:

In its policies for development, the Thatcher government has been able to give full expression to its ideological preferences. These policies reflect the power of developer interests able to convert ideas of market freedom into physical forms. The interests of the powerless, those living in squalid conditions with few amenities and substantially dependent upon the public sector, could be largely ignored since their political influence on the Conservatives was feeble.[45]

In conservation policy too, market forces have been leant upon and voluntary agreements have been the norm. Yet in other policy areas, it has been much more problematic for the government to apply its philosophy. In relation to transport policy, for instance, the Thatcherite ideological commitment to personal freedom and individual choice has encouraged car ownership and an associated programme of road building to cope with the Department of Transport's forecast of a doubling of car ownership by 2025. There surely must come a point, however, when the environmental problems associated with high levels of car ownership – an increase in greenhouse gases, physical congestion, destruction of habitat for road building, the finite nature of oil resources for running and producing cars, etc. – increase to a point where ideology must give way to the demands of the environmental movement. Such a scenario will be politically difficult for the Conservative Government to handle, having won the past three general elections on the very platform of increasing choice and individual freedom.

The environmental arena also involves many areas of loss rather than profit, and there is therefore a limit to how far the markets will respond to it. The Conservative Government have been selective in choosing sectors of the environment to be laid bare to market forces. Areas of high public risk, such as the nuclear power industry, have been steered clear of private sector control, in the knowledge that they are likely to prove major economic burdens in the long term. Furthermore, where the private sector has been encouraged to tackle environmental problems such as toxic waste disposal, public concern has made it difficult for Thatcherite ideology to translate itself into practice.

The way that Thatcherism has shaped the environmentalist challenge has been great. The 1980s saw much of the environmental movement adapt to suit Mrs Thatcher's version of popular capitalism. The rise of 'green' consumerism, the acceptability of 'green' capitalism, has to some extent been a compromised response to Thatcherite policy and philosophy. It produced a 'greenness' which suited both the markets and the Conservative Party. Private sponsorship of environmental groups, ethical investment and even the slick marketing of the Green Party 1987 election manifesto, are all signs of the strength of Thatcherism. To some within the Conservative Party, this has no doubt proved that what the environment requires is more of the same. Indeed, as a Conservative back bencher suggested playfully: 'there are some within the Party who believe that we can sell the environment off completely, let the private sector manage it as a vast going concern – air, water, land, people, the lot.'[46] The arrival of John Major has not seen the decline of Thatcherism, rather the development of a more polite and cautious version of it. The 'caring' 1990s may well produce a change of emphasis in Conservative Party ideology and how it is delivered, yet it seems highly unlikely that it will undergo the transformation necessary to tackle deep-seated, long-term environmental problems. The legacy of Thatcherite economics (something John Major is well versed in) looks scheduled to continue for some time to come, and even a re-emergence of old-fashioned Toryism appears destined to be inadequate to deal with environmental problems that relate to such questions as land ownership, social imbalance and large-scale state intervention. As environmental problems grow worse and public and political pressures continue to increase, Conservative Party ideology will have to adapt accordingly or pay the political price.

Given that much of the challenge of environmentalism involves government intervention, planning, and programmes of public expenditure, there would seem to be a great deal of philosophical common ground between the Labour Party and the environmental movement, including the Greens. What some within the environmental movement would see as ideological constraints have in effect largely disappeared. Centralised state socialism, which clearly does not match environmentalist ideals of a decentralised, community-orientated economy, is no longer the logos of a Labour Party which is looking to replace the Conservatives after over a decade of free market economics. Feelings amongst some sections of the Labour Party that environmental issues are middle-class concerns, irrelevant to the working population, have also subsided in the decade which has seen the expansion of the middle classes. Indeed, the 1980s has witnessed considerable progress in convincing the bulk of the Labour Party, and particularly the trade unions, that environmental issues are actually more relevant to the working classes than ever before: a point that the Socialist Environment Resources Association has continually focused upon with some success.

Yet the Labour Party finds itself tripping over its own ideological tail with respect to the environment in its almost subconscious belief in an industrialised society. For a party that grew up in a working-class nation, Labour now finds it has to appeal to an expanded

middle class in the non-traditional south of England where environmental issues are very much in people's minds. To such an audience,
which has flourished in the enterprise culture, Labour's philosophy
of state intervention, however toned down, is alien. It may therefore
be difficult to introduce an ideological perspective to the environment which relies upon the mechanisms of local government and has
not been applied for over a decade. Although the Labour Party's
'Statement of Democratic Aims and Values' attempts to steer party
principles toward addressing a de-industrialised society, there are
likely to remain some members amongst the hard left who are still
hostile to the process of 'greening', due to the perceived social
constituency and geographical location of many environmentalists.[47]

Of all the major parties, the Liberal Democrats have the least
problem with integrating environmental concern with party
ideology. Before merger, there were some ideological tensions
between Liberals and Owenites in the Social Democrats with regard
to the environment. One senior Liberal 'green' activist expressed his
concern with David Owen's ideological commitment to environmental matters, given 'his preoccupation with a centralised, technocratic philosophy reminiscent of his political origins'.[48] However, with the emergence of the Liberal Democrats, such potential
constraints have gone and an ideological platform has developed
which appears wholly sympathetic to environmental ideas. This is
partly a function of the flexibility of Liberal philosophy, and partly
due to the consensus the party now exhibits, with no major left/right
ideological tensions existing as in the Conservative and Labour
parties.

In the interests of whom?

The major political parties of the UK are closely aligned with a range
of formal and informal groups, whose interests are not initially
compatible with those of the environmental movement. Such groups
may be temporary pressure groups formed at local level, or locally
involved organisations who object to specific aspects of party 'greening' if it impinges upon their own operations. If it suits the interests of
government or the parties, the objections of such groups may be
inflated in order to legitimise their opposition to a given issue.

Groups which have aligned themselves to the political process in an almost permanent way are the most influential impediments to the 'greening' of the parties. The influence they hold in terms of labour, capital and the potential voters they represent, entails that government and the main opposition parties cannot afford to alienate such groups from the policy-making process, particularly that which deals with economic and employment issues, since environmental policy has a direct impact on both of these key areas.

The groups representing the interests of business, management and capital provide strong support for the Conservatives. Consultation between government departments and economic interest groups, such as the Institute of Directors and the 'City', does take place, and whereas decisions may be taken independently of such aligned interest groups, consequences may be grave in terms of lost support or party revenue.[49]

Although the CBI is a politically neutral organisation, with no formal links with the Conservative Party, the party does receive considerable financial support from the business sector it represents, and there is at least an expectation that such support will be repaid 'in kind' by the consideration of business interests, whilst the party is in office. During the 1980s, the CBI, representing the opinion of industry and commerce, recommended that a higher profile be given to an environmental approach to business, since it offered significant market opportunities.[50] This is perhaps indicative of a move away from the traditional lobbying style the CBI had developed (largely as a counter-balance to the TUC), toward, in Director John Banham's words: 'the new breed of thrusting entrepreneurs'. A spokesman for the CBI qualified the criteria for the broad support it has given the government with regard to the environment by saying:

We support the development of environmental policies by the government, so long as they are based upon a strong scientific base and not emotion, adequate consultation with those that policies are likely to affect and a realistic phase of implementation. Industry needs time to adapt to environmental policies. We have to wait for the development of new technologies.[51]

To some extent, selective support such as this amounts to passive resistance to the 'greening' process; environmental pressure groups and their ideas can be ignored, and inaction can be justified by appealing to the protection of economic interests. Furthermore, support has tended to focus upon issues which are of direct interest to business and industry. Theoretically, this should include everything, from global warming to hedgerow removal; however, in practice it focuses upon those issues which affect industrial perform-ance directly, such as air and water pollution, waste management and energy use.

Before the privatisation of electricity, powerful interest groups were active constraints on attempts to 'green' government energy policy. In 1984, Lord Marshall, then Chairman of the Central Elec-tricity Generating Board, demonstrated this through an open argu-ment with Sir Hugh Rossi MP following his Select Committee Report on Acid Rain. The argument centred upon the role of the CEGB in the acidification of Scandinavian lakes. But apart from being a disagreement about the science of the issue, it also reflected the CEGB's desire to protect itself from the immediate financial burden which would have been levied had the government accepted the report's recommendations.

Measures to introduce a higher profile for energy conservation in the UK were also thwarted by the vast institutions involved with the supply of energy.[52] The failure of the Conservative Government to back the work of the Energy Efficiency Office, established in 1983, and to give definite policy leads to the small and ineffective Depart-ment of Energy, symbolised the power of such agencies as the CEGB and, United Kingdom Atomic Energy Authority in a free-market economy, and the willingness of the government to let them exert this power.[53]

Developers, represented by the House Builders' Federation and numerous large conglomerates, have also acted as constraints in three key areas of government policy development – the attempts to regenerate 'those inner cities', the need to integrate agricultural policy with conservation, and the protection of the green belt – areas linked by the implications they carry for the release of land. In 1986, Graham Pye, Chairman of the Pye group of developers, in response to Waldegrave's courageous suggestions that land taken out of agricultural production could form the basis of a new 'conservation industry' and used to protect the encroachment of urbanism, argued that such land represented an unique opportunity for house-builders.[54] Starting from a perspective somewhat different from the then Minister, Pye argued:

Environmentalists have no right to close all doors but one to them – nor to prevent the rest of the community from taking the opportunities which are opened up to use some surplus farmland for development, in order to improve the quality of life of our urban population. Looked at realistically, the problem of agricultural surpluses then becomes an opportunity for the nation, rather than just a crisis for farming.[55]

Whatever the rhetoric, the underlying motivation of this position was to protect and expand the interests of the development lobby, and as a consequence, environmental concern as expressed by Waldegrave received short shrift from some one who was looking for business.

'Green belt' land, particularly in the south of England, has been under constant pressure from developers seeking to sell the rural environment to the urbanite. The persuasiveness and perseverence of the development lobby has inhibited even the most sympathetic Conservative members from coming out wholly on the side of the conservationist. In 1987, drawing upon a rather unstable, simplistic and outdated Tebbit-like argument, one 'crusading' Tory MP was determined to defend the position of those whose funds support his party, and suggested that development should be allowed more readily in the South of the country: 'We have got to accept the real economic pressures to build in the South where the jobs are because a lot of people in the North would like to move to the South for work but can't because there's no where to live.'[56] Although the arguments are more sophisticated than this, the constraining forces of the developers and house-builders go a long way to explain the ambiguity which has been a mark of the Conservative Government's green belt policy.[57]

Another set of interest groups long allied to the Conservative Government are the farmers and landowners represented by such groups as the National Farmers' Union, the Country Landowners' Association and the Economic Forestry Group. Such groups have the interest of their members at heart and have been traditionally viewed as enemies of the conservation groups and of policies which seek to curtail their activities. The policy context in which such groups have previously functioned has, largely under CAP, altered dramatically, and the anti-environmental block has been considerably weathered. Nevertheless, farmers and landowners still represent a major impediment to the development of environmental thinking in the government.[58]

Conservation policy is not the only concern. There is also strong reaction to pressures which seek a move away from an overuse of pesticides and herbicides, changes in animal husbandry techniques, improved public access to land and tighter controls on the development of farm buildings. Such moves not only threaten the economic interests of the farming/landowning community, but also threaten its social and political status. In terms of social status, farming interests are decidedly Tory in their view, seeing themselves as the natural conservers of the countryside and suspicious of losing control over this. Julian Byng, a farmer and landowner, in his riposte to Waldegrave's speech to the Oxford farmers, argued in heartfelt, feudal terms, that the answer lay not in political interference by pressure groups or government, but in being able to 'educate the urban electorate to realise that it is because of the stewardship of past generations of landowners, great and small, that we have inherited the countryside we now seek to conserve'.[59]

In terms of political status, many interest groups have, over the years, cultivated a niche for themselves in the political process. The National Farmers' Union (NFU) provides a good example of a group who, through its performance and relationship with the Ministry of Agriculture, continually demonstrates a high degree of political status which its members look up to and expect. Holbeche indicates that although the NFU has been an influential 'insider' group regarding some of the Ministry of Agriculture's policy decisions, it is not in the privileged position some commentators believe.[60] The fact that such a group may have participated in policy decisions at party or government level, or believes it has contributed to favourable policy outcomes, enables a group to legitimise itself in the eyes of its members and attract further support. If a group thinks its status with government or a party is under threat, this may fuel its desire to block the changes sought by the environmental movement.

In the case of the Liberal Democrats, no major interest groups are strongly aligned with the party. Although this absence of large supporting groups has always left the Liberals with an unsure financial base, it has meant that the policy process has remained largely internalised and under the control of party activists. The Labour Party, on the other hand, is strongly dependent upon the trade unions for support, and they still remain central to the party's policy-making processes, despite Labour's long period in opposition.

We have already highlighted how many of the trade unions and key members have been active in promoting the development of 'green' policies throughout the Labour Party. Unions who have seen their membership decline steeply due to the pressures exerted by the Conservative Government and the natural processes of de-industrialisation have been amongst the more ardent supporters of a 'greener' Labour Party. The interests they have actively sought to protect in the past have dwindled with the membership, threatening them with the loss of a social and political role. Where once the NUM would react vigorously to the environmental groups who criticised the pollution caused via acid rain in Europe or coal waste on the Durham coast, they have been forced to accept the government's edict that in the UK coal is no longer king, and have wound down their opposition to the environmentalists. In seeking to re-establish the unions within the context of the wider Labour Movement, Sawyer suggests that 'the way forward will be to show them that union interests are wider than the place of work. As well as defending their own members' interests, the unions must show that they care about others and have a wider political contribution to make.'[61]

Whereas the unions have had to swim with the tide of reform in the Labour Party, particularly under Neil Kinnock, uncertainties still exist about the nature and depth of environmental commitment in Labour. Before the 1987 election, with a union-dominated 'Jobs and Industry' manifesto, there was the feeling that a Labour victory and good times were around the corner, and that party statements in relation to environmental protection might be a little premature. Certainly this feeling was present amongst those unions whose membership was stable and had perhaps prospered in the growth of private development under the Tories, such as those in the EETPU, AUEW and the construction unions. Yet in the reality of election defeat, there has been even more pressure on these unions to accept the notion that Labour's environmental ambitions need not produce job losses.

In expected contrast to the view that the CBI hold – that environmental protection should stand on its own and job losses are an inevitable consequence – so long as the trade union movement remains in existence, there will be clashes between the need to protect jobs and the need for a cleaner and safer environment. Constraints will be imposed selectively, relating not to the whole process of party 'greening', but only to those dimensions which would seem to affect a particular union. Only when the whole economy is environmentally motivated in purpose and direction can such constraints be fully overcome.

Breaking down the barriers

The pressures for party 'greening' are wide-ranging, diverse, often ephemeral actions, seeking to weave their way through a maze of ritual procedures and psychological prejudices inherent to the workings of party politics. With politics being red in tooth and claw, many good intentions and ideas are lost in the process, though more than ever they keep turning up repeatedly.

Strands of greenery that are not cast by the wayside have emerged into mainstream party politics. Firstly, this is evidenced by the rhetoric that is now a central feature the majority of party politicians, from local activist to Prime Minister. The word 'green' is now sound political currency, even if there is disagreement regarding its meaning and derision from the Greens that their ideas are being stolen. Moreover, with phrases like 'sustainable development' and 'environmental audits' being bandied about, there is something new to talk about in party politics. Secondly, government and the main parties have brought environmental policies firmly on to their agendas. Action does not, of course, follow automatically, yet it is increasingly difficult to ignore the environmental policy dimension. Thirdly, there are signs that the major parties are seeking to accommodate 'green' thinking in their underlying systems of beliefs. Attention to environmental policy has instigated a process of philosophical re-evaluation, where once-forgotten ideologues are being resurrected and anti-environmental goals are being transformed.

In bringing about this range of outcomes in each of the parties, the environmentalists have had a price to pay. Politicians see themselves, quite correctly in the democratic system of the UK, as the instruments of social change. But the agents of change are not necessarily the instigators of change. However, politicians are in a position to direct and control change in line with the party political and ideological framework in which they operate.

The fact that all of the major parties have responded to environmentalist pressures may give the impression that environmental concern is somehow above party politics. Certainly, there is a strong degree of consensus. But any cohesion environmentalism possesses is rent asunder by a political system which is fuelled by party differences. Ideological purity gives way to the realities of tradition and trade-offs. Each of the parties are selective in terms of what issues they pursue and how they pursue them. They seek to find an environmentalism that is compatible with party beliefs, party interests, party unity and existing party policy. What is not compatible has to be moulded and cajoled in order to fit the parameters in which a party works. Ideological barriers, which map out the territories of the parties, are particularly difficult to surmount. Socialism, conservatism and liberalism come first. Environmentalism comes second. Jack Cunningham, as Shadow Secretary of State for the Environment, responding to the idea that the Labour Party could somehow be transformed into a type of Green Party, explained:

> The Labour Party is the Labour Party, a democratic socialist party and we're very different from the Green Party as we're very different from the Liberals and the Conservatives. We must be a party which takes greater account of the environmental pressures and concerns, and I'm in favour of that, but fundamentally we're a democratic socialist party and our policies will differ, not just in degree but sometimes in principle, from the policies of the Green Party.[62]

As the pressures for change increase from both outside and inside the parties, many of the constraints identified are beginning to wane, often due to forces which are independent of the environmental movement. Attitudes are changing, and the scent of political gain is being taken up. But the rate of change varies between the parties. Both Labour and the Liberal Democrats had nothing to lose by adopting environmental ideas and policies during the 1980s. Yet for the Conservative Government, the continued influence of powerful interest groups and powerful departments have made for a rather uncertain political will and have forced a cautious approach toward the environment. The responsibility that government carries is itself a powerful constraint and one that is difficult to argue with, given the immensity and uncertainty of the agenda. Moreover, resources required for environmental action have been difficult to secure, particularly for a government which has had priorities of tax cuts, and implementing, then dismantling, the community charge.

Selectivity has enabled the government and, to a lesser extent, the parties, to be seen to surmount some of the impediments which block environmental action, whilst at the same time respecting others. High-profile government interest in the protection of the ozone layer by Mrs Thatcher at the end of the 1980s, for instance, can be seen as an action of environmental appeasement, carefully selected to exhibit the government's environmental credentials and yet not to undermine Conservative Party priorities. Britain was obliged to join with the rest of the EEC's negotiating team at the UN-sponsored Ozone Conference held in Montreal 1987. In the case of action to prevent acid rain, however, Britain had resisted any such calls for European unity and had followed the USA in not joining the '30 per cent club'. Curbing acid rain would have cost a great deal of money the Treasury did not want to spend, and it would have infuriated the CEGB and more than likely reduced the attractiveness of the electricity industry at a time of privatisation plans. Action to reduce global production of CFCs was different. Here the USA was at the forefront of seeking cut-backs in CFC production, so the government would not be going in the opposite direction of its closest ally. The CEGB's interests would not be affected, and action of the kind the government was agreeing to would cost the Treasury very little indeed, since the costs of curtailing CFC production would have to borne by private industry, chiefly ICI.

Sophistry and illusion, as exemplified above, is part of party politics. It is one way of trying to achieve several different objectives without upsetting anyone. However, the pressures for 'greening' are growing to a point where political compromises may not be possible, and party politics may have to adopt more radical strategies to deal with the environmental challenge.

Notes and references

1 Personal Communication.

2 Rose, R. 1982. *The Territorial Dimension in Government: Understanding the United Kingdom.* Chatham and New Jersey: Chatham House Publishing.

3 Barker, A. 1986. 'Rub of the Green.' Interview with J. Cunningham. *PSLG*, April. 10–11.

4 After the 1987 General Election, Gavin Laird and Eric Hammond put forward the idea that Labour's defeat was due to its opposition to nuclear power, although it is highly unlikely that the issue was even remotely considered by the electorate. Cook, F. 'A Waste of Energy.' *Guardian.* 4.9.87.

5 Note 3, *op. cit.*

6 Ridley, N. 1987. Speech to Conservative Graduates' Association. December.

7 Meyer, M. 1989. Quoted in 'Dirty Man of Europe?' Milne, R. *Local Government Chronicle.* 15 September.

8 Those individuals within the Alliance who did not show the greatest enthusiasm for the environment were largely drawn from the SDP.

9 See for instance: Steel, D. 1984. 'Green Briefing.' Speech to the National Liberal Club. 16 February; Steel, D. 1984. 'Environment and Secrecy.' Speech to Friends of the Earth and Green Alliance. 19 March.

10 Personal Communication.

11 Steel, D. 1986. 'The Importance of Being Liberal.' An interview by M. Rutherford/M. Jacques. *Marxism Today*, October. 26–33.

12 Owen, D. 1983. Speech at SDP Environment Conference. Bedford College, London. 26 November.

13 The 1974 resolution read: 'This Assembly rejects the goal of indiscriminate economic growth as currently measured by increases in the gross national product (GNP). It also rejects the idea that the improvement and happiness of a society can be measured by the monetary value of the goods and services produced. It believes that assessment of economic activity on society must take into account social and environmental factors and include quality as well as quantity of outputs.'

14 Kinnock, N. 1983. 'Who can we Trust?' *New Ground*, No. 1. 10–11.

15 Kinnock, N. 1985. 'Turning over a new leaf.' *New Ground*, No. 5. 4–5.

16 Robinson. M. D. 1991. 'The Greening of British Party Politics: The Superficiality and the Substance.' Unpublished PhD Thesis. University of East Anglia.

17 Campbell-Savours, D. 1988. 'Shadows in a mounting greenery.' *Guardian*. 19 December. 16.

18 Carpenter, J. 1988. 'Labour's Victorian Values.' *Green Line*, No. 58. *New Year 87/88*. 13–14; Porritt, J./Winner, D. 1988. *The Coming of the Greens*. London: Fontana.

19 Personal Communication.

20 Friends of the Earth. 1990. *The Government's Environmental Record*. London: Hutchinson Radius. 6.

21 Department of Environment. 1986. *Conservation and Development: The British Approach*. The United Kingdom Government's Response to the World Conservation Strategy. London: HMSO.

22 See for instance: Paterson, T. 1985. 'Environment – does the Prime Minister care?' *Crossbow*, Summer.

23 Personal Communication.

24 Thatcher, M. 1988. Speech given at a Royal Society Dinner on Tuesday 27 September.

25 Thatcher, M. 1988. Speech to Conservative Party Conference. October.

26 Ridley, N. 1988. 'Ridley's Position.' Extract from Conservative Party Conference Speech. *The Planner*, 74, No. 11. 10.

27 Personal Communication.

28 Personal Communication.

29 Personal Communication.

30 Personal Communication.

31 Note 16, *op. cit.*

32 For example, the fitting of coal-fired power stations with desulphurisation equipment was seen to cost the UK £160 million rather than supply the benefit of 33,000 man years of work.

33   Labour Party. 1986. *Jobs and Environment*. First Interim Report, October. The Labour Party; Labour Party. 1987. *Jobs and Environment*. Second Interim Report, January. The Labour Party.

34   Note 24, *op. cit.*

35   Pearce, D. 1989. *Blueprint for a Green Economy*. London: Earthscan.

36   See for instance: Solesbury, W. 1976. 'The Environmental Agenda.' *Public Administration*, 54. Winter. 379–97; Hogwood, B. W. 1987. *From Crisis to Complacency? Shaping Public Policy in Britain*. Oxford: Oxford University Press.

37   See: Stringer, J. K./Richardson, J. J. 1980. 'Managing the Political Agenda: Problem Definition and Policy Making in Britain.' *Parliamentary Affairs*, 33, No. 1. Winter. 23–40.

38   John, B./Robertson, J. H./Randall, S. 1987. *Towards a New Agriculture: A Labour View*. The Labour Party.

39   House of Lords Select Committee on the European Communities. 1984. 'Agriculture and the Environment.' HL Paper 247. London: HMSO; House of Lords Select Committee on Science and Technology. 1984. 'Agriculture and Environmental Research.' HL Paper 272 I & II. London: HMSO.

40   Personal Communication.

41   Ryan, A. 1988. 'Party Ideologies since 1945.'. *Contemporary Record*, 1, No. 4. Winter. 17–22.

42   Personal Communication.

43   See: Wenz, P. S. 1986. 'Conservatism and Conservation.' *Philosophy*, 61. 503–12.

44   Blowers, A. 1987. 'Transition or Transformation? Environmental Policy under Thatcher.' *Public Administration*, 65. Autumn. 277–94.

45   Note 44, *op. cit.*

46   Personal Communication.

47   Labour Party. 1988. *Democratic Socialist Aims and Values*. The Labour Party.

48   In ideological terms, the Liberals struggled with SDP lack of commitment to the environment, particulary the 'greenness' of Dr David Owen. As a senior Liberal put it in 1987, 'his preoccupation with a centralised, technocratic philosophy reminiscent of his political origins' did not square with the attention that the Liberal Party wished to give the environment.

49   See for instance: Grant, W. 1988. 'Business Pressure Since 1945.' *Contemporary Record*, 2. No. 1. Spring. 5–7.

50   Elkington, J./Burke, T. 1987. *The Green Capitalists: Industry's search for Environmental Excellence*. London: Victor Gollancz Ltd.

51   Personal Communication.

52   The point is well made by: Dawkins, L. A. 1986. 'The Politics of Energy Conservation and Industrial Interests in Britain.' *Parliamentary Affairs*, 40 (2). April 1987. 250–64.

53   See: Ince, M. 1982. *Energy Policy*. London: Junction Books.

54   Waldegrave, W. 1986. Speech to Oxford Farming Conference, 7

January. Reprinted in *Policy Challenge*, August 1986. Centre for Policy Studies. 4–22.

55 Pye, G. 1986. 'Housing Land Shortage – Farmland Surplus.' *Policy Challenge*. August. CPS. 47–58.

56 Personal Communication.

57 Note 26, *op. cit.*

58 A survey carried out into farmers' attitudes to conservation, by an Oxford agricultural student, revealed that while 80 per cent of farmers recognise that conservation is an increasingly prominent issue, 42 per cent think this should not be the case. See: *Daily Telegraph*, 'Farmers Taking a Mixed View of Conservation.' 8.4.88.

59 Byng, J. 1986. 'Two Cheers for the Minister?' In *Policy Challenge*, August. CPS. 23–34.

60 See: Holbeche, B. 1986. 'Policy and Influence: MAFF and the NFU.' *Public Policy and Administration*, 1. No. 3. Winter. 40–7.

61 Sawyer, T. 1985. In Ashton, F. *Green Dreams Red Realities*. NATTA Discussion Paper, No. 2. Milton Keynes: The Open University.

62 Personal Communication.

The greening of British party politics: continuity or transformation?

With Porritt as the new Voltaire and John Button's *Green Pages* as Diderot's *Encyclopaedia*, the 1980s may well be recorded in history as the age of 'green' enlightenment: the decade which saw public concern for the environment establishing itself in the market place through green consumerism and the 'greening' of industry, and which saw the media give persistent coverage to anything bearing a tinge of green.[1] But this new age of reason has also asserted itself through an even more dramatic event – the 'greening' of the major political parties.

Public concern for the environment is centuries old, yet apart from individual pieces of legislation and the odd personal crusade, party political concern had previously not amounted to more than occasional tinkering. During the eighties, public concern was translated into political concern as the main parties took up the challenge of the environmental movement with an unprecedented seriousness. The process that is the 'greening' of British party politics is likely to be long term and almost certainly irreversible, given the ever-increasing depth of public concern and the magnitude of national and international environmental problems. It is indeed hard to envisage a return to the days when politicians would see environmental problems as little more than inconvenient by-products on the road to an ever-bounteous society.

This book has put forward a network of interlinking explanations why the main parties have undertaken to absorb selectively environmental concern into their thoughts and actions. It has also looked at the wide-ranging factors which control this process. But as the process of party 'greening' develops in the years ahead, we need to address the question of how deep party 'greenness' goes, and focus upon the implications for both the environmental movement and the parties in the 1990s and beyond.

Where were the greens?

As indicated in chapter 2, the Greens have attempted to capture the emotional and intellectual heart of environmentalism. Their efforts to knit together eclectically previously disparate groups around an ecological imperative offers a distinct intellectual system and a radical alternative focus within the environmental movement. Away from the pamphlets and promises which have characterised much of the 'greening' of the main parties during the 1980s, the Green Party was keeping alive its 'new age' philosophy; but it was also struggling with the realities of traditional party politics.

In the UK the Green Party has been the political champion of a 'green datum'. However, given the diversity of organisations and individuals the party has sought to represent, tensions with regard to policy and ideology have developed. In this sense, if in no other, the Green Party is akin to the major parties. Unlike some sections of the environmental movement, which are content passively to join groups and sign petitions, the Greens have been keen to politicise their passions. For them, the environmental pressure group forum is inadequate, and their demands too radical for conventional party politics. This has posed a fundamental problem for the Greens, not just in the UK but also in other European nations, as to how far their radicalism can be integrated into western polities and their party systems.[2] The emphasis that the Greens place on individualism and self-realisation conflicts dramatically with the bureaucratisation of contemporary living. Similarly, their long-term, socially orientated, holistic criteria as a basis of policy clashes with the traditional, short-term criteria of economic profitability which is the basis of most political decision making.

Conventional politics is challenged by the Greens who seek a transformation, not only in political outcomes, but also in the manner in which these outcomes are reached. They are therefore not ascribing to 'anti-politics', in the sense that they are against the concept of politics *per se*, but rather they stand against those forms of politics which remove or ignore basic ecological imperatives. Of course, there are some Greens that claim that the kind of fundamental changes society needs can only come about through a personal transformation of values, the inference being that if everyone did the same, changes would take place without the need for any form of political intervention.[3] For radical 'eco-anarchists', politics is about the obsession of power and the designing of structures to maintain this power. Such structures are seen to be impersonal, centralised and at the root of the ecological crisis itself. Radical Greens with a pessimistic view of society argue that it is necessary to detach oneself from the immutable system and live an alternative lifestyle. Although such positions are not widely held amongst the Greens, they do seem to attract a disproportionate amount of attention.

Instead of such 'cultural escapism', the majority of Greens would appear to accept an ultimately pragmatic definition of politics as being the primary mechanism for deciding 'who gets what, when and how', but stress that this requires updating to suit a transitional age of resource scarcity, intolerable human injustices, ecological fragility and acute public awareness.[4]

The ideological basis of a 'new politics' for the Greens is derived from an ecological worldview which stresses the role of 'grassroots' participatory democracy, together with disenchantment with traditional political activity.[5] Papworth summarises the main worry of the Greens regarding conventional politics: 'Those who choose to enter the political arena on these [traditional] terms will simply become the pawns of the non-democratic forces which dominate it.'[6]

The aim, therefore, is to create a democratic, grassroots politics which does not concentrate power in the hands of the few, nor alienates people from the decision-making processes. Grassroots democracy for the Greens revolves around two inseparable themes of 'direct' democracy and decentralisation. Direct democracy entails that political power is exercised at the lowest appropriate level within decentralised basic units, be they defined as districts or in terms of community.[7] Decentralisation is advocated as a response to the remoteness generated by conventional centralised politics. The ecologically-derived concept of community and the idea that individuals function best within our own carefully-carved-out social niche, is implicit in the politics of the Greens, with community being the most desirable social unit around which the whole of society can be restructured.

In advocating their grassroots, decentralised politics, the Greens embrace three principles. Firstly, ever keen to move away from the autocratic tones prevalent in the environmentalism of the early 1970s, the Greens emphasise a high level of individual liberty. Yet the balance between the liberty of the individual and the responsibility of the individual toward the community is a fine one. It becomes easy to see how tensions have emerged amongst Greens between those who opt for an alternative lifestyle and those wishing to adopt green principles but in a conventional way. Secondly, self-reliance is stressed for the benefits it bestows upon the community by reducing its dependence upon others and improving control over its own affairs. Self-reliance in this context does not mean isolation or selfishness, but co-operation between the able and the less able in a symbiotic sense.[8] Thirdly, and relevant to green beliefs in direct democracy, self-determination of communities is emphasised: giving communities as much autonomy as possible without transgressing primary ecological imperatives.

If, as Hayley points out, 'anarchy is the belief that government is no substitute for voluntary human relationships, and that one needs to develop at the expense of the other', then on initial reflection the Greens would seem to be following an anarchistic line.[9] Yet despite the recognition of anarchistic influences, the state would still seem to have a controlling role in the 'new politics' of the Greens so long as it was fully representative of the community base.[10] This sort of tension is not easily resolved, either for the analyst or for the Greens themselves, making it difficult to assess what kind of politics the Greens are seeking. As one Green put it: 'We are the politics of the twenty-first century and cannot be assessed by today's terms.'[11]

Despite problems of categorisation, green parties seeking to advance 'green' principles became part of the political map of Europe during the 1980s.[12] By far the most successful in political terms have been the West German Green Party who, only three years after formation, entered the Bundestag in March 1983, with twenty-seven delegates (5·6 per cent of the vote). In the 1987 German federal election this performance was improved and the German Green Party (Die Grunen) held forty-four seats (8·3 per cent of the vote). In both national and European elections, the green parties of Belgium, Luxemburg, Italy and the Netherlands can also claim some success for making inroads into the traditional vote.[13] Reasons for the electoral successes of these green parties through the 1980s are varied. On the surface, the very formation of political parties to advance 'green' policies would seem to substantiate ideas of fundamental value changes sweeping European democracies.[14] Moreover, party dealignment, where motivation for voting as a function of class has declined in line with the breakdown of class boundaries, has helped smaller parties with alternative policy positions develop.[15] Yet it would seem that success or failure of a green party is invariably related to the particular political culture, electoral system and historical circumstances of the country involved.[16]

In the UK, since its inception as the 'People' Party in 1973, and through most of its lifetime as the Ecology Party, the Green Party has desired to be an 'alternative' political party in British politics. Despite an increase in Green Party votes at local government level and a significant increase in the percentage share of the vote in the European elections of June 1989, electoral success at the national level has never materialised. In the General Election of 1987, for instance, the UK Green Party total vote increased, but still remained at less than 1·5 per cent of the national vote.[17] Table 4 illustrates the

Table 4 *Green Party election results, 1974–1989*

Election	No. of candidates	Percentage of vote (average)	Highest individual result (per cent)
General Election 28 Feb. 1974	5	1·8	3·9 (Coventry, N.W.)
General Election 10 Oct. 1974	4	0·7	0·8 (Coventry, N.W.)
General Election 5 May 1979	53	1·5	2·8 (London St. Marylebone & Worcestershire S.)
European Election 7 June 1979	3	3·7	4·1 (London Central)
General Election 6 June 1983	106	1·0	2·9 (Ogmore)
European Election 14 June 1984	16	2·6	4·7 (Hereford & Worcester)
General Election 11 June 1987	133	1·3	3·6 (Weston-super-Mare)
European Election 16 June 1989	79	14·9	Not Known

Sources: Rudig and Lowe (1984), Rudig (1985), Rose (1987)

performance of the Green Party in the National and European elections between the years 1974 and 1989.

The conventions of the British electoral system are central to the lack of success of the Green Party. The traditional representative 'seat' system, dominated by two parties and the first-past-the-post manner in which one of these political parties is elected, militates against the election hopes of smaller parties such as the Green Party. A further factor has been the financial threshold of the deposit, currently at £500, which makes it difficult for small parties with limited resources to mount an expensive and sophisticated electoral challenge. Of the 650 contestable seats in the 1987 General Election, the Green Party could only target 133 due to an acute lack of funds. In doing so, they lost close to £75,000, merely for the opportunity of telling the electorate that we face a serious environmental challenge.[18]

A further reason for the poor performance of the Green Party in the UK is that there already exists a strong tradition of political influence by the environmental pressure groups. The Green Party, despite their protestations, are still perceived by the electorate as a party of solely environmental/ecological issues with little concern for other matters. Most environmental pressure groups have become well integrated into the established political system and largely function in a politically neutral way. This, together with an implicit British aversion to radicalism, the preference for consensus rather than conflict, and, unlike the German Greens, a failure to mobilise other relevant social movements, accounts for the external constraints acting upon the attempt to express 'green' principles through the medium of a single political party.

However, there are internal reasons for the Green Party's lack of impact on British politics – reasons which reach beyond the political and cultural context and reveal fundamental ambiguities in the 'green' dimension of environmentalism. These derive from the duality of 'green' ideology, which hovers between anarchistic and pantheistic traditions and can loosely be described as phobias toward concepts of political power, personalities, organisation and tradition. Such fears are at the root of a two-way split in both the German and UK Green Parties, which arguably is detracting from a higher level of political success. The split has been labelled as being between 'Fundamentalists' and 'Realists' (Fundis and Realos in West Germany): those who resolutely seek to defend the purity of their 'green' principles, and those who are willing selectively to forsake some of these in the interests of pragmatism.[19]

Characterisations of the contemporary Green Party as a band of enlightened despots seeking environmental reform through a Hobbesian-like state still appear in the media and have perhaps induced an element of 'power paranoia' within Green Party ranks. In their efforts to move away from an elite view of political power to a more radical notion of power sharing, the concept of leadership, together with associated images and individual charisma, have become suspicious entities to many Greens. In the UK Green Party, there is no elected leader or spokesperson, but rather three co-chairs elected by Party Council each year. The latter is an elected body consisting of twenty-two members whose job it is to organise the party. The co-chairs exist to speak on the party's behalf when necessary and are not there to 'lead' from the front. Similarly, Die Grunen have long operated a 'rotation' system of leadership to prevent members from becoming too removed from the grassroots and to exclude careerists.[20] Leadership is linked with bureaucratic organisation and is therefore viewed as a manifestation of structured power and the antithesis of localised grassroots expression and self-determination. Since the 1987 General Election, however, the Green Party have begun to attract public attention via key figures such as Sara Parkin, Jean Lambert and, recently, former TV sports personality David Icke (until his embarrassing claim to be the Son of God!).

Fundamentalist Green Party members reject any notion of 'selling-out' to the big power game of politics. Papworth, for instance, identifies the fundamentalist position in a characteristically evangelical and moralistic way, by a process of lengthy elimination:

Our immediate opponents are those who own private motor cars, who spend hours watching advertisement t.v. programmes, who buy goodies in big supermarkets and help to keep all those monster lorries on the road, who buy 60-page Sunday newspapers, who ignore local health food shops, who grow none of their own food when they have ground on which to do so, who eat chickens, veal and beef from animals whose lives are a horrendous man-made process of mind-screaming torture, whose homes are littered with all the latest consumer gadgets, who help to promote unemployment by using postcodes, who totter around from one national rally, conference or gathering to another dealing with national concerns whilst making no attempt to define local problems, nor to help create local community power or to give a lead to local people on possible forms of local action using local resources in order to achieve local solutions based on local power; people who will bank with the big banks instead of starting a local one and who generally live passively and contentedly on the goodies of mass consumerism (as most of us still do) even though the destination of such living is a world of starving millions drowned in blood and radioactive ashes.[21]

Traditional politics is perceived as a reflection of a traditional society, and if the aim is radically to change society in terms of its consciousness and structure, then tradition is not for the Green Party fundamentalists. They argue for 'personal politics' outside the constricts of mass institutions: a politics of sincerity which walks the tightrope between individualism and communitarianism, attracting some members and repelling others. For Rudolf Bahro, a leading ideologue of the West German Green Movement, the position of Die Grunen on the issue of animal experiments in particular, and of their increasingly pragmatic and conventional politics in general, caused his resignation in June 1985. He commented:

What people are trying to do here is to save a party no matter what kind of party, and no matter for what purpose. The main thing is for it to get re-elected to parliament in 1987. It has no basic ecological position; it is not a party for the protection of life and I now know it never will be, for it is rapidly distancing itself from that position.[22]

Against the often frustrating adherence to 'green' principles by the fundamentalists, realists argue that they wish to achieve something sooner and more tangible than a change in consciousness. Although they may hold the same beliefs and visions, realists are prepared to compromise, participate and think in conventional political terms. However, the problems of developing a pragmatic UK Green Party was ideally illustrated through what became known as the 'Maingreen' debate.[23]

In April 1986, after a conference at Malvern had rejected ideas to make the UK Green Party more professional, a group of members suggested reforming the party through the idea of a forum called 'Maingreen'. This was due to be launched at a quietly organised meeting of selected guests, centred around two advance personal papers by Paul Ekins (ex-secretary of the Ecology Party) and Jonathan Tyler (Working Group Convenor and former parliamentary candidate). In Tyler's paper he attacked the apathy and paranoia of the anarchistic faction of the party toward all government, and the overall 'collective incompetence' that it showed in wanting to be a political party. In Tyler's own words:

There is a disproportionate representation of people who have never been part of, or who have kept out of the formal economy – which is fine in terms of keeping the green conscience polished but does little to prepare the Party for the realities of participation in government (which readers of this paper will not need reminding is the Party's function but which too many readers need to be reminded of).[24]

Ekins too was keen to stress that the Green Party's taboos on basic political concepts were holding it back from any chance of success: 'Organisation, image, leadership: these are the the substance and backbone of real-world politics. We may wish they were not. Our reward for continuing to pretend there are not will be eternal marginality.'[25]

The 'Maingreen' debate revealed deep-seated frustration amongst pragmatists toward the fundamentalist position. At the time there was much private sympathy for the 'Maingreen' proposals, which seemed to be seeking the creation of a new organisational core of pragmatists. Yet publicly the Green Party Council reacted angrily toward Tyler's and Ekin's suggestions. Although some of the anger was due to the selective and undemocratic way a factional meeting had been arranged, there was considerable upset at the very political direction of the proposals. 'Maingreen' pointed toward the formation of a breakaway, centralised, top-down party, and although it is difficult to assess accurately the response of all Green Party members (itself a source of frustration for the pragmatists), feedback at the time of the suggestions was defensive and on the whole tended to encourage a re-emphasis of the fundamentalists.

The disruption caused by the 'Maingreen' debate did, however, begin to stimulate a process of introspection by the UK Green Party leading up to and beyond the General Election of 1987. The 1987 election manifesto was a glossy affair, and similarly 'glossy' appearances were made on TV and radio, perhaps reflecting not just a change in media attitudes to the party, but also the willingness of the party to respond, albeit uneasily, to the challenges of being a mainstream political party.[26]

The dividing line between fundamentalism and realism within the politics of the UK Green Party is perhaps more flexible than the above example shows, and in the long term damaging splits have developed, as in Die Grunen. However, even at its most pragmatic, the UK Green Party, in its attempts to change society, has come up against the accommodatory side of the environmental movement which has tended to reflect wider developments in British politics and society. The result is an ongoing search for an identity.

Porritt and Winner suggest a number of roles the Green Party may adopt in the future. As they put it: 'Given the unremittingly harsh nature of the electoral set-up in Britain, it is hardly surprising if its role remains a little unclear. A pressure group? Conscience-prickers and conscience-raisers? A conventional political party? An extra-parliamentary catalyst? All of these at the same time?'[27] It is inconceivable that despite the media charm of Sara Parkin, the Green Party will ever be a conventional political party. Apart from the fact that the political system struggles to cope with more than two parties, the Green Party will not give way on its fundamental push for a 'greenness' that is complete and lasting rather than anything that is superficial and ephemeral. If it loses this message, it loses everything.

Political coalitions appear to be a closed road for the Green Party. The Conservatives have certainly no time, nor need, for 'environmental zealots' or 'closet Marxists'.[28] In the Labour Party, where amongst the left there appears some sympathy for the ideas of the Green Party, the tendency is still to see them as middle-class, misguided socialists, and talk of a 'red/green' political coalition of the sort which emerged in West Germany in the mid 1980s is fanciful.[29] Of those on the left who have talked of links, no-one has influence within the dominant PLP, and even in a hung Parliament situation, the Green Party would have in terms of voters, little political capital to offer Labour. Only the Liberal Democrats would seem to possess the ideological flexibility and the political need to forge links with the Green Party. Yet despite 'green' sympathies amongst members such as Simon Hughes, links would have to be on Liberal Democrat terms.

A system of proportional representation would perhaps help the Green Party gain a parliamentary voice, although the party is never likely to be in a position to exert much in the way of direct political influence. It is an interesting to think how Green Party MPs would react in the House of Commons with all of its attendant idiosyncrasies of tradition and history.

Green Party members have often claimed that when it comes to politics, they are neither left, right, nor centre, but in front.[30] However, conventional party politics is too fast for the Green Party. As an increasing number of issues become politicised, the political agenda of Parliament and the parties has become packed to capacity. Politicians have to move swiftly between issues; some are ignored and some are scaled down in order to fit busy timetables. There is little time to intellectualise. The Green Party in Britain, perhaps more so than its European allies, is intellectually very strong, with the concept of 'greenness' well developed and increasingly philosophically sound. One can guess that this position has been reached precisely due to the party's existence outside of mainstream politics, where it has had time to contemplate the vastness of the environmental idea. It may well be that an overdependence on theory implies that the Green Party would always find it difficult to cope with the practicalities of politics – a point accentuated by its lack of practice at the conventional political game.

Porritt and Winner suggest that the best thing that the Green Party can do in the near future is not to panic and 'carry on doing better what it already does'.[31] In many respects, this is all the Green Party can do, perhaps with a more pressure-group-like approach or perhaps by lobbying politicians of the main parties more overtly. Green Party ideology is unique but unco-ordinated, and its comparatively small resource base is unreliable.[32] Green Party membership is riven with tensions between eco-anarchists, eco-socialists, residual eco-fascists and political realists, and organisation is problematic in a party that does not like to be organised. Moreover, the party is uncertain whether it actually wants to exist in a system where it is always likely to be excluded.

As we saw in chapter 3, social movements in Britain, unlike those in Europe, rarely develop any lasting identity in political culture. Instead, the existing political parties have tended to absorb the pressures for social change and channel them through the conventional political system, encouraged by the pressure groups. Environmentalism is still undergoing a similar process. As the movement grows, the rate of absorption will increase and the very reason for the existence of a Green Party may well disappear. Ironically, the long-term and ultimate challenge for the Green Party is not to survive as a political force. The short-term challenge is to see that the existing parties take the principles of the Green Party to heart in order that it can self-destruct, leaving the true 'green' message to rise pheonix-like from the ashes.

Against the green datum

The process of 'greening' the main political parties may now be established, but, as we have seen, it is highly selective. New issues and new ideas are chosen to fit established structures of party thought and action, and the reasons why party politicians respond to the challenge of the environmental movement have as much to do with the intricacies of politicking and the desire for political power, as with genuine environmental concern. Any genuine concern for the environment is inevitably coloured by sets of motivations which are specific to individuals and party ideologies. As such, we must expect that 'greenness' to the Conservatives is different from that advocated by the Labour Party and the Liberal Democrats and vice versa. But how different are these conceptions of 'greenness' to those advocated by the Greens and the Green Party?

The answer is that 'greenness' for the three main political parties is vastly different to that which the Green Party is trying to advance. Although some broad similarities exist between the 'green datum' and policy positions of the Labour Party and the Liberal Democrats, the belief systems of all the parties fall short, despite their rhetoric.

The theme of ecological interdependence, central to 'green' thinking, is largely missing from the major parties. Amongst the environmental crusaders of the parties, it is increasingly recognised that environmental matters impinge upon all policy sectors and all stages of policy making – a point increasingly recognised by the parties during the 1980s when calls for co-ordinating environmental ministries were loud in both the Labour Party and among the Liberals. Indeed, the need for better co-ordination amongst departments has penetrated party thinking which previously relied on a system which divides policy up, both intellectually and physically, through the departmental system of government. The depth of commitment behind ensuring that environmental thinking influences all areas of policy remains to be tested, though it is unlikely that any of the parties could master the holistic approach to policy advocated by the Green Party. The main parties still have to treat the environment as one issue among many others, and any attempt at holistic thinking is immediately choked by a system of departments and shadow departments where competition always seems to have the edge over co-ordination.

To some extent, growing awareness of ecological interdependence has been shown in the parties' recognition that environmental problems do not respect geographical or political boundaries. The threat of global warming and the destruction of the ozone layer is forcing politicians to establish global mechanisms for dealing with such mega-issues. However, a high degree of co-operation and consensus in the international scientific community is proving difficult to achieve in political terms, as the 1987 Montreal Protocol and 1989 International Ozone Conference have illustrated. Holistic approaches to solving world problems are thwarted by the immense variation in the levels of development between nations being asked to sign the protocols. Getting everyone to agree a time-scale which correlates with their present and projected levels of economic development, together with distractions of other political differences, makes reaching total agreement a Herculean task.

Behind the Greens' idea of global interdependence is the notion of global equity; the major parties have still to address this question, which necessitates a fundamental reassessment of the relations between North and South. Promises of increased aid for developing countries have been forthcoming in party manifestos and were a feature of Mrs Thatcher's speech to the United Nations in November 1989.[33] But this is far removed from any major reform of the international monetary system, a reassessment of trading relations (including arms), or an emphasis on Third World self-reliance as called for by the Green Party. Commitment to tackling global warming is still seen in the light of British interests, not in the interests of the already poor Third World nations where the effects would be radically more devastating than the loss of some areas of lowland Britain through flooding.

The main political parties are still chained to the idea that the natural ecosystem exists primarily as a resource for man's exploitation. Although, as a review of environmental policy documents of recent years show, the parties have begun to address issues of resource planning, future energy policy, recycling and the nascent concept of sustainability, the sacred cow of economic growth has not been sacrificed, nor is it likely to be in the near future. The Greens may call for greater emphasis on non-material values and qualitative assessments of people's needs rather than wants, yet this is still outweighed by the idea that a growing economy is the panacea for the world's ills. It is the apparently blinkered efforts to achieve ever-higher levels of economic growth which worry Greens most of all.[34] Achieving economic growth is the traditional clarion call of the main parties. Although opinion polls continue to indicate that the British public seek improved environmental quality, the parties would be foolish to ignore the public's inherent desire to live within an expanding economy.

The notion that the earth's resource base is finite has not, it seems, permeated the thinking of the Conservative Government over the past decade. During the most of the 1980s, the environment was generally seen to be more about the issue of straw-burning than the burning of the Brazilian rainforest. Policies to cope with a world without oil have been shaped to meet wider political objectives, rather than environmental ones. Government investment in long-talked-about alternative energy sources has been minuscule, despite the rundown of the UK's coal industry, a lack of public confidence in nuclear power and a lifespan for oil of perhaps forty years. Where in this rationality is the Burkean idea of continuity and responsibility to future generations, potentially so close to a Green Party perspective? All the Conservatives have offered in terms of tangible policy has been a commitment to more nuclear power, the radioactive waste from which counters any 'High Tory' thoughts towards future generations.

The major parties are still well behind the Greens in grasping the connections between events such as the destruction of the Amazonian rainforest, Macdonalds, company car tax allowances, and the price of the weekly family shopping. They are not driven intellectually by the holistic imperative that lies at the heart of the Green position. Although accepting that environmental problems undoubtedly exist, they either do not share the prognosis that an environmental crisis is as imminent as the Green Party would have us believe, or they are confident that it can be met by technological ingenuity. In the Conservative Party both views are prevalent. On the one hand, there is a genuine, deep-seated, almost patriotic belief that Britain's environmental record is actually second to only a handful of other nations. In the words of one conservative journalist: 'Britain's air is relatively fresh. There are more fish each year in the Thames. We lead the world in toxic waste treatment. We scrub our buildings and tend our public gardens. We are, by and large, a neat fastidious race, proud to eschew the macho squalor and Bohemian scruffiness of much of America, Italy or Spain'.[35] On the other hand, Mrs Thatcher's claim made during her television interview with Michael Buerk in 1989 that 'in the next five years we will have got rid of most of our problems' is deep-seated in the Conservative Party. Good science, a propensity for common sense, a dash of the stiff-upper-lip spirit, and the knowledge that prominent technological corporations are important sources of support, seem to hold sway amongst important sections of the party.

In the Labour Party, the technocrats, once so dominant, have receded with de-industrialisation, the sustained pressures for a non-nuclear power policy and an active alternative technology/energy lobby. Other preoccupations, none more than the desire to win a general election, have prevailed in the Labour Party, but it remains unlikely that there will be a return to the dominance of a technocractic, management approach to the environment.

If one sees the 'green datum' merely as a comprehensive catalogue of environmental policies, then it may be only a matter of time before the mainstream political parties adopt those policies. As values change and new expectations emerge, social coalitions are formed around them, forcing the parties to take note and adopt policies accordingly. To a large extent, world events have diluted the peace imperative of the Greens and Labour's left, although the demands of the women's movement, health issues and animal welfare issues have risen in prominence within all the parties. The links between these issues and global environmental problems were once the force of the Greens, but now they are finding their way into conventional party politics, albeit slowly. However, there is still a long way to go before there is any hint of demise in the anthropocentric, patriarchal politics of the main parties.

The idea of a 'green datum' has little in the way of policy implications for the main parties, given that policy is constructed on a multitude of factors other than environmental concern. It is first and foremost an emergent ideology which looks not only to change society via the mechanisms of policy and legislation, but also seeks to change core belief systems. The Greens are not content merely to treat the symptoms of environmental problems; their aim is to tackle the root causes. The green datum puts forward a framework for this. However, party politics already works within a framework which is wholly different. It is largely reactive, non-anticipatory and short-term. It is also well established as a distinctive system of human activity. Spirituality, emotion, inner feelings and individual value changes are, by and large, kept apart from day-to-day politicking, the conventional wisdom being that they are not a firm base for making hard political decisions.

The Greens may point to the failure of any of the mainstream UK political parties to match up to a 'green datum', but 'green' politics as advocated by the Green Party is itself an intellectual con-trick. It is not politics as we know it. It involves new motivations and goals which go far beyond the protection of party interests, short-term economic objectives and the pacifying of social want. It is not the politics of tradition, for there is no coherent tradition to 'green' politics. It is neither politics from the point of view of institutional dogma and organisation, nor is it the politics of power, given the distrust Greens associate with this. Indeed, the Greens seek to change the nature of politics to such an extent that it would not be politics at all![36]

There may well be connections between conservation and conservatism, but the basic tenets of Conservative Party ideology are well removed from the radicalism at the centre of 'green' politics; 'greenness' for the Conservatives appears as little more than a cosy, nostalgic feeling about countryside past-times and thatched cottages.

Traditional class-based socialism can also claim some common ground with the Greens with regard to a concern with community, participatory politics, egalitarianism in resource distribution and activism within a number of complementary social movements. Yet the Labour Party of Neil Kinnock has not recognised the unified system of values that characterises 'being green'. Unlike the West German Greens, the Green Party in the UK have not joined with the Labour Party, partly because there has been no need on Labour's part, but also because radicalism is no longer a hallmark of the majority of the British Labour Party, and it is a radicalism of vision which is a trait of the Greens. For Labour, 'greenness' appears as an environmentally-aware brand of socialism still, strongly tied to its industrial roots.

Within the Liberal tradition of middle-class radicalism, ideas of decentralisation, political reform and community politics would all seem to link the Liberal Democrats with the Greens. But even under a self-declared environmental enthusiast such as Paddy Ashdown, the Liberal Democrats still appear to seek the safe middle ground of party politics, unable to jettison their party tradition in favour of any real alternative form of politics. For the Liberal Democrats, 'greenness' is a worthy, philanthropic, middle-class activity.

We could then argue that against the 'green datum', UK party politics amounts to nothing more than shallow, ephemeral tinkering with global realities. However, it would be artificial to make a direct comparison for numerous reasons. Firstly, although the idea of the 'green datum' is useful for highlighting the differences between the Greens and the mainstream political parties, it is not realistic to set any absolute standard of 'greenness'. Indeed, variety and eclecticism are actually promoted by the Greens. Because of this diversity there is always likely to be considerable fluctuation in 'green' ideology between the realists and fundamentalists, contributing to the debate as to whether 'greenness' can be defined by a fixed set of principles.

Secondly, although the Greens may claim the moral high ground, they have no automatic right to it. There is no single way in which the environment affects society, and no single way in which it can be approached. The fact that each of the main parties have historical and ideological claims to environmental concern, each legitimate within their own terms of reference, indicates that there are other ways of addressing environmental issues apart from the 'pure green' approach. The environment is, and needs to remain, a 'free-for-all' issue, as a mark of its importance. Its relevance would surely be lost should it ever become the prerogative of one political or social group, who would claim to have found the right path.

Thirdly, and related to the above, it should be remembered that the Greens are only part of the wider environmental movement. They may make the connections between emergent social values and the environment, providing an increasingly articulate, intellectual base for much of the environmental movement, yet their failure to come to terms with political realities gives them less influence than those within the environmental movement able to speak the language of compromise. Indeed, we can argue that the Greens and concepts such as 'deep ecology' and 'Gaianism' are far from being vital organs in the complex structure of environmentalism. Without the Greens, the Green Party, or any notion of a 'green datum', the social movement of environmentalism would be virtually just as strong in political terms – a point recognised by the majority of politicians in the mainstream parties.

Fourthly, it is both too early and too easy to sit in judgement of the main political parties and their claims to 'greenness'. The politicians of the main parties and the vast majority of society are still at the base of a great learning curve. This is borne out by the many environmental problems still to be faced. The 1980s may come to be known as the period when the main parties began to take environmental

issues seriously, but this seemingly large step is really only very small
in comparision to those which have to be consistently taken to solve
environmental problems. With society's generally poor understanding of the environment, should we be so eager to dismiss the Conservative Government's, Labour's, or the Liberal Democrats'
environmental efforts as cynical marketing exercises? No-one has
really got to grips with the question, let alone provided an answer.

The triumph of accommodation

Even under a system of proportional representation, the Green Party
in the UK is unlikely to achieve political power. It may well remain in
some form as a moral conscience, but there is neither the social need
for a separate party to handle environmental issues, nor the political
drive to establish one, independent of the lack of opportunity
afforded by the present electoral system. The environmental movement is therefore forced to use existing channels to politicise its
messages, rather than attempt to cut new channels through the
traditional political strata.

The rapid growth in membership of the environmental pressure
groups, particularly since the mid-1980s, and their increasingly
sophisticated organisation, reflects the continued potency of the
environmental cause. Through the groups and the attentive public,
the major political parties have come to appreciate that such a social
and moral force cannot be ignored.

The 'pressure-response' model of party 'greening' highlights the
power of the environmental movement and the role that national
and international environmental disasters can play in bringing issues
on to party agendas. The intensity of the pressures which have
emerged as part of Britain's Europeanisation have forced issues such
as water and air quality higher up the government's policy agenda.
However, despite the build-up of organised pressure, the responses
of the Conservative, Labour and Liberal Democrat parties have been
cautious ones.

A model which relies on outside pressures being applied to the
political parties does not suggest any major ideological change. It
suggests an approach which is politically acceptable to the constitutional framework in which the major parties operate; policies can be
altered, the majority of environmental 'cause' groups can be satisfied

for a short period of time, but core political values and beliefs remain unchallenged.

The 'intentional' model of party 'greening' put forward in chapter 5 offers an insight into how environmental concern is growing within the parties themselves, touching both politicians and policies, and challenging the belief systems which the parties are based on. Internal pressures, in the form of key personalities and informal groups, can be powerful, as Mrs Thatcher's 'green' conversion demonstrated, but they are also inherently unstable and susceptible to wider political constraints. However, overall there appears an increasingly more receptive climate for environmental issues in all of the main parties. The environmental crusaders and allies are very much aware that although skirmishes will continue to take place with the environmental pressure groups, the major battles still have to be fought within the parties themselves. The 1990 White Paper on the Environment and the Environmental Protection Act are indications that some victories can be gained, although other battles are being lost.

Caution is a watchword for the Conservative Party, particularly when it is the party of government. Following Mrs Thatcher's speech to the Royal Society in 1988, and her subsequent flirtations with global environmental politics, it seemed caution was being thrown to the wind. Indeed, the environmental movement was plunged into a sea of excitement when Chris Patten, as Secretary of State for the Environment, announced at the 1989 Conservative Party Conference that a White Paper was to be produced which would 'bring together the Government's whole strategy and set the environmental agenda until the end of the century'.[37] This charismatic man who had demonstrated his environmental credentials as Minister for Overseas Development looked set to build upon the work of Waldegrave and transform the Conservative Party into true 'friends of the earth'. The reality was something different, with the production of the White Paper demonstrating that despite good intentions and support in some sections of the party, powerful constraints, as identified in chapter 6, were active.

The establishment of Cabinet Committee Misc. 141, chaired by Mrs Thatcher as Prime Minister, was given the task to produce the White Paper. This in itself seemed to indicate an unprecedented shift in emphasis from a concern for litter, to a long-term commitment to the future of the planet. In December 1989, Committee Misc. 141

requested costed plans regarding what each government department could do. Detailed costings were provided in February 1990, and immediately worries spread in Whitehall regarding the costs and the possible emergence of an over-powerful DOE. Patten himself had already warned of the possible high costs involved in the exercise.[38] However, Patten, influenced by his personal adviser David Pearce, put his faith in the use of market and various price mechanisms as the answer to the high costs involved. This faith it seems was not shared by John Major, then Chancellor of the Exchequer, when in his March budget he re-emphasised the government's commitment to bringing down inflation, effectively ruling out unilateral introduction of the so-called 'carbon tax', to combat growing pollution and congestion problems caused by the car.[39]

Many in the environmental movement had hoped that the White Paper would release much-needed resources for environmental improvement. However, in competition for a share of the Chancellor's financial cake, the environment was destined to lose out. For example, in February 1989 gross over-estimates were submitted to the Treasury from the Department of Energy, of £200 per household, regarding proposals for undertaking home energy audits. The actual cost was something of the order of £50 per household, but the first set of figures had been enough to do the damage, and the policy for undertaking energy audits was lost.

Despite Patten's high profile role in the compilation of the White Paper, his 'high Tory' principles were swamped by the then Prime Minister's own brand of Conservative ideology, her political instincts, and those of some of her 'dry' cabinet colleagues. In addition to wanting a carbon tax, Patten had been keen to see an end to tax concessions on company cars. However, against a Thatcher/ Parkinson alliance determined to uphold their beliefs in a 'free-for-all' motoring policy (at least until after the next general election), Patten's attempts to introduce a minimum of intervention was thwarted. This was borne out by a leaked minute from the Department of Transport (then headed by Cecil Parkinson) responding to Patten's pressure for a change in policy, which said that this would place 'intolerable restrictions on society'.[40]

At the time the White Paper was being put together, the environment lagged behind a range of other issues on the policy agenda, not least the privatisation of the electricity industry and the implementation of the community charge. Indeed, it is likely that Chris Patten's then responsibility for the community charge deflected him from the key debates behind the drafting of the White Paper. Moreover, ideas of a carbon tax on all fossil fuels would have made coal-fired power stations as unattractive to the market as nuclear ones. A full agenda, and possible clashes of interests, added to the erosion of Patten's efforts to secure the political will he needed to shape the White Paper into the radical document the environmental movement was seeking.

Although 'Our Common Inheritance', published on 25 September 1990, contained over 350 commitments, these were heavily diluted to measure up to a 'greenness' which suited the government at the time. Notably absent was any primary coverage of the ideas of David Pearce regarding the use of the price mechanism to prevent environmental damage.[41] It appeared that the government, and the Chancellor in particular, was not ready to make the bold political step of attaching a price to environmental improvement. The White Paper took the important step of taking the environmental economics debate to the politicians, but in the build-up to a potential general election in 1991, it refrained from explicitly pointing out that preventing damage to and improving the environment will cost the public (already under the strain of high interest rates) money. Instead, the document emphasised voluntarism as the way to deal with many environmental problems, and shrouded many of its suggestions with well-presented 'put-offs' and ministerial side-steps, such as, 'consider', 'explore', 'study', 'work towards'.[42]

Criticisms of the 1990 White Paper are all too easily made, yet it was a landmark in the 'greening' of party politics: not for its radicalism, but for the fact that it was the first document to seriously attempt to co-ordinate environmental policy. This in itself was a significant achievement, particularly for a government which had previously seemed unconcerned with environmental matters. The establishment of a permanent Cabinet Committee on the environment chaired by the Prime Minister was an important step in gearing up the machinery of government for a 'greener' approach; so too was the nomination of a minister in each department to take responsibility for the environment and publish an annual report on achieving environmental objectives. However, it remains to be seen whether these low-cost institutional measures will eliminate the constraints to 'greening' that relate to inter-departmental rivalries and lack of policy co-ordination.

The politicisation of the environment during the 1980s has opened up a Pandora's box of issues which are waiting to be tackled. Indeed, there are just too many environmental issues and too many interests for party politics to handle. Agendas can only be expanded so far, and the constitutional system is already straining to cope with far more than it was ever designed to do. The 1990 Environmental Protection Act, for instance, heralded as the most comprehensive piece of environmental legislation since the Clean Air Act of 1956, is 120 clauses long, but not long enough. Focusing mainly on establishing integrated policies on pollution control, litter, waste disposal and the reorganisation of the Nature Conservancy Council, the Act goes some way in tackling important domestic issues. Yet it has been criticised by environmental groups for tackling the more superficial environmental problems such as straw-burning, rather than global issues. But however long the Act is, and how many issues it addresses, it can never be adequate to deal with the backlog of environmental problems, plus many others that are revealed almost daily. Environmental issues may well rise and fall, but they will never go away, and legislation can never keep pace: a point often forgotten by some sectors of the environmental movement in their clamour for change, and highlighted to various degrees by the major parties who know the limitations of politics in the process of social change.

As well as limits to the length of agendas of government and the parties, there are also limits to the amount of political will needed to deal with environmental questions, dictated by the significant number of powerful interest groups who do not wish to see any dramatic transformation in the way the parties deal with the environment – who fear they will lose out. Paradoxically, whilst the Thatcher years witnessed the most dramatic upsurge of environmental concern via increased membership of environmental groups, they also saw an entrenchment of groups representing private capital, often accumulated from the most short-term, anti-environmental practices. Action taken by the trade unions, the CBI and many large companies to examine their own environmental policies and investment strategies has gone some way to changing this. Yet despite the promises of 'green capitalism' and 'green consumerism', the market is still not geared up to handling such a vital and often intangible commodity as the environment. It is under the influence of the open market economics of the 1980s that the major parties are forced to address environmental issues in the short term.

Party ideologies are at the root of the 'greening' of British politics.

Belief systems with origins almost exclusively in an era of industrial and colonial expansion, and which have, by and large, worked well for most of the late twentieth century, are clearly problematic for the environmental movement which, as a coherent force, has only been operating for some twenty-five years. Thatcherism demonstrated that political ideology is far from at an end. Indeed, its links to government policy over the past decade have been explicit. In each of the major parties there has tended to be an affirmation of the importance of principles, even though there have been questions raised as to their relevance. The rediscovery of environmentalist ideologues within each of the parties, and the introspection of party beliefs against a backdrop of post-industrial values, has gone some way in widening ideological goal posts, but they remain basically unchanged. Moreover, the political system itself demands that they remain unchanged and uncompromising, so as to map out distinct choices between the parties for the electorate. The environmental movement may alter party philosophies at the margins, but it cannot change them to suit itself rather, it must work around them, or wait a long time for them to change.

Given these 'natural' limits to the 'greening' of the main parties, can we expect anything more than the processes of continuity and accommodation to dominate the 'greening' of party politics in the 1990s and beyond? The answer is bound up with the future of the political parties and the political system in which they operate. It is hard to imagine a Britain without its parties and the ideological tensions on which they are founded.[43] Arguably, the strength of the British party system is based neither on rationality nor on tradition, but on its flexibility and its 'capacity to absorb social changes and to adapt itself to a form appropriate for the articulation of the new social pressures'.[44] This view is certainly compatible with the way in which the 'greening' of the parties has developed so far; a process of policy manipulation, ideological capture and much rhetoric. Yet ultimately the environmental movement is such a powerful force for social change that political structures and the present system that holds them together may *have* to be dramatically altered in order to cope with the enormity of the changes needed. This is the most dramatic of messages from the Greens; any transition to a truly sustainable global economy has to be built upon radical political change.

However, in entering the debate about which alternative political

system would be more responsive to the challenge of environmentalism, we are in danger of overestimating the nature of social
change itself. For despite what the Greens may believe, social
change in the UK is characterised more by small-scale, incremental
adjustments and piecemeal alteration than by radical transformation. The majority of environmentalists seek a multitude of
minor changes relating to a range of fragmented issues, rather than
working to some 'mega-plan' for a 'deep green' future. As such, the
framework of the existing party political system is appropriate, and
broadly speaking, the diversity amongst environmental groups is
well matched with the variety of political ideologies. Each of the
parties may have a long way to go before they are fully responsive to
the needs and desires of the environmental movement, but this is not
to say that they can never be responsive; it merely reflects early days
in the courtship between the parties and environmentalists.

On reflection, it appears ridiculous to suggest that the major
parties would, or could, suddenly sweep their traditions and beliefs
away in response to the challenge of environmentalism, particularly
when the environmental movement itself has no clear ideological
position to offer as a substitute. The processes of continuity and
adaptation dominate British party politics, and environmentalism is
very much a Cheshire Cat phenomenon, appearing never as a
whole, but in parts, at various times and under various conditions.
It will have to continue to materialise at the right time and place,
amongst the myriad of issues that occupy politicians for most of the
time. The environment is not above party politics. Like any other
social phenomenon, it has to be part of it.

Behind the dissatisfaction of many environmentalists regarding
the failure of the major political parties to handle environmental
questions is an inate over-reliance on political mechanisms to solve
what are ostensibly social problems. Politicians, at national or local
level, are there to respond to the public. But although they can
formalise public concern and legislate for it, ultimately it is the
public who has to bear the costs of a better environment – costs not
only in monetary terms, such as how much of a price increase we are
willing to accept in our electricity bills in order to have cleaner air,
but costs relating to our personal liberty, freedom as to where we
live and the choices we have in society. These difficult choices will
continue to be articulated by politicians in the years ahead,
reflecting real limits on what politics can achieve in such an impor-

tant and all-embracing area.

In the short term, the future of the environment as a party political issue is bound up with the political future of each of the main parties and the individuals of influence within each. Clearly, we can only speculate as to how the environment will fare given the range of variables that can affect outcomes, but some brief and broad indicators are offered here for consideration.

Personalities are powerful forces in the process of political change. In a relatively short time, at the end of 1988, with well-chosen speeches and her political charisma, Mrs Thatcher, when Prime Minister, did much to accelerate the 'greening' process in all of the main parties. Ironically, with the departure of the woman who for so long had been recognised as the most formidable of impediments to a better environment, went much of the momentum for environmental action which had been building up. Indeed, the dramatic downfall of Mrs Thatcher was itself a distraction from environmental matters.

Chris Patten, as Secretary of State for the Environment, did not have the forcefulness to make anything other than a superficial impression upon his Cabinet colleagues. His crusading efforts were unable to overcome the empires of an inherently competitive departmental system of government, nor the ideological dragons in the Cabinet. As a good Conservative, Patten talked down much of the criticism which was hurled at the White Paper. In his own words, it 'was not the last word but a very good first word' on the environment – recognition of the immensity of the task facing any Secretary of State for the Environment involved in matching environmental ideals to political realities.

As Patten's successor, with Mrs Thatcher removed and the community charge rumpus fading way, Michael Heseltine has the capacity to make a positive contribution to the development of Conservative environmental policy. During his first years as Secretary of State for the Environment between 1979 and 1983, apart from his drive for inner-city regeneration, Heseltine made little impression upon the environmental front. However, he has exhibited some of his interest in 'green' matters since. In November 1988, Michael Heseltine addressed the Royal Institute for Environmental Affairs on the links between foreign policy and the environment, calling for a readiness to engage in 'green geopolitics'.[45] The speech was seen by some at the time as Heseltine's way of matching Mrs Thatcher's Royal Society speech delivered two months earlier, and indicating that he was able to challenge the then Prime Minister.

Michael Heseltine's first major speech on countryside and planning matters as John Major's Secretary of State for the Environment early in 1991 was generally welcomed by environmental groups such as the Council for the Protection of Rural England. Indeed, Mr Heseltine seems to understand what needs to be done to address environmental issues. In the words of the former Director of Christien Salvesen, Tom Baron, who has known the man for many years: 'Heseltine is a do-er and environment is where the big jobs need doing now.'[46] Even with the benefit of the framework established by the 1990 Environment White Paper and the Environmental Protection Act, the real challenge for Michael Heseltine, as it was for Chris Patten, is to convince the party interest groups, others in the Cabinet, and particularly John Major, what needs to be done.

It remains to be seen whether John Major as Prime Minister has sufficient interest in the environment or the necessary political courage to take some of the important decisions which will inevitably face a UK government in the years ahead. His mild manner and apparent concern for social issues would seem to suggest that he is someone the environmental movement can do business with. However, the signs are that, unlike his predecessor in her later years, he neither understands the issues, nor possesses the political skill and authority to raise them high on the agenda and keep them there. During his time as Chancellor, Mr Major, in league with the Departments of Energy and Transport, helped emasculate some of Chris Patten's more adventurous Environment White Paper proposals. Indeed, as Chancellor, John Major exhibited a commitment to Thatcherite economics which still appears to dominate his view of the environment.

In July of 1991, John Major gave his first speech on the environment at the *Sunday Times* Environment Exhibition, indicating that, as a policy issue, the environment had not been lost forever. However, it contained little to suggest that Mr Major's approach to the environment was to be any different to that of his predecessor. The main thrust of the speech was the announcement of a new environmental protection agency which would unite the National Rivers Authority and Her Majesty's Inspectorate of Pollution; in the words of Mr Major: 'It is right that the integrity and indivisibility of the environment should now be reflected in a unified agency.'[47] Given that the Labour Party and the Liberal Democrats have long-established policies on establishing such a body, this was hardly a new idea. However, with an election scheduled for 1992, it may well prove to be a centrepiece for the next Conservative manifesto.

After removing the standard rhetoric, John Major's speech neither confirmed nor denied any personal commitment to the environment but, significantly, it did explicitly reaffirm the ideological approach to tackling environmental questions which has dominated British politics throughout the 1980s. The emphasis remains firmly upon market forces and a partnership between business and individual consumers to regulate and improve the environment. Moreover, Mr Major's speech focused upon those issues which readily allied themselves to this approach – litter, recycling and energy conservation – in much the same way as Mrs Thatcher's did. This continuity in approach to the environment confirms that, whereas personalities are important in the 'greening' process, they are themselves dominated by party ideology. Whereas the legacy of Thatcher-style market economics undoubtedly has a role to play in the 'greening' of an advanced capitalist economy, Conservative Party ideology, as it presently stands, is not flexible enough to deal with big environmental issues, and policy measures such as introducing higher petrol duty is likely to make little impact on an anticipated 125 per cent increase in road transport over the next twenty-five years.

Since the election of Paddy Ashdown as leader of the Liberal Democrats in July 1988, the environmental resolve of the party has been strengthened. It may well have been the agonies of merger with the SDP that focused the minds of both parties on the ideals they needed to present to the public. In the lead-up to merger, many Liberals followed Simon Hughes MP in striving to make the environment a central, rather than peripheral, issue of the party. It was for some Liberals a make-or-break issue. As Hughes put it: 'Unless these ideals of one world, peace, stewardship, and justice are incorporated into and welcomed in the new party, I – and I believe many other Liberals – will not be able to join.'[48]

Paddy Ashdown, eager to prove himself as a dynamic leader in touch with the future, has built on this Liberal commitment and has made the environment a central issue in his party. Partly in search of a profile which will distinguish the Liberal Democrats from the other major parties, and partly under the influence a well-established network of Liberal greens at the grassroots, Ashdown has manoeuvered his party to a position of credibility with environmentalists. In his own words, taken from his foreword to the 1990 Liberal Democrat Agenda for Environmental Action, 'What Price our Planet?':

Our persistent advocacy over many years of a new economic order in harmony with our environment has been influential in bringing politicians in this country to realise their importance too. But Liberal Democrats say that it is necessary to be far more imaginative then either Tory or Labour have ever been. We also say that it is necessary to be more realistic than the Green Party. It must fall to those of us, now Liberal Democrats, who have been for the longest time in the forefront of green politics, to be the predominant national force with the power to bring our policies into practice.[49]

This document draws heavily on ideas long advocated by the Green Party, and puts together an agenda for the 1990s and beyond which effectively makes the links between global environmental policy, the role of the UK in Europe with regard to the environment, local community action and personal action. It also leans upon the Pearce Report and puts together a credible policy platform resting on sustainable economics. For all of its foresight and intention, the document could come to mean very little unless Ashdown can lead the Liberal Democrats to political power. Ashdown has signalled that he would not consider any pre-electoral pacts, but would wish to hold out for total victory. The future of the party is heavily dependent upon the fortunes of the Tories and Labour, but it seems highly unlikely that in the foreseeable future the Liberal Democrats will find themselves in a position where they can do anything more than marginally influence national environmental policy. However, at the local level the Liberal Democrats will no doubt continue to undertake sound environmental action where it is needed.

After more than a decade of Thatcherism, democratic socialism still offers itself as the one major ideology which offers the most complete analysis, not only of how an environmental crisis has emerged, but how it can be tackled realistically within the existing political culture. With issues of class likely to fade within the Red/ Green debate, the Labour Party may be in a strong position to absorb defectors from the Green Party. This position is strengthened now that Cunningham, and his legacy of supporting nuclear power, has been replaced by Bryan Gould as Shadow Secretary for the Environment. However, in order to win a future election, the Labour Party needs to attract not Green Party supporters, but disenchanted Conservatives.

In Labour's challenge for political power, it remains to be seen whether the type of socialism which would go a long a way to tackling some fundamental environmental issues will be the same type of socialism that will appeal to the electorate and the majority of party members. Labour's 1990 policy statement on the environment, 'An Earthly Chance', contains an interesting admixture of conventional socialist solutions to environmental problems, such as bringing the water industry and the electricity industry back into public sector ownership, and dealing with the legacy of a property-owning, popular capitalist democracy.[50] 'An Earthly Chance' adopts some new positions on the environment, but stops well short of offering a full-blooded socialist approach, reflecting caution. The party's opposition to the construction of further nuclear power stations is emphasised, though the document does not promise to halt work on the thermal oxide reprocessing plant at Sellafield and the Sizewell B nuclear power station. Administrative reform to establish an Environmental Protection Executive is proposed, together with the establishment of a Food Standards Authority. Such reforms would be unlikely to upset industry to any degree, and may be seen as inevitable moves. State intervention is present in the document as a pro-environment mechanism, but in an effort not to alienate potential voters, measures such as the introduction of a carbon tax are omitted from the document.

The Labour Party, including Kinnock and the unions, appear fully committed to a high profile for environmental policy in the long term. But, despite the rhetoric, there is always likely to be a nagging doubt regarding any future relationship between promises to rebuild the manufacturing base of the UK and environmental policy. The 1980s witnessed a sea change amongst the trade unions with regard to the environment/economic growth interface, but this newly-cultivated attitude still remains to be tested under a Labour government in an economic recession.

A further key issue for the Labour Party's environmental profile is their commitment to Europe. A Labour victory at the next election would push this issue to the fore, with direct implications for Labour environmental policy. But, as with the Liberal Democrats, the most pressing question for the Labour Party in the short term is whether or not they can overturn the Tories at the next general election with a working majority. This in itself is a major hurdle. The longer the party goes without a general election victory, the more the pressures will increase for policies of expediency and populism; it may well be, for instance, that in economic recession, under a fourth successive Conservative administration, much of the work done to 'green' the PLP and the trade unions would be lost.

Without the responsibilty of government, Labour and the Liberal Democrats have been provided with valuable time for introspection and the development of environmental policies. The 1980s saw major upheavals for both parties, and in many ways they have each started the 1990s with a clean sheet. Their future, and to an extent that of the Green Party, is firmly bound up with that of the Conservatives. Should political will and party understanding ubiquitously emerge and override all other issues, interests and prejudices, then a fourth term for the Conservatives could see radical follow-ups to the 1990 White Paper. For a government rapidly running out of the radicalism on which it has prided itself, the environment could provide a popular vehicle through which the essence of Thatcherism could be kept alive. But this is highly unlikely, for under the corporate style of government they have cultivated, and with their inherent ideological antagonism to interventionist politics, the Conservatives can only deal with the worst environmental problems in a marginal way.

National and international environmental problems have developed to such an extent that all of the major parties will need to rethink substantively their ideologies to allow environmental concern to pervade all areas of policy and political action. Indeed, this is what the 'greening' of British party politics is about: a process which forces deep-seated ideological changes on all of the major parties. This process, which came to the fore during the 1980s, is scheduled to continue, and there are a number of wider developments that will assist its progression.

The first is the de-intellectualisation of the environmental movement. In any social movement, the emphasis is on action, and while important academic debates will continue to develop, environmentalism has become a pragmatic movement with a new political awareness. The second is the decline in environmental radicalism. This is a natural development which has helped to propel the mainstream politicisation of the environment, although in some ways it threatens to weaken the position of environmentalists by focusing upon low-profile reformists instead of on the radicals. Thirdly, there is a new maturity emerging in the phenomenon of green consumerism. As the attentive public continue their own environmental crusade, there is increasing sophistication which helps keep the politicians alert to the validity of claims made in the market place regarding the depth of concern exhibited by companies. Fourthly, there is a whirlwind of new-found internationalism, focusing not just upon East/West relations, weapons control and the opening up of new markets, but also upon North/South relations, resource allocation and debt default. All of the major UK parties will increasingly find themselves looking at such global issues with an environmental perspective.

The 'greening' of British party politics promises no transformation in society. The political manoeuvring of the main parties over a decade or so cannot hope to do much more than create a more responsive climate for environmental and social change. But this in itself is an optimistic development. Accommodation, adaptation and integration are at its heart. Departmental integration and co-ordination now underpin each of the main parties' approach to environmental issues, in recognition that the environment is the most 'lateral' of concepts. Further progress is likely to materialise where environmental concerns can be integrated with economic interests. Yet while anachronistic party ideologies strive to come to terms with environmental issues, while politicians attempt to learn various dialects of the new language of 'greenery', and politics itself struggles to cope with unprecedented global change, time – the one resource we believe to be infinite – moves on.

Notes and references

1   Button, J. 1988. *Green Pages: A Directory of Natural Products, Services, Resources and Ideas.* London: Optima.
2   See: Poguntke, T. 1987. 'New Politics and Party Systems: The Emergence of a New Type of Party?' *West European Politics*, 10, No. 1. Jan. 76–88.
3   This perspective of shifting personal values from the so-called Dominant Social Paradigm to the New Ecological Paradigm is explored by Dunlap, R. E./Van Liere, K. D. 1978. 'The "New Environmental Paradigm": A Proposed Measuring Instrument and Preliminary Results.' *Journal of Environmental Education*, IX. 10–19.
4   The use of the phrase 'who gets what, when and how' to define politics is usually credited to Laswell, H. D. 1951. *Power and Personality.* Oxford: Oxford University Press.
5   See for instance: Cotgrove, S. 1982. *Catastrophe or Cornucopia.*

Chichester: John Wiley.
  6   Papworth, J. 1987. 'Ghosts in the Megamachine.' *Green Line*, No. 49. February. 14–15.
  7   The possible relationship between land 'units' and political power is outlined by Sale, K. 1984. 'Bioregionalism: A New Way to Treat the Land.' *The Ecologist*, 14, No. 4. 167–73.
  8   See: Robertson, J. 1986. 'Health, Wealth and the New Economics.' The Other Economic Summit.
  9   Hayley, R. 1986. 'Anarchy for Beginners.' *Green Line*, No. 42. May. 14–17.
  10 The Greens' acceptance of the principles of individual freedom, self-reliance and self-determination are reminiscent of Marcusian 'New Leftism', though the Greens are quick to point out that any political ideology which neglects the importance of ecology bears no relation to Green politics.
  11 Personal Communication.
  12 See for instance: Galtung, J. 1986. 'The Green Movement: A Socio-Historical Exploration.' *International Sociology*, 1, No. 1. March. 75–90; Rudig, W./Lowe, P. D. 1984. 'The Withered "Greening" of British Politics: A Study of the Ecology Party.' Paper presented at the United Kingdom Political Science Association Conference, Southampton, 3–5 April.
  13 See: Rudig, W. 1985. 'The Greens in Europe: Ecological Parties and the European Elections of 1984.' *Parliamentary Affairs*, 38, No. 1. Winter. 56–72.
  14 As put forward by: Inglehart, R. 1981. 'Post-Materialism in an Environment of Insecurity.' *American Political Science Review*, 75. 880–900.
  15 See: Dalton, R. J./Flanagan, S. C./Beck, P. A. (Eds.) 1984. *Electoral Change in Advanced Industrial Democracies: Realignment or Dealignment?* Princeton: Princeton University Press.
  16 A point made by Rudig & Lowe, Note 12, *op. cit.* and by: Mewes, H. 1983. 'The West German Green Party.' *The New German Critique*, 28. 51–85.
  17 For an outline see: Rose, C. 1987. 'Analysis '87: The General Election.' Eco News, 35. 8.
  18 Personal Communication.
  19 See: Johnstone, D. 1986. 'Realo, trulio green?' *New Socialist*, October. 10–11.
  20 When Petra Kelly (a vociferous figure in Die Grunen and ironically a supporter of the rotational system at its inception) refused to 'rotate', on the basis that she was too important a media figure for the party, she lost considerable credibility with many activists. For an overview of the German Green Party's organisation see: Shaw-Taylor, L. 1987. 'How Die-Grunen are organised.' *Green Line*, 55. September. 7.
  21 Papworth, J. 1986. Letter in Econews, No. 30. May. 5.
  22 Reported in: Bahro, R. 1986. 'The Party and Beyond.' (Interview.) *Green Line*. 39. 3–6.
  23 See: Benton, S. 1986. 'Problems of a Party Without Politics.' *New Statesman*, 26 September. 20–21; Carpenter, J. 1986. 'Maingreens for the

Mainstream.' *Green Line*, No. 43. June. 17.

24 Tyler, A. 1986. 'A Personal Introduction.' Discussion Paper for the Green Strategy Meeting, 10th May.

25 Ekins, P. 1986. 'Maingreen.' Discussion Paper for the Green Strategy Meeting, 10th May.

26 Pressures for sharpening the political profile of the Green Party have been ever-present at its party conferences since the 1987 General Election. As then spokesman David Icke commented in 1988: 'It is time for us to adopt a new and sharper image. We must show the electorate that we are the people who mean business.' From: Icke, D. 1988. In Walker, T. 'Greens Prepare for Less Woolly Image.' *Observer*, 16.10.88. 7.

27 Porritt, J./Winner, D. 1988. *The Coming of the Greens*. London: Fontana.

28 Reactionary positions against the environmentalists are exemplified by: Bowman, J. 1989. 'Green Grows the Rousseau-o!' *The Spectator*, 12 August. 9–11; Ferguson, C. 1989. 'The peril in the Greens' pie in the sky.' *Daily Mail*. 17 June. 6.

29 See for instance: Dyson, K. 1987. 'The Challenged Consensus: the 1987 German Federal Elections.' *Political Quarterly*, 58, No. 2. 152–66.

30 A term first used by Porritt. See: Porritt, J. 1984. *Seeing Green – The Politics of Ecology Explained*. Oxford: Basil Blackwell.

31 Note 27, *op. cit.*

32 Estimated at only £4,738 in 1987.

33 In her speech, Mrs Thatcher emphasised her commitment to good science and stressed the role that 'sound economics' can play in solving global environmental problems. She also focused upon the pressures of world over-population. But whereas the speech may have furthered her own 'green' credentials, it contributed little to altering the even economic balance between first and third worlds.

34 The concept of sustainable development as outlined in the Brundtland Report goes some way in alleviating this worry, although some radical Greens have not yet moved away from positions of 'no-growth' or 'zero growth'.

35 Jenkins, S. 1988. 'How Green are our Politics?' *Sunday Times*, 'Week in Review'. 4 September. 1.

36 The very activity of politics, as we would traditionally view it, would not seem to marry well with central 'green' ideas of co-operation and openness.

37 Department of Environment, 1990. White Paper: *Our Common Inheritance*. Although a first brave attempt to co-ordinate environmental policy in the UK, other nations such as the Netherlands and Canada have had national environmental policy plans for several years previous to this date.

38 Interview with Chris Patten, BBC1, 'On the Record', November 1989.

39 A persistent argument used by the Conservatives against introducing a carbon tax to curb UK contributions to global warming has been that unilateral action would have little impact on the global situation, and would

instead put British industry at an economic disadvantage in a competitive world.

40   As reported on BBC 2, 'Newsnight', 25.9.90.

41   The ideas of David Pearce on using market policy instruments to tackle environmental questions were largely relegated to an 'Environmental Protection' appendix in the White Paper, indicating a reluctance, at the time, to use them.

42   See for example: Paragraph 5.52: 'The Government is exploring the possibility of a code of advertising practice which would encourage car manufacturers to lay less stress on power, speed and acceleration, and more on effiency, economy and safety.' (Emphasis added.)

43   A useful point made by:Rose, R. 1974. *The Problem of Party Government*. London: Macmillan Press. (1st ed.).

44   Ingle, S. 1989. 'Change, Politics and the Party System.' *Parliamentary Affairs*, 42. January. 23–37.

45   Heseltine, M. 1988. Speech to the Royal Institute for International Affairs, Chatham House, London. 23 November.

46   From: Davis-Colman, C. 1990. 'Highwayman or Buccaneer?' *Municipal Journal*. 49, 12–13.

47   Major, J. Speech, *Sunday Times* Environment Conference. London. 8.7.91. Mr Major's speech was in effect a policy turnaround, given that Patten as Environment Secretary had rejected the idea of a unified environmental protection agency.

48   Hughes, S. Quoted in: *Guardian*. 22.01.88.

49   Ashdown, P. 1990. Foreword. *What Price Our Planet? A Liberal Democrat Agenda for Environmental Action*. The Liberal Democrats.

50   Labour Party. 1990. *An Earthly Chance*. The Labour Party.

Index